THE 21 MOST POWERFUL
MINUTES
in a
LEADER'S DAY

REVITALIZE
YOUR SPIRIT AND
EMPOWER
YOUR LEADERSHIP

JOHN C. MAXWELL

Publishers Since 1798

THOMAS NELSON PUBLISHERS®
Nashville

Published in Nashville, Tennessee, by Thomas Nelson, Inc.

Scripture quotations noted NKJV are from THE NEW KING JAMES VERSION. Copyright ©
1979, 1980, 1982, Thomas Nelson, Inc., Publishers.

Scripture quotations noted *The Message* are from *The Message: The New Testament in
Contemporary English.* Copyright © 1993 by Eugene H. Peterson.

Scripture quotations noted NIV are from the HOLY BIBLE: NEW INTERNATIONAL VER-
SION®. Copyright © 1973, 1978, 1984 by International Bible Society. Used by permission of
Zondervan Publishing House. All rights reserved.

Scripture quotations noted NASB are from the NEW AMERICAN STANDARD BIBLE ®,
Copyright © The Lockman Foundation 1960, 1962, 1963, 1968, 1971, 1972, 1973, 1975,
1977. Used by permission.

Scripture quotations noted KJV are from the KING JAMES VERSION.

Scripture quotations noted CEV are from THE CONTEMPORARY ENGLISH VERSION.
Copyright © 1991 by the American Bible Society. Used by permission.

Library of Congress Cataloging-in-Publication Data

Maxwell, John C.
    The 21 most powerful minutes in a leader's day
    ISBN 0-7852-7432-4 (HC)
    ISBN 0-7852-6785-9 (IE)
    00-134098

Printed in the United States of America

2 3 4 5 6 BVG 05 04 03 02 01 00

This book is dedicated to the following people who serve with me on the *EQUIP* board. Together we have a dream to raise up leaders who will make a difference in the lives of millions of people.

Ron McManns
Gerald Brooks
David Burdine
Jim Campbell
Jim Dornan
Larry Maxwell
Bill McCartney
Mac McQuiston
Kevin Miller
Ray Moats
Tom Phillippe
Mitch Sala

CONTENTS

ACKNOWLEDGMENTS

Thank you to the team of people who helped me work on this book:

Charlie Wetzel—for his writing skill and wisdom
Dan Reiland—for his creativity and leadership insight
Tim Elmore—for his biblical insight and keen perception
Brent Cole—for his assistance with research
Stephanie Wetzel—for her assistance with proofreading and editing
Linda Eggers—for the way she runs my life

INTRODUCTION

How can I become a better leader? That's a question I ask myself every day of my life. I'm constantly searching for new things to learn and ways to grow. But sometimes the best way to learn is to return to the fundamentals. After all, that's what championship coaches do when they want to sharpen the skills of their players, whether they're rookies or seasoned veterans.

That's what prompted me to go back to the Source, to the greatest leadership book ever written: the Bible. Every leadership lesson I've ever taught has been based on scriptural principles. Now in *The 21 Most Powerful Minutes in a Leader's Day*, I'm bringing the leadership contained in the Bible to the forefront. By examining the lives of the Bible's great leaders, we can learn more about leadership and apply the principles we learn to our daily lives.

This book is a leadership development tool. It's not meant to be read through in a sitting. It's designed to be consumed in daily bites and digested slowly, so put it someplace where you can conveniently read it five days a week.

If you go through the process as I've intended, you will spend the next twenty-one weeks working your way through the material. The book is organized around *The 21 Irrefutable Laws of Leadership*. Each week you will spend four days learning leadership from a different biblical figure. Every day focuses on one predominant leadership thought, contains a lesson learned from the biblical leader, and poses a question for you to meditate on all day long. The fifth day will help you change your focus from *thinking* about leadership to *acting on it* as you take steps to help you become a better leader.

I hope you enjoy the next few months living with some of the greatest leaders in mankind's history—and with a few who should have been but weren't. I've learned some wonderful leadership lessons from them, and I hope you do too.

Week 1

THE LAW OF THE LID

LEADERSHIP ABILITY DETERMINES A PERSON'S LEVEL OF EFFECTIVENESS

Success is within the reach of just about everyone. But . . . personal success without leadership ability brings only limited effectiveness. A person's impact is only a fraction of what it could be with good leadership. The higher you want to climb, the more you need leadership. The greater the impact you want to make, the greater your influence needs to be . . .

Leadership ability is the lid that determines a person's level of effectiveness. The lower an individual's ability to lead, the lower the lid on his potential. The higher the leadership, the greater the effectiveness . . . Your leadership ability—for better or for worse—always determines your effectiveness and the potential impact of your organization . . . To reach the highest level of effectiveness, you have to raise the lid on your leadership ability.

FROM "THE LAW OF THE LID" IN *The 21 Irrefutable Laws of Leadership*

Day 1

Saul and David
and the
Law of the Lid

LEADERSHIP THOUGHT FOR TODAY:
Every person has the potential to become a leader.

Read
1 Samuel 10:17–24; 13:5–15; 15:10–16:13; 17:32–18:16;
2 Samuel 5:1–5; 11:1–5, 14–15, 26–27; 12:1–15

Looks can be deceiving. Sometimes we look at a person, and we assume that he has everything it takes to be a great leader. That was the case with Saul. Scripture tells us,

> There was a man of Benjamin whose name was Kish . . . a mighty man of power. And he had a choice and handsome son whose name was Saul. There was not a more handsome person than he among the children of Israel. From his shoulders upward he was taller than any of the people. (1 Sam. 9:1–2 NKJV)

When the people of Israel asked for a king, God gave them Saul, and everyone expected him to be a great leader. But the people looked at his outer appearance while God looked at his heart. It wasn't long before Saul, a man of power and potential, discredited himself and his leadership, and God chose a new leader in his place. He picked David, a man after God's own heart.

TWO KINGS WITH DIFFERENT LEADERSHIP LIDS

Why did Saul fail as Israel's king while David, who appeared to be weaker, succeeded? The answer can be found in the Law of the Lid: Leadership ability determines a

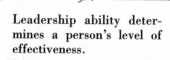

> Leadership ability determines a person's level of effectiveness.

person's level of effectiveness. While David tried to become a better leader and had many lid-lifting experiences, Saul's attitude kept the lid clamped down firmly on his leadership.

Take a look at the similar paths the men traveled:

1. BOTH RECEIVED COUNSEL FROM GODLY MEN

The anointing and opportunity given to Saul and David were strikingly similar. Both were anointed by Samuel, the last judge of the Hebrew nation. And both received the benefit of godly counsel—Saul received his from Samuel, and David from Samuel and later Nathan the prophet. But look at how different their reigns were as monarchs.

Saul never really understood the nature of leadership. The day he was appointed king, he actually hid from the people. I believe he did that because he recognized his inability to lead. But after he tasted success in battle, he mistook his *position* as king for real leadership. Though he had the title, power, and crown of a king, he never moved the monarchy beyond a charisma-based judgeship. He was made a general, but he never attracted a large standing army. He created no organized government to preserve his gains. And when God no longer favored him, he thought the title of king entitled him to continue leading.

David, on the other hand, seized opportunities to grow in his leadership. He learned to be a warrior. He built a standing army and conquered his enemies. He chose a city and captured it to become the nation's new capital, and then he built a lasting government there. Much of that he did before he sat on the throne. From the beginning, all the people of Israel and Judah loved him (1 Sam. 18:16). David attracted citizens, warriors, and leaders alike, and he led them well. As the result of his leadership, the people flourished.

2. BOTH FACED GREAT CHALLENGES

Every leader faces obstacles, tests, and trials. Saul and David sometimes faced the same ones. Take Goliath, for example. When the huge Philistine offered to fight Israel's champion, both Saul and David heard the warrior's challenge. Saul, Israel's greatest warrior who rightfully should have faced the giant in battle, reacted by hiding in fear. But David, a mere boy, was eager to face the challenge and win honor for God.

What was Saul's reaction? He offered David his armor. (Why not—*Saul* wasn't going to be using it!) While others wait to see what's going to happen, leaders step forward and rise to a challenge.

3. BOTH HAD THE CHOICE TO CHANGE AND GROW

The two men's very different reactions when confronted with their short-comings capture the two natures of Saul and David. When Saul disobediently made a burnt offering to God, Samuel rebuked him. The Scripture is silent on what followed. There is no record of sorrow or repentance by Saul. Instead, the narrative continues with Saul's campaign against the Philistines. Evidently he kept going on the same course.

David's reaction to his sin, on the other hand, was remarkably different. After David committed adultery with Bathsheba and sent her husband to his death, Nathan confronted him, and the king sorrowfully repented.

THE ONE WHO LIFTED THE LID

David's interaction with Nathan is representative of his attitude during his life. He was never afraid to admit his shortcomings, ask for God's forgiveness and blessing, and improve himself. It is the reason the lid on his leadership kept getting lifted higher and higher.

We can all learn from David. If we want to reach our potential and become the person God would have us be, then we need to lift the lids on our lives. That's the only way we can go to the next level.

TODAY'S QUESTION FOR REFLECTION:
In your leadership, have you been more like David or Saul?

Day 2

Samuel said to Saul, "You have done foolishly. You have not kept the commandment of the LORD your God, which He commanded you. For now the LORD would have established your kingdom over Israel forever. But now your kingdom shall not continue."

1 Samuel 13:13–14 (NKJV)

Every leader has lids on his life. Nobody is born without them. And they don't disappear when a person receives a title, achieves a position, or is invested with power. The issue is never whether you have lids. The issue is what you are going to do about them.

THE LIDS THAT LIMITED SAUL

When God made Saul king of Israel, He removed all the external lids from the new ruler's life. Saul received God's anointing, took the position of king, and had the potential to become a great leader. But even though he had no external lids to his leadership, there still remained *internal* lids in Saul. There were many:

> Every leader has lids on his life. The issue is never whether you have lids. The issue is what you are going to do about them.

- *Fear.* He began his reign by hiding among the equipment, and he was afraid to face Goliath.

- *Impatience.* He refused to wait for Samuel and presumed upon God by taking matters into his own hands when he offered the sacrifice that was to be presented only by a priest.

- *Denial.* After Samuel told Saul that he'd been rejected as king, Saul continued as though all was well.

- *Impulsiveness.* He was reckless and rashly made an oath that almost cost him the life of his son, Jonathan.

- *Deceit.* He used his daughter Michal as a bribe by offering her in marriage to David if he would fight the Philistines, but Saul's real hope was that David would die in battle.

- *Jealousy.* He became enraged when the people compared him to David. From then on he kept a jealous eye on the man he considered his enemy.

- *Anger.* More than once he attempted to kill David with a spear as David played the harp for him.

The majority of Saul's lids had to do with his weak character. Unfortunately he was always more concerned with keeping up appearances than cleaning up his character. Even when he was rejected as king, Saul was most concerned about what others would think of him. He begged Samuel, "I have sinned; yet honor me now, please, before the elders of my people and before Israel" (1 Sam. 15:30 NKJV). Because he never removed the lids from his leadership, God had to remove him from the throne of Israel.

THE LIDS THAT DID *NOT* LIMIT DAVID

When you look at the life of David, you see that he also had many lids on his life, both internal and external:

1. HIS FAMILY

David's limitations started at home. When his father, Jesse, was asked to gather all his sons so that Samuel could select the next king of Israel, David wasn't invited to attend. His father overlooked and underappreciated him.

The same was true of his brothers. When David went to the battlefront to visit them, their contempt for him was clear. When David spoke out against Goliath's blasphemous challenges, his brothers insulted him and told him to go home.

2. HIS LEADER

Saul was continually trying to inhibit David's leadership and effectiveness. When David offered to fight Goliath, Saul told him, "You are not able to go against this Philistine to fight with him" (1 Sam. 17:33 NKJV). Then he tried to put his heavy armor on the boy. Later, Saul declared that David was his enemy. For many years, Saul repeatedly tried to kill him.

3. HIS BACKGROUND

Saul came from a good and powerful family. His father is described as "Kish the son of Abiel, the son of Zeror, the son of Bechorath, the son of Aphiah, a Benjamite, a mighty man of power" (1 Sam. 9:1 NKJV). He was undoubtedly a landowner, leader in his tribe, and military commander during times of war. David, on the other hand, was from a family of poor shepherds. He is described as the son of "Jesse the Bethlehemite," a man without lofty lineage or powerful position. And David wasn't the eldest son. He was the eighth and youngest in his family.

4. HIS YOUTHFULNESS AND INEXPERIENCE

When David was anointed by Samuel, he was merely a boy, and he had no experience leading anyone or anything but sheep. When he stepped forward to fight Goliath, he was considered "only a youth," and he had never fought in a battle. Time and again, people underestimated and disrespected him for those reasons.

Ultimately David became a great leader, yet it wasn't because he had no limitations in his life. He achieved much because he became a lid lifter. And that's the subject of tomorrow's lesson.

❧

TODAY'S QUESTION FOR REFLECTION:
What lids exist in your life?

Day 3

LEADERSHIP THOUGHT FOR TODAY:
Some lids can be lifted by the leader.

> Saul clothed David with his armor, and he put a bronze helmet on his head; he also clothed him with a coat of mail. David fastened his sword to his armor and tried to walk, for he had not tested them. And David said to Saul, "I cannot walk with these, for I have not tested them." So David took them off.
>
> 1 Samuel 17:38–39 (NKJV)

David was able to go far despite difficult circumstances and many limiting lids. Why? Because unlike Saul, he became a lid lifter. When you look at David's life, you see a pattern of lid lifting that helped him to continue growing and keep going to the next level. And the lifting of a leader's lids not only releases his personal potential but also lifts the lid on the potential of his people and the whole organization.

LIDS THAT DAVID LIFTED

1. DAVID LIFTED THE LID FOR HIMSELF FIRST

David's life demonstrates the practice of demanding personal improvement first. Look at his attitude toward Goliath. Even though he had never fought in battle, he used his previous experiences as a shepherd as preparation. He had learned to use a sling, and he had faced attacks from a lion and a bear, both dangerous beasts much more powerful than he was. From those experiences he grew in valor, confidence, and faith. So on the day he faced Goliath—when he faced the lid of his inexperience in warfare—he lifted his lid.

> To grow the organization, grow the leader.

People often ask me what it takes to grow an organization. And to that question I always give the same response: to grow the organization, grow the leader. Everything starts and ends with him. Because David first lifted his lid and grew, he removed what is the first and often the most limiting lid from the organization—the leader.

2. DAVID LIFTED THE LID FOR OTHERS CLOSE TO HIM

As soon as a leader lifts his lid, incredible things can start to happen. Before David arrived, the entire army of Israel stood in fear of the Philistines. They drew up their battle lines at the Elah Valley and listened to Goliath's abuse every morning and evening for *forty days*! And what did Saul, their leader, do? He hid. Saul was a lid on the entire army of Israel.

But as soon as David stepped in and exercised lid-lifting leadership by killing Goliath, he lifted the lid off the whole army: "When the Philistines saw that their champion was dead, they fled. Now the men of Israel and Judah arose and shouted, and pursued the Philistines . . . And the wounded of the Philistines fell along the road" (1 Sam. 17:51–52 NKJV). Israel's warriors handed them a resounding defeat.

3. DAVID LIFTED THE LID FOR THE WHOLE NATION

In time, as David continued to exercise deep faith and sound leadership, he lifted the lid for the entire nation. That process began almost immediately as the people observed, "Saul has slain his thousands, and David his ten thousands" (1 Sam. 18:7 NKJV). With David's leadership, the people finally began to believe that with God's favor, they could do anything. And Israel's victories over its enemies grew. By the end of David's reign, his kingdom solidified the regions of Israel and Judah, and also incorporated the powers of Edom, Moab, Ammon, and Zobah. The nation grew in power, and David's kingdom was second only to that of his son, Solomon.

Everyone loves an opportunity. But many people want an opportunity to come to them before they start improving themselves to capitalize on it. They think, *When I get the position, then I'll start growing.* That's doing things backward. David had it right. He grew first, lifting his personal lids, and by the time his big opportunity came, he was ready for it. And when he was confronted with a lid that he couldn't remove by himself, he allowed others to help him. More about that tomorrow.

TODAY'S QUESTION FOR REFLECTION:
What lids can you lift?

Day 4

LEADERSHIP THOUGHT FOR TODAY:
Few leaders let others lift lids in their lives.

Then Jonathan and David made a covenant, because he loved him as his own soul. And Jonathan took off the robe that was on him and gave it to David, with his armor, even to his sword and his bow and his belt . . . Now Saul spoke to Jonathan his son and to all his servants, that they should kill David; but Jonathan, Saul's son, delighted greatly in David. So Jonathan told David, saying, "My father Saul seeks to kill you. Therefore please be on your guard until morning, and stay in a secret place and hide. And I will go out and stand beside my father in the field where you are, and I will speak with my father about you. Then what I observe, I will tell you."

1 Samuel 18:3–4; 19:1–3

There are times when leaders face a problem or limitation that they cannot remove on their own. When some leaders hit those lids, they give up, and they stop growing. That's the beginning of the end for their organizations. But a few leaders, those with the courage and the humility to learn, get together with other leaders who are able to be lid lifters in their lives. That was the case for David, and the person who lifted the lid for him was none other than the son of Saul: Jonathan.

WHAT'S UP WITH LID LIFTERS?

Lid lifters always demonstrate three qualities that help others go to another level. They can always be counted on to . . .

1. LIFT UP OTHERS WITH THEIR WORDS

Lid lifters are encouragers. Scripture records that Jonathan and David made a covenant with each other:

Jonathan said to David: "The LORD God of Israel is witness! . . . If it pleases my father to do you evil, then I will report it to you and send you away, that you may go in safety. And the LORD be with you as He has been with my father. And you shall not only show me the kindness of the LORD while I still live, that I may not die; but you shall not cut off your kindness from my house forever, no, not when the LORD has cut off every one of the enemies of David from the face of the earth." So Jonathan made a covenant with the house of David, saying, "Let the LORD require it at the hand of David's enemies." (1 Sam. 20:12–16 NKJV)

Jonathan constantly lifted up David. And he was an encouragement to David when his future looked darkest. He gave David hope and helped him find the courage to keep going despite his desperate circumstances.

2. RAISE UP OTHERS WITH THEIR ACTIONS

Speaking positive words to someone is fairly easy. It takes commitment to back up words with actions. Jonathan was willing to do that—even though he nearly lost his life.

Jonathan was true to his word and reported his father's intention to kill David to his friend. But even before then, Jonathan had taken an active role in David's promotion and well-being. When he gave David his robe, armor, sword, bow, and belt, he was making a statement. The royal robe would make David, a commoner, stand out among all the other people of Israel. And the giving of his armor not only equipped David, but also honored him and indicated Jonathan's willingness to be vulnerable to him.

When Jonathan told David, "Whatever you yourself desire, I will do it for you" (1 Sam. 20:4 NKJV), he really meant it. And he backed it up with action.

3. GIVE UP SO OTHERS CAN GO UP

It's one thing to give encouragement and resources to people in order to lift them up. But it's another to sacrifice for them so that they can go to another level. Yet that's what Jonathan did.

As Saul's eldest son, Jonathan was the next in line for the throne of Israel. Jonathan should have hated David, the man God had anointed to displace him. But Jonathan was willing to give up everything for his friend:

David saw that Saul had come out to seek his life. And David was in the Wilderness of Ziph in a forest. Then Jonathan, Saul's son, arose and went to David in the woods and strengthened his hand in God. And he said to him, "Do not fear, for the hand of Saul my father shall not find you. *You shall be king over Israel,* and I shall be next to you. Even my father Saul knows that." So the two of them made a covenant before the LORD. (1 Sam. 23:15–18 NKJV, emphasis added)

> **Jonathan, whom anyone would expect to be a heavy lid on David's life, was instead determined to be his lid lifter.**

Jonathan, whom anyone would expect to be a heavy lid on David's life, was instead determined to be his lid lifter.

Without Jonathan's help, David would never have survived and made it to the throne.

There are some lids in life that you can't lift on your own. Sometimes, as in the case of David, a lid lifter looks for you. Other times, you have to go out and find one. But no matter what, if you want to go to the highest level, you can't get there alone.

TODAY'S QUESTION FOR REFLECTION:
Who are the lid lifters in your life?

Day 5

Bringing the Law to Life

TAKING IT IN

Think about the following statements:

1. Every person has the potential to become a leader.
2. Every leader has lids.
3. Some lids can be lifted by the leader.
4. Few leaders let others lift lids in their lives.

How aware are you of the various lids in your life? What is your attitude concerning them? Are you taking responsibility for lifting them as David did? And are you willing to be humble and vulnerable enough to allow a lid lifter into your life?

SORTING IT OUT

If you're not sure where you stand when it comes to understanding and applying the Law of the Lid, visit the Web site www.injoy.com/21 Minutes to take a free twenty-five-question assessment quiz that will help you measure your ability.

PRAYING IT THROUGH

Use the following words to begin your time of prayer:

Dear God, I want to be a better leader. Give me a teachable attitude. Then show me the lids in my life. Reveal my character flaws to me, and help me to

repair them. Show me where I need to grow. And as I come up against lids that
are outside me and beyond my control, please send me a lid lifter like Jonathan.
I place myself in Your hands. Amen.

LIVING IT OUT

Take some time today to write down all the lids you detect in your life. Start
by focusing on internal characteristics, which may include character qualities, leadership skills, and relational capabilities. Then move on to list external lids, which may be related to your circumstances, age, and so on.

Now sort the lids into three categories: (1) lids I can lift (plan how you
will address these needs personally); (2) lids others can lift (look for mentors
to help you with them); and (3) facts of life (get used to them because you
can't change them).

PASSING IT ON

Which one leadership concept, insight, or practice that you've learned this
week will you pass on to another leader in the next two days?

Week 2

THE LAW OF INFLUENCE

THE TRUE MEASURE OF LEADERSHIP IS INFLUENCE—NOTHING MORE, NOTHING LESS

Leadership is influence—nothing more, nothing less. When you become a student of leaders, as I am, you begin to recognize people's level of influence in everyday situations all around you . . . One of the people I admire and respect most as a leader is my good friend Bill Hybels, the senior pastor of Willow Creek Community Church in South Barrington, Illinois, the largest church in North America. Bill says he believes that the church is the most leadership-intensive enterprise in society . . . What is the basis of his belief? Positional leadership doesn't work in volunteer organizations . . . In other organizations, the person who has position has incredible leverage . . . in the form of salary, benefits, and perks . . . But in voluntary organizations, such as churches, the only thing that works is leadership in its purest form. Leaders have only their influence to aid them. And as Harry A. Overstreet observed, "The very essence of all power to influence lies in getting the other person to participate." Followers in voluntary organizations cannot be forced to get on board. If the leader has no influence with them, then they won't follow.

FROM "THE LAW OF INFLUENCE" IN *The 21 Irrefutable Laws of Leadership*

Day 1

Joshua
and the
Law of Influence

LEADERSHIP THOUGHT FOR TODAY:
Leadership impact increases as influence increases.

Read
Numbers 13:1–33; 14:1–38; 27:12–23;
Joshua 1:1–18

The day that Joshua and Caleb stood before the children of Israel and tried to get them to enter the promised land, I doubt the two men really understood all that was at stake. They certainly possessed the vision of God for His people to enter the promised land. When the people resisted their rallying cry, the two men told them, "The land we passed through to spy out is an exceedingly good land. If the LORD delights in us, then He will bring us into this land and give it to us, a land which flows with milk and honey" (Num. 14:7–8 NKJV).

They also recognized the power of God to defeat their enemies. Both Joshua and Caleb had been present when God had closed the Red Sea over Pharoah's army. But did they truly understand that their ability (or, rather, their inability) to lead the people in that moment would determine whether an entire generation of people would enjoy the land of milk and honey promised to their ancestors—or die in the desert?

Obedience to God is important. Because Joshua and Caleb were obedient, they alone of the adult Jewish population entered the promised land. But for leaders, obedience isn't enough. If they can't take others on the trip, they fail their God-given mission.

THE NATURE OF LEADERSHIP

1. LEADERSHIP IS INFLUENCE

Joshua came face-to-face with the true nature of leadership when he failed to influence the people to do what they should have done alone. His *position* as tribal leader did nothing to help him influence others.

2. LEADERS DO NOT POSSESS INFLUENCE IN EVERY AREA

According to Numbers 13:2, those selected to spy out the promised land were "every one a leader." That means Joshua was a leader and had influence. But evidently his influence didn't reach beyond his tribe.

3. OUR INFLUENCE IS EITHER POSITIVE OR NEGATIVE

The Scripture says nothing about the mood of the people as they waited for the return of the spies from the promised land, but they must have been in a state of anticipation. I believe that if all of the spies had given a good report, the people of Israel would have obeyed God and crossed into the land. But influence is a two-edged sword. It cuts both positively and negatively. The ten unfaithful tribal leaders used their influence to lead the people astray, and the result was disaster, not only for those leaders, but also for all of the followers.

4. FAITHFUL LEADERS USE THEIR INFLUENCE TO ADD VALUE

Influencers who lead because they desire to advance their own agendas manipulate the people for their own gain. That's what the other ten spies did. They were afraid, and they used their influence to create fear in the people of Israel. They lied to the people, saying the land "devours its inhabitants." On the other hand, Joshua and Caleb desired to motivate the people to do what was right for the benefit of everyone. That is always the agenda of great leaders.

5. WITH INFLUENCE COMES RESPONSIBILITY

Maybe the ten unfaithful tribal leaders didn't desire to start a rebellion. But that's what they did. Following their negative report about the promised land, the people sought to depose Moses and Aaron and return to the slavery of Egypt. As a result, those ten leaders died of plague, and all of their follow-ers died in the desert.

INFLUENCING OTHERS IS A CHOICE

Many people who experience ineffectiveness as leaders give up and never try to lead again. Fortunately for the children of Israel, Joshua was not that type of person. He desired to become a better leader. And he would later receive a second chance. Meanwhile, he continued to be faithful to God and to learn as much as he could from Moses, who became his mentor.

❧

TODAY'S QUESTION FOR REFLECTION:
What are you currently doing to increase your influence?

Day 2

LEADERSHIP THOUGHT FOR TODAY:
When a leader has little influence,
little can be accomplished.

All the congregation lifted up their voices and cried, and the people wept that night . . . [They cried,] "Why has the LORD brought us to this land to fall by the sword, that our wives and children should become victims? Would it not be better for us to return to Egypt?" So they said to one another, "Let us select a leader and return to Egypt." . . . But Joshua the son of Nun and Caleb the son of Jephunneh, who were among those who had spied out the land, tore their clothes . . . And the LORD spoke to Moses and Aaron, saying, "How long shall I bear with this evil congregation who complain against Me? . . . Say to them, 'As I live,' says the LORD, 'just as you have spoken in My hearing, so I will do to you: The carcasses of you who have complained against Me shall fall in this wilderness, all of you who were numbered, according to your entire number, from twenty years old and above. Except for Caleb the son of Jephunneh and Joshua the son of Nun, you shall by no means enter the land . . . But your little ones, whom you said would be victims, I will bring in, and they shall know the land which you have despised.'"

Numbers 14:1, 3–4, 6, 26–31 (NKJV)

Gaining influence with people takes time. It isn't achieved overnight. Joshua discovered that when he and Caleb tried to get the people to go into the promised land. Scripture indicates that no one followed their leadership.

A leader's influence must be greater than the people's resistance. That is especially important when the people face a formidable challenge or extremely difficult circumstances.

As my friend Andy Stanley says, "You can't resist the will of God and receive the grace of God at the same time." In the case of Joshua, the people's resistance was huge, and Joshua's influence was small.

> "You can't resist the will of God and receive the grace of God at the same time."
>
> —ANDY STANLEY

WHY THE PEOPLE RESISTED JOSHUA

Three major factors caused the people to disregard Joshua and Caleb's advice and resist their leadership:

1. THEY FORGOT THE PAST

When the Jews were in Egypt, the Egyptians "made their lives bitter with hard bondage" (Ex. 1:14 NKJV). Though they hadn't been gone from Egypt long, they had already forgotten how miserable their lives had been there.

2. THEY WERE SETTLED IN WITH THE PRESENT

God had answered the people's cries for help by sending them a leader to take them out of Egypt, out of slavery. Then in their disobedience, they refused to enter Canaan, and they actually looked for a leader who would take them back.

3. THEY FEARED THE FUTURE

The root of their problems was fear. Joshua and Caleb looked at the land of Canaan and saw only potential. The rest of the people looked and saw only pitfalls, even though God Himself had *promised* them the land.

When followers are faced with the prospect of taking unknown territory, they always experience fear. The greater the challenge, the greater their fear is likely to be. What causes them to overcome that fear and move forward in spite of it? Leadership. It's the size of the leader, not the size of the challenge, that determines whether people conquer new territory. If a leader's influence is great enough, the people will follow.

When Joshua and Caleb tried to lead the people into the promised land the first time, they lacked influence, and as a result, they accomplished little. But forty years later, when Joshua tried again, the people gladly followed. Why? Because he had become a person of great influence. And leadership is influence—nothing more, nothing less.

TODAY'S QUESTION FOR REFLECTION:
Is there an area where you aren't accomplishing as much as you could?

Day 3

LEADERSHIP THOUGHT FOR TODAY:
*When a leader has much influence,
much can be accomplished.*

We make it our goal to please him, whether we are at home in the body or away from it. For we must all appear before the judgment seat of Christ, that each one may receive what is due him for the things done while in the body, whether good or bad. Since, then, we know what it is to fear the Lord, *we try to persuade men.* What we are is plain to God, and I hope it is also plain to your conscience.

2 Corinthians 5:9–11 (NIV, emphasis added)

How was Joshua, once a tribal leader incapable of persuading the people, transformed into a leader able to take the children of Israel into the land promised to their forefathers? Why did his influence grow so much?

JOSHUA'S INFLUENCE GREW
BECAUSE HE WAS RIGHT

From the beginning, Joshua had tried to do the right thing. He had tried to lead the people in the direction they should go. The first generation missed their opportunity to obey God and prosper. The next generation didn't.

Not only was Joshua right, but he also tried to model right living. As a result, he consistently lived beyond his ability as a leader. If you desire to do great things in your leadership, then try to live according to this pattern that Joshua modeled.

1. PRAYER

Joshua was a man of prayer. When Moses returned to camp following his times with God, "Joshua the son of Nun, a young man, did not depart from the tabernacle" (Ex. 33:11 NKJV). He didn't ride his mentor's coattails. He developed his own relationship with God.

> "Never try to explain God until you've obeyed him. The only part of God we understand is the part we have obeyed."
>
> —OSWALD CHAMBERS

2. OBEDIENCE

Preacher and missionary Oswald Chambers said, "Never try to explain God until you've obeyed him. The only part of God we understand is the part we have obeyed." Joshua obeyed God as a servant, a warrior, and a leader. When he spoke to the children of Israel to persuade them to enter Canaan, he did so as someone who understood God. The Hebrews did not share that same understanding.

3. FAITH

Joshua's life was marked by courage—as he stood up against the other spies, as he fought the Amalekites. And courage is nothing more than faith in action. He lived his life by this formula:

$$\text{Courage} + \text{Obedience Today} = \text{Success Tomorrow}$$

When a leader's faith is great, he or she can do anything. As the saying goes: "God puts no limitation on faith; and faith puts no limitation on God."

4. COMMITMENT

Joshua's level of commitment can be seen in his willingness to risk his life. He fought in battles where he was vastly outnumbered, and the Israelites wanted to stone him when he stood up to them. But he never failed to give his best for what he believed. And as football legend George Halas remarked, "Nobody who ever gave his best regretted it."

5. PARTNERSHIP

During World War II, King George VI of England encouraged his people with the following words:

And I said to a man who stood at the gate of the yard, "Give me a light, that I may tread safely into the unknown." And he replied: "Go out into the darkness, and put your hand into the hand of God, that will be to you better than a light, and safer than a known way."

Through partnership with God, Joshua and the children of Israel were able to conquer Canaan. The conquest of Jericho most clearly shows that partnership with God outweighs any other advantage.

Joshua's first order of priority was his character. He always valued what was right over what was popular. That provided a strong foundation upon which to build greater influence.

JOSHUA'S INFLUENCE GREW BECAUSE OF HIS RELATIONSHIP WITH MOSES

The other major factor in Joshua's increase in influence was the impact of Moses on his life. Not long after the children of Israel escaped from Egypt, Moses selected Joshua to be his assistant. He was described as one of Moses' "choice men" (Num. 11:28 NKJV). Wherever Moses went, Joshua went with him, whether it was to go up Mount Sinai or to meet with God in the tabernacle.

After the Hebrews refused to enter the promised land, the mentoring relationship between the two men continued. The process lasted forty years and culminated with Moses imparting his authority to the younger man. We read in Deuteronomy 31:7 (NKJV): "Then Moses called Joshua and said to him in the sight of all Israel, 'Be strong and of good courage, for you must go with this people to the land which the LORD has sworn to their fathers to give them, and you shall cause them to inherit it.'" After Moses died, no one questioned Joshua's leadership.

> "God is looking for people through whom He can do the impossible—what a pity that we plan only the things we can do by ourselves."
>
> —A. W. TOZER

Preacher and writer A. W. Tozer said, "God is looking for people through whom He can do the impossible—what a pity that we plan only the things we can do by ourselves." Crossing over into the promised land and conquering its people was a humanly impossible task, yet Joshua was willing to take on that challenge. And by the time he got his second chance to do it, he had enough influence with the people to take them along.

❧

TODAY'S QUESTION FOR REFLECTION:
In what areas are you accomplishing much through your influence?

Day 4

LEADERSHIP THOUGHT FOR TODAY:
When a leader places family first, future generations will be blessed.

[Joshua said,] "Now therefore, fear the LORD, serve Him in sincerity and in truth, and put away the gods which your fathers served on the other side of the River and in Egypt. Serve the LORD! And if it seems evil to you to serve the LORD, choose for yourselves this day whom you will serve, whether the gods which your fathers served that were on the other side of the River, or the gods of the Amorites, in whose land you dwell. *But as for me and my house, we will serve the LORD.*" So the people answered and said: "Far be it from us that we should forsake the LORD to serve other gods; for the LORD our God is He who brought us and our fathers up out of the land of Egypt, from the house of bondage, who did those great signs in our sight, and preserved us in all the way that we went and among all the people through whom we passed. And the LORD drove out from before us all the people, including the Amorites who dwelt in the land. We also will serve the LORD, for He is our God."

Joshua 24:14–18 (NKJV, emphasis added)

As a leader, where should your influence begin? A good answer can be drawn from the life of Joshua. For him—as for other leaders wanting to make an impact beyond their lifetimes—it began at home. Before anything else, Joshua took responsibility for the spiritual life of his family. Take a look at Joshua's values when it came to leadership:

❧

When a leader puts his family first, the community benefits. When a leader puts the community first, both his family and the community suffer.

---

1. JOSHUA'S LEADERSHIP OF HIS FAMILY WAS GREATER THAN HIS LEADERSHIP OF THE COUNTRY

It may sound ironic, but when a leader puts his family first, the community benefits. When a leader puts the community first, both his family and the community suffer. Starting at home is always the key to affecting others in a positive way. Because Joshua had his priorities right and had led his household well, he gained credibility to lead the entire house of Israel.

2. REGARDLESS OF WHAT OTHERS DID, JOSHUA DIDN'T WAIT FOR THE CROWD

When Joshua stood before the people of Israel and declared that no matter what the rest of the people did, he would follow God, he wasn't bluffing or grandstanding. I believe he meant it. When the people responded that they would follow God, Joshua tested and warned them:

> Joshua said to the people, "You cannot serve the LORD, for He is a holy God. He is a jealous God; He will not forgive your transgressions nor your sins. If you forsake the LORD and serve foreign gods, then He will turn and do you harm and consume you, after He has done you good." (Josh. 24:19–20 NKJV)

Joshua didn't follow the crowd at the beginning of his career when the spies rebelled against God and Moses, and he didn't follow the crowd when his career was at its end. He led his family with integrity and encouraged them to do what was right.

3. JOSHUA MODELED FAITH-FILLED LEADERSHIP AS A PARENT

Yesterday I discussed the kind of life Joshua lived, a life of prayer, faith, and obedience. For the health of a family, nothing can replace the modeling of a spiritual leader.

I was privileged to have virtuous parental models at home. My parents, Melvin and Laura Maxwell, influenced the path of my life because I consistently

- heard them pray earnestly and often.

- listened as they talked about the things of God.

- heard them share their faith with others.

- saw them put God first in their finances.

- went with them to visit the unfortunate.

- heard them say only positive things about other people.

- watched them grow mentally and spiritually.

- sensed their deep love and commitment for each other.

- sensed their relationship of intimacy with God.

If you have a family, I want to encourage you to put them first in your leadership. There is no legacy like that of the positive influence a leader can exercise with his family.

A wonderful example of this kind of influence can be found in the early years of American history. Jonathan Edwards, the notable preacher of the early eighteenth century, and his wife, Sarah, left an incredible legacy based on their influence. Their descendants include the following:

- Thirteen college presidents

- Sixty-five college professors

- One hundred lawyers, including the dean of a law school

- Thirty judges

- Sixty-six physicians, including the dean of a medical school

- Eighty holders of public office, including three U.S. senators, three mayors of large cities, three governors, a U.S. vice president, and a controller of the U.S. Treasury

If you want to impact your community, your country, or your world, the place to start is in your home.

⚬⟞

TODAY'S QUESTION FOR REFLECTION:
Are you truly placing your family first?

Day 5

Bringing the Law to Life

TAKING IT IN

You've spent the last few days reading about the Law of Influence and Joshua's leadership. Take five to ten minutes and meditate on the following statements and their implications for the way you approach leadership:

1. Leadership impact increases as influence increases.

2. When a leader has little influence, little can be accomplished.

3. When a leader has much influence, much can be accomplished.

4. When a leader places family first, future generations will be blessed.

SORTING IT OUT

If you're not sure where you stand when it comes to understanding and applying the Law of Influence, visit the Web site www.injoy.com/21 Minutes to take a free twenty-five-question assessment quiz that will help you measure your ability.

PRAYING IT THROUGH

Use the following words to begin your time of prayer:

Dear God, reveal to me my true level of influence on others. Show me my weaknesses so that I may submit them to You for Your grace. Strengthen me so that I can better serve You through leadership, and increase my influence with others. Teach me to be salt and light to others, not to benefit myself, but to add value to others. And above all, empower me to place my family first when it comes to leadership. Let my influence begin with the modeling of a faithful life. Amen.

LIVING IT OUT

What must you do to increase your influence, to be more like Joshua? Do you need to realign your moral compass so that you do what's right? Do you need to develop better relationships with the people you lead? Should you find a mentor to be your "Moses"? Or do you need to reorder your priorities to put your family first? What concrete, specific action can you take immediately to improve your ability to live the Law of Influence?

PASSING IT ON

Which one leadership concept, insight, or practice that you've learned this week will you pass on to another leader in the next two days?

Week 3

THE LAW OF PROCESS

LEADERSHIP DEVELOPS DAILY, NOT IN A DAY

Becoming a leader is a lot like investing successfully in the stock market. If your hope is to make a fortune in a day, you're not going to be successful. What matters most is what you do day by day over the long haul. My friend Tag Short maintains, "The secret of our success is found in our daily agenda." If you continually invest in your leadership development, letting your "assets" compound, the inevitable result is growth over time . . .

Although it's true that some people are born with greater natural gifts than others, the ability to lead is really a collection of skills, nearly all of which can be learned and improved. But that process doesn't happen overnight. Leadership is complicated. It has so many facets: respect, experience, emotional strength, people skills, discipline, vision, momentum, timing—the list goes on . . . That's why leaders require so much seasoning to be effective . . .

The good news is that your leadership ability is not static. No matter where you're starting from, you can get better.

FROM "THE LAW OF PROCESS" IN *The 21 Irrefutable Laws of Leadership*

Day 1

Joseph
and the
Law of Process

LEADERSHIP THOUGHT FOR TODAY:
It's not the dream of a lifetime; it's the dream that takes a lifetime.

Read
Genesis 37:1–36; 39:1–42:6; 47:13–26

In many ways, Joseph was like other great leaders. First, all leaders have a dream, a vision of a better future. In Joseph's case, he experienced literal *visions*. Second, the vision and the person who has the vision are inseparable. The leader's heart beats for the vision, and he won't be content until it is fulfilled. Another person cannot fulfill that leader's dream for him. Joseph and his vision were divinely destined to be intertwined. Third, no leader's vision can be kept secret. When vision is shared in the right way, it can enhance a person's leadership. But when it's done in the wrong way, it creates problems. And that, of course, is what got Joseph in trouble.

INTO THE FIRE

Like most great leaders, Joseph had a vision long before he had the leadership ability to make it happen. He had a divine leadership destiny, but he didn't start out as an effective leader. He held

> Before God could use him, Joseph had to be prepared, purified, and forged into the leader he had the potential to become.

no influence with his brothers, or with anyone other than his father, for that matter. Before God could use him, Joseph had to be prepared, purified, and forged into the leader he had the potential to become.

All great leaders need three things to prepare them:

1. TIME TO MATURE

Like most great leaders, Joseph labored in obscurity for a season of his life before becoming qualified to lead others. Sold into slavery at only seventeen, he finally stood before Pharaoh for the first time at age thirty. He required thirteen years to be prepared. By the time he interpreted the monarch's dream, he was a changed man. He was equipped. He was humble. He was a great leader.

2. TRIALS TO STRENGTHEN

Gold is purified only after it passes repeatedly through the fire. Diamonds are created only under extreme pressure. And great leaders are formed only through trials. Joseph would never have reached his potential if he had stayed at home. To become a great leader, he had to become a slave and a prisoner.

3. GOD TO BLESS

Without God, a leader can do nothing of real value. Jesus declared, "He who abides in Me, and I in him, bears much fruit; for without Me you can do nothing" (John 15:5 NKJV).

God blessed Joseph as he worked in Potiphar's house as a slave. Then He blessed him as he worked in the prison. Four times in chapter 39 of Genesis the Bible expresses God's favor. For example, Genesis 39:23 states, "The LORD was with him; and whatever he did, the LORD made it prosper." If you're on God's side, you can't lose.

TODAY'S QUESTION FOR REFLECTION:
Are you willing to pay the price to accomplish your dream?

Day 2

LEADERSHIP THOUGHT FOR TODAY:
It takes time to grow as a leader.

> While the earth remains,
> Seedtime and harvest,
> Cold and heat,
> Winter and summer,
> And day and night
> Shall not cease.
>
> Genesis 8:22 (NKJV)

Joseph was a cocky kid. That's not unusual for a boy of seventeen. It seems he lived out the saying that goes, "Solve the world's problems before you turn twenty—while you still know everything." But Joseph was worse than that. He was too arrogant for his own good. It wasn't enough for him to be the favorite of his father, Jacob, and to be the "son of his old age," the child who received special favor and treatment above all of his older brothers. Joseph had to rub it in.

When God gave Joseph a dream revealing that he would one day become the leader of his family—not only of his eleven brothers but also of his parents—Joseph thoughtlessly told everyone about it. Twice. His father rebuked him. His brothers wanted revenge. And they got it.

JOSEPH AND THE FOUR PHASES OF LEADERSHIP GROWTH

Early in his life, Joseph's skill at working with people was weak. Worse, he lacked experience, wisdom, and humility—three qualities that can be gained only with the passage of time. If you look at Joseph's life, you can see how time and experience contributed to his daily leadership development as he went through the following four phases:

> Early in his life, Joseph lacked experience, wisdom, and humility—three qualities that can be gained only with the passage of time.

PHASE 1: I DON'T KNOW WHAT I DON'T KNOW

Everyone starts out in a state of ignorance. That's where Joseph began. He didn't understand the dynamics of his family. Either he was ignorant of how his brothers would react when he shared his dream about the sheaves bowing down, or he didn't care about the damage he would do to their relationships. The Scripture says his brothers already hated him; when he shared his dream, they hated him even more.

Joseph didn't know what he was doing. He was doing and saying things without understanding the existing interpersonal issues. The cost was alienation from his family for more than two decades.

PHASE 2: I KNOW WHAT I DON'T KNOW

It took a life-changing incident to arrest Joseph's attention and start him on the road to change. Thrust into slavery in Egypt, he began to learn about what he didn't know. He came to understand that leadership is difficult and carries a huge weight of responsibility. Over the years, Joseph experienced betrayal, and he received lessons in human nature, relationships, and leadership. The process molded his character. He developed patience and humility. And he began to recognize that God was his Source of blessing and power.

PHASE 3: I GROW AND KNOW AND IT STARTS TO SHOW

Leaders who show great skill when opportunity presents itself do so only because they've paid the price to prepare for that opportunity. When Joseph was finally called before Pharaoh, he performed with excellence and wisdom. He didn't succeed because he suddenly got good at age thirty. He succeeded because he had been paying the price for thirteen years. Because of his wisdom and discernment, Joseph was made second in command of what was then the most powerful nation on earth.

PHASE 4: I SIMPLY GO BECAUSE OF WHAT I KNOW

For seven years, during the time of plenty in Egypt, Joseph skillfully executed his leadership plan. He filled the cities of Egypt with grain, and he prepared the country for the coming famine. His previous years of pain and growth were paying off in a big way. But you can really see how far his leadership had come only by observing what he did during the lean years that followed. His primary goal was to feed the people of Egypt during the seven difficult years. But because of the strength of his leadership, Joseph fed his monarch's nation, and he sustained the people of other lands. In the process, he brought all the money, livestock, and land of Egypt into his master's possession. He also fulfilled the prophecy of his teenage dreams.

To become an effective leader, a person needs time. But time alone doesn't make someone an effective leader. Some people never discover the Law of Process. They don't work at growth, and they remain in phase 1 their entire lives.

❧

TODAY'S QUESTION FOR REFLECTION:
Which phase of leadership growth are you in?

Day 3

Therefore be patient, brethren, until the coming of the Lord. See how the farmer waits for the precious fruit of the earth, waiting patiently for it until it receives the early and latter rain. You also be patient. Establish your hearts, for the coming of the Lord is at hand . . . My brethren, take the prophets, who spoke in the name of the Lord, as an example of suffering and patience. Indeed we count them blessed who endure. You have heard of the perseverance of Job and seen the end intended by the Lord—that the Lord is very compassionate and merciful.

James 5:7–11 (*NKJV*)

When the future leadership responsibilities are especially difficult (or the potential leader is particularly hardheaded), God uses time to pass for the maturation process. He also allows trials. The larger the task ahead, the more difficult the trials. That was true for many prominent leaders in Scripture: Moses, Daniel, Job, Naomi, David, Esther, Peter, Paul, and many others. Joseph was among that group.

When faced with adversity, people become either bitter or better. Joseph chose the latter. He certainly had plenty of opportunities to become negative. He could have held a grudge against many individuals: his brothers, the slave traders, Potiphar's wife, and the chief butler. But instead he turned to God in the midst of his struggle and viewed the people who offended him as instruments of divine sovereignty.

THE POSITIVE OUTCOME OF NEGATIVE EXPERIENCES

Why were Joseph's problems such an integral part of his growth as a leader? When people react positively to trials, many remarkable things result.

1. THEY GLORIFY GOD

Joseph didn't mope, rebel, or curse God for his troubles. Instead, he gave God credit for his victories. As God received the glory, Joseph received God's blessing.

2. THEY RECEIVE OPPORTUNITIES

What could be worse than being sold into slavery and taken by force to another country? As bad as that experience was for Joseph, it was the key to every other opportunity he received. Without the trial of slavery, Joseph never would have experienced the triumph of leadership in such a powerful nation.

3. THEY DEVELOP INTEGRITY

Joseph wasn't long in Potiphar's house before he faced a difficult decision. He was already enjoying all the comforts of Potiphar's household. But then he had the opportunity to enjoy the man's wife. He refused, even though it meant he would go to prison.

Only in testing do people discover the nature and depth of their character. People can *say* anything they want about their values, but when the pressure is on, they discover what their values really are.

4. THEY GROW SPIRITUALLY

Psalm 105:17–19 speaks about Joseph's time of trials:

> He sent a man before them—
> Joseph—who was sold as a slave.
> They hurt his feet with fetters,
> He was laid in irons.
> Until the time that his word came to pass,
> The word of the LORD tested him. (NKIV).

An older English translation of that passage states that "iron came into his soul." Adversity shows a person his mettle.

5. THEY BECOME PREPARED IN MIND AND HEART FOR LEADERSHIP

It took more than a decade, but Joseph eventually learned to value difficult people and awful situations, seeing them as divine instruments in his development. Joseph became a leader in Egypt only after he passed each test that he faced in life. By the time he became second in command to Pharaoh, he was a proven leader. He had experienced personal calamity, remained true to God, and learned to lead under difficult circumstances. That gave him the wisdom and experience he needed for what lay ahead.

Joseph learned that God could not use him until he had been tested and proved. As he told his brothers, "Do not therefore be grieved or angry with yourselves because you sold me here; for God sent me before you to preserve life . . . So now it was not you who sent me here, but God" (Gen. 45:5, 8 NKJV).

TODAY'S QUESTION FOR REFLECTION:
Do you make a practice of learning from the trials in your life?

Day 4

LEADERSHIP THOUGHT FOR TODAY:
It takes God's help to grow as a leader.

Trust in the LORD, and do good;
Dwell in the land and cultivate faithfulness.
. . . .
Rest in the LORD and wait patiently for Him;
Do not fret.
. . . .
For evildoers will be cut off,
But those who wait for the LORD, they will inherit the land.
. . . .
The steps of a man are established by the LORD;
And He delights in his way.

Psalm 37:3, 7–9, 23 (NASB)

Like most great leaders, Joseph labored in obscurity for a season of his life before he became qualified to lead others. And it is during this period that God most often works to prepare a potential leader. That was true for Abraham, Jacob, Nehemiah, and many others.

Nearly twenty-three years passed from the pit to the palace before he was reunited with his brothers and his own vision was fulfilled. But by then, he had come to learn that true progress occurs only when God orchestrates it. He understood that self-promotion can never replace divine promotion. And he learned that lesson the hard way. His self-promotion with his brothers failed miserably. Only when he finally became submissive—as a slave—and chose to work faithfully

> True progress occurs only when God orchestrates it. Joseph understood that self-promotion can never replace divine promotion.

for Potiphar did it become evident that the Lord was with him. In prison, he served the jail's keeper, and again God showed him favor and mercy. It didn't take long for the prisoners to be put under Joseph's authority. And his work prospered.

When Joseph tried to take self-promotion back into his hands—by recommending himself to Pharaoh's chief butler—God again made him wait. Two years passed before Joseph got an audience with the monarch. By then, Joseph had learned his lesson. He was content to recognize that God was in charge. When Pharaoh asked him to interpret his dreams, Joseph answered, "It is not in me; God will give Pharaoh an answer of peace" (Gen. 41:16 NKJV).

JOSEPH GAINED AN ETERNAL PERSPECTIVE

It took a lot of growth, but Joseph eventually realized that God was directing the process of his leadership development. And he recognized that he was being grown as a leader for a much greater purpose than he could have imagined.

By the time Jacob, his father, died, Joseph had learned to see things more from God's perspective. When his brothers feared for their lives, Joseph summed up his life using the following words: "Do not be afraid, for am I in the place of God? But as for you, you meant evil against me; but God meant it for good, in order to bring it about as it is this day, to save many people alive" (Gen. 50:19–20 NKJV).

Joseph could trace God's hand though his entire life. And he understood God's long-term plan for his people. At age 110, he told his family, "I am dying; but God will surely visit you, and bring you out of this land to the land of which He swore to Abraham, to Isaac, and to Jacob" (Gen. 50:24 NKJV). He understood how God had impacted his life and how He intended to help future generations.

TODAY'S QUESTION FOR REFLECTION:
How has God helped you as a leader?

Day 5

Bringing the Law to Life

TAKING IT IN

As you read through the following statements related to the Law of Process, think about how they apply to your life and leadership development:

1. It's not the dream of a lifetime; it's the dream that takes a lifetime.
2. It takes time to grow as a leader.
3. It takes trials to grow as a leader.
4. It takes God's help to grow as a leader.

Many factors in your leadership development are beyond your control. Others are not. Joseph didn't choose the timing of his life, the trials he faced, or the way in which God would bless him. But he did choose to learn and grow. That choice is also yours.

SORTING IT OUT

If you're not sure where you stand when it comes to understanding and applying the Law of Process, visit the Web site www.injoy.com/21 Minutes to take a free twenty-five-question assessment quiz that will help you measure your ability.

PRAYING IT THROUGH

Use the following words to begin your time of prayer:

Dear God, please put me on the road to greater leadership development. Reveal the dream You have for my life. Place it in my heart, and kindle my passion for it. While You help me to grow, teach me to embrace the whole development process. Give me patience when I need it and passion when it's appropriate. Teach me to look beyond my life and desires. And when I'm ready, show me the big picture as You did for Joseph. Amen.

LIVING IT OUT

Where are you in the leadership development process? Are you in the dream-development stage? Or do you already possess a dream that you desire to live out? Either way, you need to grow as a leader. The greater the vision, the greater the need for good leadership. Everything rises and falls on leadership.

Develop a personal growth plan for yourself.

- Identify the next three books on leadership you will read, and write on your calendar when you will read them.

- Select one conference to attend this year. Pay for the registration immediately, and put the conference on your calendar. Or start saving the money now by skipping luxuries in the coming weeks or months.

- Subscribe to one magazine or tape service that will sharpen your skills on a monthly basis.

- Pick a growth partner. Find someone with whom you can trade resources, discuss leadership, and solve problems as you meet them.

PASSING IT ON

What one leadership concept, insight, or practice that you've learned this week will you pass on to another leader in the next two days?

Week 4

THE LAW OF NAVIGATION

ANYONE CAN STEER THE SHIP,
BUT IT TAKES A LEADER TO CHART THE COURSE

Leaders who navigate do even more than control the direction in which they and their people travel. They see the whole trip in their minds before they leave the dock. They have a vision for their destination, they understand what it will take to get there, they know who they'll need on the team to be successful, and they recognize the obstacles long before they appear on the horizon . . . Sometimes it's difficult balancing optimism and realism, intuition and planning, faith and fact. But that's what it takes to be effective as a navigating leader . . .

Above everything else . . . the secret to the Law of Navigation is preparation. When you prepare well, you convey confidence and trust to the people . . . You see, it's not the size of the project that determines its acceptance, support, and success. It's the size of the leader . . . Leaders who are good navigators are capable of taking their people just about anywhere.

FROM "THE LAW OF NAVIGATION" IN *The 21 Irrefutable Laws of Leadership*

Day 1

Nehemiah
and the
Law of Navigation

LEADERSHIP THOUGHT FOR TODAY:
Leaders not only know where they're going;
they also know how to get there.

Read
Nehemiah 1:1–11; 2:1–20; 4:1–23; 6:15–16

When poet Robert Frost wrote, "Something there is that doesn't love a wall," he was commenting on how walls tend to fall down over time when left to the elements. Knowing that, imagine the condition of a wall after being ripped down by a conquering army and then allowed to sit unrepaired for more than a century. That describes the wall surrounding Jerusalem when Hanani returned to see his brother Nehemiah in the city of Shushan.

A city wall in ruins was a bad thing in those days. Not only did it leave a city open to attack, but it also prompted ridicule from neighboring powers. With Jerusalem, the unrepaired wall also gave foreigners a reason to scorn God, whose holy city it was. That is why Nehemiah wept, mourned, fasted, and prayed when he heard the news of the wall's condition.

During the 120 years after the walls were torn down by the Chaldeans (2 Chron. 36:19), literally tens of thousands of Jerusalem's people had seen the walls and done nothing. Maybe to them, rebuilding the wall seemed an impossible challenge, even in the city with plenty of workers. What the people needed was someone to rally them, plan their course of action, and take them through the rebuilding process. They needed a leader.

WHAT ONLY A NAVIGATOR CAN SEE

One of the most remarkable things about Nehemiah is that he could see the problem and the solution even though he had never been to Jerusalem. That's an incredible characteristic of all great leaders: they have vision unlike that of other people. And that's why they are capable of navigating groups of people. A leader sees . . .

- *Farther than others see.* Nehemiah was able to see the problem even though he was hundreds of miles away from Jerusalem. And he could picture the solution in his head.

- *More than others see.* Nehemiah knew that the wall could and should be rebuilt, and he knew what it would take to do it. Before he left Shushan, he asked the king to provide him with letters allowing him to gather materials and granting him safe passage to Judah.

- *Before others see.* None of Jerusalem's neighbors wanted to see the Jews rebuild their wall, and several enemy leaders conspired against Nehemiah and the people. But Nehemiah saw the danger coming and planned accordingly. He didn't give in to the plots of his enemies. And when the people sensed danger, he formulated strategies to defend the city and keep the people working at the same time.

The people needed only fifty-two days to rebuild a city wall that had lain in ruins for 120 years. And they were able to do it because they had a great leader to navigate for them.

Nehemiah knew his purpose, made his plans, and led the people through the process. His is truly one of the most remarkable stories of leadership ever recorded.

❧

TODAY'S QUESTION FOR REFLECTION:
Do you like to plan the trip, or are you content to just take it?

Day 2

LEADERSHIP THOUGHT FOR TODAY:
Leaders find purpose in the needs around them.

Where there is no vision, the people perish.
Proverbs 29:18 (KJV)

Have you ever thought about what prompts a leader to step forward and champion a cause? What starts that process? What brings the vision to life in the leader so that he can bring the people to life to fulfill it? The answer can be found in the life of Nehemiah.

HIS BURDEN TO BEAR

When Nehemiah heard his brother's report that the walls of Jerusalem were in ruins, he was devastated. After weeping for days, he was compelled to pray:

> "I pray, LORD God of heaven, O great and awesome God, You who keep Your covenant and mercy with those who love You and observe Your commandments, please let Your ear be attentive and Your eyes open, that You may hear the prayer of Your servant which I pray before You now, day and night, for the children of Israel Your servants, and confess the sins of the children of Israel which we have sinned against You . . . Now these are Your servants and Your people, whom You have redeemed by Your great power, and by Your strong hand. O Lord, I pray, please let Your ear be attentive to the prayer of Your servant, and to the prayer of Your servants who desire to fear Your name; and let Your servant prosper this day, I pray, and grant him mercy in the sight of this man." For I was the king's cupbearer. (Neh. 1:5–6, 10–11 NKJV)

In Nehemiah's time, being anything but happy in the presence of a Persian king was an offense punishable by death. Yet he felt compelled to speak to the king about the state of Jerusalem. Why? Because he had a burden for the city and people of Jerusalem.

THE POWER OF A BURDEN

Nehemiah didn't discover his purpose until he was confronted with a problem. That's the way it works for most godly leaders. They don't have to go looking for something that captures their hearts. The calling comes as the result of obediently seizing an opportunity that is close at hand. The burden precedes their vision for their leadership.

When leaders experience a burden prior to receiving a vision, it has many positive effects.

1. A BURDEN PURIFIES MOTIVES

The essence of a burden is the desire to do something beneficial for others. When you are drawn to serve, it's difficult to be self-seeking at the same time. Nehemiah had a good position at the luxurious court of the king. Traveling hundreds of miles to a ruined city would guarantee sacrifice, not personal gain.

2. A BURDEN CULTIVATES PERSISTENCE

Leadership is difficult. If you don't have persistence, you are likely to drop out of the race before the end. Nehemiah faced various challenges, and persistence carried him through.

3. A BURDEN CEMENTS CONVICTION

Lots of worthwhile activities clamor for a leader's attention. But a need is not necessarily a call. A burden helps a leader *know* that he

> Lots of worthwhile activities clamor for a leader's attention. But a need is not necessarily a call. A burden helps a leader *know* that he must take on a task.

must take on a task. Nehemiah put his life on the line more than once to fulfill his vision to rebuild Jerusalem.

In the case of Nehemiah, the report created the burden, and the burden led to the vision. Most people desire to have the vision first, but God doesn't often work that way in our lives.

I have found that when people have a burden, they experience particular emotions. Take a look at these questions:

- Does a person or a project constantly come to your mind as a concern?

- Do you seem unable to escape the needs of this concern?

- Are you constantly trying to challenge others to be concerned for this person or project?

- Do you migrate to books, sermons, or people that focus on your concern?

- Do you repeatedly give time and resources to meet this particular need?

- Does your concern move you to the point of tears?

- Do you have gifts and abilities to meet the needs associated with this concern?

- Does your concern increase or decrease with time?

If you look at the Scripture, I believe you can see that Nehemiah would have answered yes to all of these questions. Clearly the task of rebuilding Jerusalem's walls stirred his heart. And acting on that burden revealed the purpose of his life.

∞

TODAY'S QUESTION FOR REFLECTION:
What need around you stirs your heart?

Day 3

A leader follows the carpenter's rule: measure twice, saw once.

For which one of you, when he wants to build a tower, does not first sit down and calculate the cost, to see if he has enough to complete it? Otherwise, when he has laid a foundation, and is not able to finish, all who observe it begin to ridicule him, saying, "This man began to build and was not able to finish."

Luke 14:28–30 (NASB)

Nehemiah is rightfully considered one of the great planners and leaders in the Bible. He could be called Nehemiah the Navigator. If you look at the way he approached the planning of the rebuilding project, you can learn a lot from the way he did things.

NEHEMIAH'S NAVIGATION

Before the actual building process began, Nehemiah spent time getting himself and his people ready.

1. HE IDENTIFIED WITH THE PROBLEM

Nehemiah's first step was to inquire about the status of the Jews and the wall around Jerusalem. When he heard that the wall was rubble and that God's name was being mocked, he wept. The people's problem became his problem. It was his burden to bear.

2. HE SPENT TIME IN PRAYER

Almost immediately Nehemiah went to his knees to pray. He confessed his wrongdoing and that of the people. And he interceded for them. Then he asked for God's favor. I believe that it was during his time of connection with God that he got the vision and plan to rebuild the wall.

3. HE APPROACHED THE KEY INFLUENCERS

There is an incredible phrase in the Scripture where Nehemiah recounted, "So I prayed to the God of heaven. And I said to the king . . ." (Neh. 2:4–5 NKJV). In any leadership endeavor, key people of influence can make or break the whole undertaking. In this case, it was Persia's King Artaxerxes. From him, Nehemiah received not only permission to rebuild the wall, but also resources and support. And then Nehemiah undoubtedly selected and approached the other key people whom he took with him on the journey.

4. HE ASSESSED THE SITUATION

When he finally arrived in Jerusalem, Nehemiah surveyed firsthand the challenge he was facing. He did it quietly at night, personally assessing the damage and planning the project without unwanted interference or advice from others.

5. HE MET WITH THE PEOPLE AND CAST THE VISION

We don't know exactly how Nehemiah approached the people or with whom he met first, but we do know he communicated with the Jews, the priests, the nobles, the officials, and the people who did the work. He shared his vision for rebuilding the wall and the spiritual ramifications of the project.

6. HE ENCOURAGED THEM WITH PAST SUCCESSES

With a task as daunting as the rebuilding of the wall, Nehemiah knew he needed to encourage the people. He recalled, "I told them of the hand of my God which had been good upon me, and also of the king's words that he had spoken to me" (Neh. 2:18 NKJV).

7. HE RECEIVED BUY-IN FROM THE PEOPLE

Two short sentences record what happened next, but it was the turning point for the whole rebuilding process: "So they said, 'Let us rise up and build.' Then they set their hands to this good work" (Neh. 2:18). The people had bought in. They were willing to dedicate themselves to Nehemiah's leadership and his vision.

8. HE ORGANIZED THE PEOPLE AND GOT THEM WORKING

When the people worked, they didn't do it haphazardly. Nehemiah organized them by family and set them to work according to planned priorities, beginning with the city's gates.

A lot of work went into Nehemiah's approach to realizing his vision. He was a great leader of people, but without careful planning the wall never would have been built.

≫←

TODAY'S QUESTION FOR REFLECTION:
Do you make your plan before you make your move?

Day 4

LEADERSHIP THOUGHT FOR TODAY:
Leaders not only know where they're going;
they also take people with them.

We built the wall, and the entire wall was joined together up to half its height, for the people had a mind to work . . . Then Judah said, "The strength of the laborers is failing, and there is so much rubbish that we are not able to build the wall." And our adversaries said, "They will neither know nor see anything, till we come into their midst and kill them and cause the work to cease." So it was, when the Jews who dwelt near them came, that they told us ten times, :From whatever place you turn, they will be upon us." Therefore I positioned men behind the lower parts of the wall, at the openings; and I set the people according to their families, with their swords, their spears, and their bows . . . Those who built on the wall, and those who carried burdens, loaded themselves so that with one hand they worked at construction, and with the other held a weapon . . . And the one who sounded the trumpet was beside me.

Nehemiah 4:6, 10–11, 13, 17–18 (NKJV)

It's one thing to have a vision for a project. It's another to rally an entire city to undertake the task despite threats and fierce opposition from your enemies. Yet that's what Nehemiah did.

NEHEMIAH'S PEOPLE PRINCIPLES

The walls of Jerusalem were rebuilt because of Nehemiah's ability to work with people and lead them where they needed to go. If you look at the process of rebuilding, you can see that he practiced the following principles when working with people:

1. SIMPLIFICATION

He expressed the vision in the simplest terms possible. The people's goal was to rebuild the wall.

2. PARTICIPATION

He attempted to include as many people in the process as he could and moved forward with those who were ready. And he organized them in natural groupings based on relationships. They worked together by family.

3. DELEGATION

Nehemiah matched tasks with workers. He noted that "half of my servants worked at construction, while the other half held the spears, the shields, the bows, and wore armor; and the leaders were behind all the house of Judah" (Neh. 4:16 NKJV).

4. MOTIVATION

Nehemiah understood how to motivate people. He made sure they knew what they were fighting for, saying, "Remember the Lord, great and awesome, and fight for your brethren, your sons, your daughters, your wives, and your houses" (Neh. 4:14 NKJV). Then to make sure they didn't forget, he stationed them in front of their own houses.

5. PREPARATION

Because they faced the danger of attack at any time, Nehemiah prepared for the worst. He posted guards around the clock, and he kept the trumpeter with him. He let the people know what he had done so that they would feel more secure. He announced to everyone, "The work is great and extensive, and we are separated far from one another on the wall. Wherever you hear the sound of the trumpet, rally to us there. Our God will fight for us" (Neh. 4:19–20 NKJV).

6. COOPERATION

Nehemiah continually cultivated cooperation among the people. He stopped the practice of usury and created unity between the wealthy rulers and the people who felt oppressed. He also brought people together and fed them at his expense. Without cooperation, the wall would not have come together. That the entire work was completed in fifty-two days is a testament to the teamwork Nehemiah fostered among the people.

7. CELEBRATION

After the wall was completed, Nehemiah helped the people to celebrate. He arranged for thanksgiving choirs to sing, a huge feast to be prepared, and the Book of the Law to be read. And when Ezra finished reading and the people wept, Nehemiah told them, "Go your way, eat the fat, drink the sweet, and send portions to those for whom nothing is prepared; for this day is holy to our LORD. Do not sorrow, for the joy of the LORD is your strength" (Neh. 8:10 NKJV). Even Nehemiah's written recollection of the rebuilding of the wall is a celebration and encouragement to those who participated.

No great task is accomplished without both people to do the work and a leader to guide them. And when there is a convergence of the opportunity of the moment, the need of the people, the purpose of the leader, and the calling of God, even the impossible becomes possible.

> No great task is accomplished without both people to do the work and a leader to guide them.

TODAY'S QUESTION FOR REFLECTION:
Whom are you gathering for your leadership journey?

Day 5

Bringing the Law to Life

TAKING IT IN

Review the four leadership thoughts from this week:

1. Leaders not only know where they're going; they also know how to get there.
2. Leaders find purpose in the needs around them.
3. A leader follows the carpenter's rule: measure twice, saw once.
4. Leaders not only know where they're going; they also take people with them.

Think about which statement best describes your personal strength as a leader. Which reveals an area of weakness? Spend several minutes thinking about the reasons for each.

SORTING IT OUT

If you're not sure where you stand when it comes to understanding and applying the Law of Navigation, visit the Web site www.injoy.com/21 Minutes to take a free twenty-five-question assessment quiz that will help you measure your ability.

PRAYING IT THROUGH

Use the following words to begin your time of prayer:

Dear God, I know that You have a purpose for my life. I ask that You reveal or confirm that purpose in me day by day. Help me to be fully engaged in the sit-

uation You've placed me in at this season of my life and to connect with the burden You would place on my heart. Draw me forward in obedience to Your calling. And I ask that You would place in me the navigational ability of Nehemiah so that I am able to lead and guide the people to fulfill Your vision. Amen.

LIVING IT OUT

What project or process that you are currently facing do you need to be able to navigate others through? It can be something you are facing at home, at work, in ministry, or elsewhere. Set aside an appropriate amount of time to focus entirely on planning. A relatively simple task may require a few hours of planning. Something major may require a few days. Remember, the key to the Law of Navigation is preparation.

PASSING IT ON

Which one leadership concept, insight, or practice that you've learned this week will you pass on to another leader in the next two days?

Week 5

THE LAW OF E. F. HUTTON

WHEN THE REAL LEADER SPEAKS, PEOPLE LISTEN

Once you learn the Law of E. F. Hutton, you'll never have trouble figuring out who the real leader is in just about any situation . . . Go to a meeting with a group of people you've never met before and watch them for five minutes . . . When somebody asks a question, whom do people watch [for the answer]? Whom do they wait to hear? The person they look to is the real leader . . .

People listen to what someone has to say not necessarily because of the truth being communicated in the message, but because of their respect for the speaker . . . When Martin Luther King Jr. was alive . . . no matter where or when he spoke, people—black and white—listened. Today, Billy Graham gets a similar kind of respect because of his unquestionable integrity and lifetime of service. For nearly fifty years, his advice has been heeded by world leaders . . .

When it comes to identifying a real leader . . . the proof of leadership is found in the followers . . . When the real leader speaks, people listen.

FROM "THE LAW OF E. F. HUTTON" IN *The 21 Irrefutable Laws of Leadership*

Day 1

Samuel
and the
Law of E. F. Hutton

LEADERSHIP THOUGHT FOR TODAY:
Leaders earn the right to be heard.

Read
1 Samuel 1:8–28; 3:1–21; 7:2–15; 8:1–4; 10:1;
12:1–25; 13:1–15

Like any other leader, Samuel didn't start life as an E. F. Hutton. His ability to speak into the lives of others grew and developed over the course of time. But he did start unusually early. People began listening to him when he was just a boy. And once he was established as a voice of authority, he retained that level of influence throughout his life.

Samuel was special from the time he was born because he was an answer to prayer. As a very young child, he was placed in the care of Eli, the high priest and judge of Israel. The first record we have of his speaking as an E. F. Hutton occurred when Samuel told Eli of the prophecy he had received concerning the older priest's family. As young Samuel grew, his authority increased. Scripture tells us, "Samuel grew, and the LORD was with him and let none of his words fall to the ground" (1 Sam. 3:19 NKJV).

LEADERSHIP AT THE HIGHEST LEVEL

Samuel's level of influence with the people continued to increase throughout his lifetime. As a prophet, he was respected because he spoke for God. But in time, Samuel also became Israel's judge, a position similar to that of king. He was the nation's civil and military leader. We read in 1 Samuel 7:15 (NKJV), "Samuel judged Israel all the days of his life."

That put Samuel in a truly unique position. Before Christ, Samuel is the only person in Israel's history who functioned as prophet, priest, and king. No wonder people listened to him and followed his leadership.

Because Samuel occupied such well-established offices, you may be tempted to think that people listened to him only because of his position. But his leadership wasn't positional, despite his impressive titles. Without a doubt, he was an E. F. Hutton. You can be sure of that by observing the events that followed the one time the people *didn't* listen to him—when they asked him for a king.

God gave Samuel the authority to anoint a king for Israel. And in obedience to God, Samuel placed Saul on the throne, thus replacing himself as civil and military leader. But even though Samuel didn't sit on the throne, the people still listened to him and recognized his voice as that of the leader. When he spoke, *everyone* listened: laypeople and prophets, leaders and followers, peasants and kings. When he called warriors of Israel to battle, they fought. When he called the people of God to repent, they repented. When he called a king to come forward, he came. He was the greatest influencer of his generation. And when he died, the people lamented (1 Sam. 25:1). They knew they had lost a true leader and a great man of God.

TODAY'S QUESTION FOR REFLECTION:
Is anyone listening to you?

Day 2

Leaders should listen to God before asking others to listen to them.

Then Moses and the priests, the Levites, spoke to all Israel, saying, "Take heed and listen, O Israel: This day you have become the people of the LORD your God. Therefore you shall obey the voice of the LORD your God, and observe His commandments and His statutes which I command you today."

Deuteronomy 27:9–10 (NKJV)

What started Samuel on the path of great leadership? Was there a moment when the seeds of leadership were sown in his life, giving him hope for positive influence in the lives of others? I believe the answer is yes. Author Stephen R. Covey says, "Because you listen, you become influenceable. And being influence-

> "Because you listen, you become influenceable. And being influenceable is the key to influencing others."
> —STEPHEN R. COVEY

able is the key to influencing others." The turning point for Samuel occurred when he was only a boy, when he opened his heart to God and decided to be influenced by Him.

THE MAKING OF AN E. F. HUTTON

We can learn much from Samuel, not the least of which is how to be in a position to hear God's voice. Looking at what happened in Samuel's encounter with God, we can observe three things. Samuel assumed . . .

1. THE PROPER PRACTICE

Before God spoke to Samuel, he was doing what was right in God's eyes. The Scripture reports, "Samuel ministered before the LORD, even as a child"

(1 Sam. 2:18 NKJV), and goes on, "The child Samuel grew in stature, and in favor both with the LORD and men" (1 Sam. 2:26 NKJV). God blessed him because of his obedience.

As a leader, you must never neglect to do the right things in God's eyes, no matter what your other responsibilities require.

2. THE PROPER POSTURE

I once heard that someone asked Joan of Arc why God spoke only to her. She is said to have responded, "Sir, you are wrong. God speaks to everyone. I just listen."

A proper posture of quieting oneself and listening is essential to learning to recognize God's voice:

> Behold, the LORD passed by, and a great and strong wind tore into the mountains and broke the rocks in pieces before the LORD, but the LORD was not in the wind; and after the wind an earthquake, but the LORD was not in the earthquake; and after the earthquake a fire, but the LORD was not in the fire; and after the fire a still small voice. So it was, when Elijah heard it. (1 Kings 19:11–13 NKJV)

When God spoke to Samuel, it was as the boy lay down quietly in the middle of the night. Even then, Samuel did not at first recognize that the voice belonged to God. He needed the advice and wisdom of his experienced mentor, Eli, to understand who was communicating with him. But based on how often Samuel heard God's voice as an adult, it's clear that he learned to identify, listen to, and obey God's voice.

Leaders are often very busy people. And they can easily get caught up in the activity of their obligations. If you're a leader, that's why it's important to set aside times to quiet yourself and listen for God's direction. My friend Bill Hybels asserts, "Leaders need to ask God to give them Samuel's ear."

> "Leaders need to ask God to give them Samuel's ear."
> —BILL HYBELS

3. THE PROPER PLACE

Scripture records that when Samuel first heard God's voice, he was "in the tabernacle of the LORD where the ark of God was" (1 Sam. 3:3 NKJV). That was a good place to be because that location was as close to the presence of God as a person could be in those days—unless he was the high priest who entered the Holy of Holies once a year.

Every leader belongs close to God. That doesn't mean you have to be in a place of formal worship. It just means you need to have an attitude of worship wherever you are. It's a posture of the heart.

That's a lesson I learned back when I was in college, and I took it with me into the ministry. When I was attending Circleville Bible College, I used to go out to an old deserted blockhouse after my classes were finished and spend time with God every afternoon. It became my special place to connect with Him.

Since then, I've always had a special place I visit to listen to God. In Hillham, Indiana, at my first pastorate, it was a huge rock in the woods behind our house. In Lancaster, Ohio, it was Rising Park Mountain. At Skyline Church in San Diego, it was the upper room in the old sanctuary. Today, there's a special overstuffed armchair in my home office where I often sit and connect with God. When He awakens me in the middle of the night, I slip out of my bedroom so that I don't wake my wife, Margaret, and I go down to that chair.

If you want to become the kind of person that others listen to, then get better acquainted with God. Connect with Him on a consistent basis, and you will increase the likelihood that you will connect with others.

TODAY'S QUESTION FOR REFLECTION:
Do you spend enough time listening to God?

Day 3

The impact of the voice is determined by the influence of the leader.

The lips of the righteous feed many.
Proverbs 10:21 (NKJV)

What is the greatest measure of an E. F. Hutton? The answer is the ability to lead other leaders. That's the toughest job of any leader because most leaders don't like to be led. They want to go their own way, not fall in line behind another leader.

> **What is the greatest measure of an E. F. Hutton? The answer is the ability to lead other leaders.**

WHEN SAMUEL SPOKE . . .

Samuel was a leader of leaders. He displayed influence with the nobles and elders of Israel. And he displayed influence with its highest leader, the king. What made people want to listen to Samuel? They listened to him because . . .

1. SAMUEL WAS SECURE IN HIS CALLING

People are more likely to listen to confident, secure leaders. Samuel never doubted his worth or his calling from God. Though he appointed and anointed Saul, Samuel was never intimidated by him—not by his position, his power, his handsome appearance, or his stature. Samuel wasn't intimidated when Saul became a powerful warrior either. When Saul failed to kill King Agag as God ordered him to, Samuel himself executed Agag (1 Sam. 15:33 NKJV).

2. SAMUEL WAS WILLING TO SHARE HIS AUTHORITY

As judge over Israel, Samuel was its most visible leader, yet he gave his civil and military authority to Saul when God directed him to do so. And he honored Saul publicly, reserving special food and a special place at the table for him (1 Sam. 9:22–24 NKJV). Samuel practiced a principle of leadership that is expressed well by my friend Bill McCartney, who says, "We are not here to compete with each other, but to complete each other."

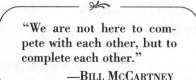

"We are not here to compete with each other, but to complete each other."

—BILL MCCARTNEY

3. SAMUEL DESIRED TO HELP OTHERS DEVELOP THEIR POTENTIAL

Although Samuel recognized that the people's request for a king was a mark of disobedience to God and that they were courting disaster, he did his best to advise the people and to try to make Saul successful as king. He saw Saul's potential and encouraged him. Samuel told the new leader, "Then the Spirit of the LORD will come upon you, and you will prophesy with them and be turned into another man. And let it be, when these signs come to you, that you do as the occasion demands; for God is with you" (1 Sam. 10:6–7 NKJV). Samuel tried to develop Saul into the spiritual leader God had called him to be.

4. SAMUEL SPOKE THE TRUTH INTO PEOPLE'S LIVES

Samuel never hesitated to speak the truth with love to anyone who needed to hear it. When the people clamored for a king, he told them how a king would treat them (1 Sam. 8:10–18). When Saul became impatient and offered a sacrifice instead of waiting as directed, Samuel told him he had acted foolishly (1 Sam. 13:13). And when Saul disobeyed God's command to destroy the Amalekites, Samuel called him to account and informed Saul that God had rejected him as king (1 Sam. 15:10–29). Samuel never spoke out of spite or superiority, but he never backed away from the truth either.

5. SAMUEL HAD A HEART FOR BOTH GOD AND THE PEOPLE

Samuel genuinely desired the best for all the people and tried to direct them so that they would enjoy God's blessing. That desire extended to Saul, Samuel's replacement as the nation's leader. And even after Samuel denounced Saul as king, he mourned for him (1 Sam. 15:35). He still had a heart for him and the people.

Ultimately the leaders that people listen to most carefully are the ones who have their people's best interest in mind, not their own. That's what it takes to become an E. F. Hutton.

❧

TODAY'S QUESTION FOR REFLECTION:
Why should people listen to you?

Day 4

Either make the tree good and its fruit good, or else make the tree bad and its fruit bad; for a tree is known by its fruit . . . For out of the abundance of the heart the mouth speaks. A good man out of the good treasure of his heart brings forth good things, and an evil man out of the evil treasure brings forth evil things.

Matthew 12:33–35 (NKJV)

You will never find a disparity between the words and the actions of an E. F. Hutton. Great leaders have integrity. Anyone who displays inconsistency of character will not remain a voice of influence in the lives of others. When you

> You will never find a disparity between the words and the actions of an E. F. Hutton. Great leaders have integrity.

look at the life of Samuel, you see that consistency. Two things come shining through: character and competence. He lived according to his values and practiced solid leadership without wavering. And people listened to him as a result.

GAINING CREDIBILITY

If you desire to become an E. F. Hutton, first check your motives to be sure your desire isn't driven by ego or the desire for personal gain. Then recognize that the following must happen for your message to have credibility:

1. YOU MUST LIVE YOUR MESSAGE FIRST
The effectiveness of any message relies more on the character of the

messenger than on the content of the message. Or as the old saying goes, "Your character speaks so loudly that I can't hear your words."

People listened to Samuel because he demonstrated with his life everything that he asked others to do. That is why he was able to say this to the people at Saul's coronation:

> "And now here is the king, walking before you; and I am old and grayheaded, and look, my sons are with you. I have walked before you from my childhood to this day. Here I am. Witness against me before the LORD and before His anointed: Whose ox have I taken, or whose donkey have I taken, or whom have I cheated? Whom have I oppressed, or from whose hand have I received any bribe with which to blind my eyes? I will restore it to you." And they said, "You have not cheated us or oppressed us, nor have you taken anything from any man's hand." Then he said to them, "The LORD is witness against you, and His anointed is witness this day, that you have not found anything in my hand." And they answered, "He is witness." (1 Sam. 12:2–5 NKJV)

2. YOU MUST BE MORE THAN THE MESSENGER

For anything you say to really connect with others, the message must contain a piece of you. You can't deliver something you haven't given your heart to. As a prophet, Samuel was a messenger of God. But he was much more than that. Like David, Samuel truly had a heart for God. God's desires became his desires.

As you speak to people, do it with passion. The conviction of your message must be apparent in your words and in your life.

3. YOUR MESSAGE MUST BE MORE THAN A MESSAGE

One reason that people listen to an E. F. Hutton is that his words carry a message that has the potential to change lives. They're not merely communication that perpetuates the status quo.

Samuel's words frequently carried that kind of weight. Listen to the advice he gave the people as they prepared to accept their new king:

> If you fear the LORD and serve Him and obey His voice, and do not rebel against the commandment of the LORD, then both you and the king who

reigns over you will continue following the LORD your God. However, if you do not obey the voice of the LORD, but rebel against the commandment of the LORD, then the hand of the LORD will be against you, as it was against your fathers. (1 Sam. 12:14–15 NKJV)

The message Samuel delivered had the potential to change the life of every person listening to his voice. It also contained truth that could change the course of the nation's history. Although the people listened to Samuel's message, they didn't possess the character to obey it in the long run.

4. YOU MUST HAVE A STAKE IN THE OUTCOME

People can tell the difference between a leader who is a spectator on the sideline and one who is a participant in the game. They have greater respect for someone who has a stake in the outcome of his message. A good leader may send his people into battle, but a great leader leads them there—and the people respect him for putting himself on the line with them.

To be a credible leader, you must make your life match your message. If your character is inconsistent with your communication, it underlines the reality that you are a phony. In contrast, if your character is consistent with your communication, it underlines what you have to say. And it makes everyone want to listen.

TODAY'S QUESTION FOR REFLECTION:
Does your character complement your message?

Day 5

Bringing the Law to Life

TAKING IT IN

It's true that a group of people will listen to the most credible leader among them. But to become the kind of E. F. Hutton who can make a positive impact on people's lives, you must embrace these truths:

1. Leaders earn the right to be heard.
2. Leaders should listen to God before asking others to listen to them.
3. The impact of the voice is determined by the influence of the leader.
4. The character of the leader underlines the content of the message.

SORTING IT OUT

If you're not sure where you stand when it comes to understanding and applying the Law of E. F. Hutton, visit the Web site www.injoy.com/21 Minutes to take a free twenty-five-question assessment quiz that will help you measure your ability.

PRAYING IT THROUGH

Use the following words to begin your time of prayer:

Dear God, give me Samuel's ear, a listening ear. Help me to quiet myself before You so that I may hear Your still, small voice. And give me a pure, obedient heart, one that compels me to live a life of character before my people. And once I've listened to You, when I have something worth saying, please give me favor with my people so that I am able to add value to their lives. Amen.

LIVING IT OUT

If people dismiss your words, it may be because of a problem with credibility in the area of competence or character. Make a list of the possible reasons people could have to doubt your words. Which area do they fall into? What will you do to begin building your credibility in those areas to increase your ability to become an E. F. Hutton?

If people *do* listen to your words, think of ways to increase your credibility. Build on a personal strength to revise your level of influence.

PASSING IT ON

Which one leadership concept, insight, or practice that you've learned this week will you pass on to another leader in the next two days?

Week 6

THE LAW OF SOLID GROUND

TRUST IS THE FOUNDATION OF LEADERSHIP

A leader's history of successes and failures makes a big difference in his credibility. It's a little like earning and spending pocket change. Each time you make a good leadership decision, it puts change into your pocket. Each time you make a poor one, you have to pay out some of your change to the people.

Every leader has a certain amount of change in his pocket when he starts in a new leadership position. From then on, he either builds up his change or pays it out . . .

To build trust, a leader must exemplify these qualities: competence, connection, and character. People will forgive occasional mistakes based on ability, especially if they can see that you're still growing as a leader. But they won't trust someone who has slips in character. In that area, even occasional lapses are lethal . . .

No leader can break trust with his people and expect to keep influencing them . . . Trust makes leadership possible.

FROM "THE LAW OF SOLID GROUND" IN *The 21 Irrefutable Laws of Leadership*

Day 1

Samson
and the
Law of Solid Ground

LEADERSHIP THOUGHT FOR TODAY:
Trust is formed by a leader's character and credibility.

Read
Judges 13:1–16:31

How could someone who was given such a strong start in life finish so poorly? By all accounts, Samson could have been one of Israel's greatest leaders, yet when all was said and done, he turned out to be one of the worst.

STRONG START—WEAK FINISH

Samson had everything going for him. He was a special child, foretold by the angel of the Lord to his parents. He had a divine destiny and purpose. Scripture reports that the angel said, "The child shall be a Nazirite to God from the womb; and he shall begin to deliver Israel out of the hand of the Philistines" (Judg. 13:5 NKJV). And even as a child, Samson was blessed by God, and the Spirit of God was on him (Judg. 13:24–25).

Samson performed many feats of strength during his life, and he judged Israel for twenty years. Yet despite his good start, Samson got himself into trouble many times, and in the end he finished poorly: he was weak, blind, and enslaved to the Philistines from whom he was supposed to deliver his people.

Why didn't Samson become the great leader he had the potential to be?

His despicable character made him untrustworthy, and that destroyed his leadership. He was impetuous, volatile, lustful, moody, emotional, and unpredictable. No one could figure out his intentions, not his new wife, his father-in-law, or the Israelites. His people bound him up and delivered him to the Philistines to save their own necks.

Samson's untrustworthiness extended to God. Before he had finished, he broke the vows of a Nazirite. First, before his marriage, he touched a dead animal (Judg. 14:9). Second, he gave a wedding feast that included much drinking (Judg. 14:10). And when he finally broke the third vow, by allowing his hair to be cut, God removed the anointing from his life (Judg. 16:19–20). Samson repeatedly flirted with disaster, and it overtook him.

HOW MANY WILL FINISH WELL?

A few years ago, I did a leadership conference for pastors in Albuquerque, New Mexico. While I was there, I talked with a pastor friend from Houston, Texas, named John Basagno about the subject of finishing well. As we chatted, he showed me an old, well-worn Bible and said, "John, I received the call to preach when I was twenty-one years old. I told my father-in-law about it soon after receiving the call, and do you know what he told me? He said, 'This is how it's going to be. Only one person out of every ten who enter the ministry will still be in it when he reaches age sixty-five.'"

I could see that John was getting emotional as he opened up that old Bible and showed me the inside front cover. "I wrote down in this Bible the names of twenty-five friends I went to college with. All of us were in our early twenties. I'm not sixty-five yet, but I'm sorry to say that twenty of them have already dropped out."

Then he looked me in the eye and said, "I'm fighting hard to be one of those who make it. I want to finish well."

I think many people believe that if they had been given a start like Samson's, they would find it easy to lead and to finish well. But God gives every one of us a good-enough start to be able to finish well. It's up to us to see to our character and build trust with others so that God can use our leadership.

Samson's lack of integrity was his undoing. When leaders lose that, they also lose the people's trust. And when that's gone, they're finished. Samson might have taken down a few hundred Philistines in the end, but not without losing his authority and leadership as judge as well as his life.

❧

TODAY'S QUESTION FOR REFLECTION:
Do your people consider you trustworthy?

Day 2

There are always signs when a leader is not on solid ground.

> He who walks with integrity walks securely,
> But he who perverts his ways will become known.
>
> Proverbs 10:9 (NKJV)

Samson had time to turn himself around, yet he didn't. Judges 14–15 outlines much of his impetuous behavior and the fruit of his poor character, yet the passage ends saying of Samson, "He judged Israel twenty years in the days of the Philistines" (Judg. 15:20 NKJV).

Look at Samson's life, and you see a pattern of negative behavior that spelled trouble—in terms of his relationship with God and his leadership of his people. In fact, no leader ends up out of bounds without first passing signposts that indicate he is straying into dangerous territory.

> No leader ends up out of bounds without first passing signposts that indicate that he is straying into dangerous territory.

SIGNS OF LEADERS IN TROUBLE

When leaders start to erode the solid ground of trustworthy leadership, they usually exhibit one or more of the following signs that they are headed for trouble. Like Samson, leaders in trouble . . .

1. FAIL TO ADDRESS GLARING CHARACTER WEAKNESSES

From early in his life, Samson struggled with sexual impurity. And because he didn't try to restrain his desire, it continually caused him to go out of bounds. Instead of honoring God's command against marrying non-Hebrews, he requested a Philistine wife from his parents because, as he said, "she pleases me well" (Judg. 14:3 NKJV). Later he slept with prostitutes. And his ultimate destruction came as the result of his relationship with Delilah.

Anytime a leader neglects to repair flaws in his character, they become worse. And the flaws inevitably lead to a downward spiral culminating in the destruction of the leader's moral foundation.

2. COUNT ON DECEPTION TO SAFEGUARD THEMSELVES

When people flirt with disobedience, they often find themselves using deception to protect themselves. That was certainly true of Samson. He was fond of using riddles to try to trick others. And when he stepped completely over the line of obedience by having an affair with Delilah, he out and out lied. Three times he lied to her about the source of his strength to protect himself. Whenever a leader twists the truth in any way, it's a sure sign that he is in trouble.

3. ACT IMPULSIVELY

Time after time, Samson displayed his impetuosity. He chose his wife rashly. He didn't consider the possible consequences of posing his riddle to the wedding guests or of revealing the answer to his Philistine wife. And more than once he found himself in bloody battle as the result of his impulsive spirit. A leader who cannot control his temper is a danger to himself and others.

4. MISUSE THEIR GOD-GIVEN GIFTS

Samson possessed immense strength and godly anointing, but he took both for granted. In fact, he sometimes used his influence to play games for his amusement. After his father-in-law gave Samson's wife to Samson's best man, Samson exploited what God intended to be used for the deliverance of His people for the purpose of personal revenge. That led to the deaths of Samson's father-in-law and the Philistine man's daughter.

God gives gifts for His own purposes, and the gifts are always greater than the person who possesses them. But when a leader misuses the gifts and resources God provides, there are always unwanted consequences.

5. ARE OVERCOME BECAUSE OF AN AREA OF WEAKNESS

Those who give free rein to their sins eventually are consumed by them.

When Samson encountered Delilah, he finally met his match. The deceiver was deceived; the seducer, seduced. He toyed with her, knowing that she was working for the enemy. But she got the better of him, enticing him to tell her all that was in his heart (Judg. 16:18). It was a dangerous game, which he lost, and it cost him everything.

Some people like to believe that their private imperfections won't have public consequences, but they always do. Leaders cannot escape who they truly are, and what they do in the dark comes out in the light. If what they do is good, it builds character in the leader and trust in the people. If it's bad, then it undermines everything they do until there's no solid ground left for them to stand on.

❧

TODAY'S QUESTION FOR REFLECTION:
Are any of these signs of trouble present in your life?

Day 3

When a leader is out of touch with God and his people,
he loses his teachability.

He who keeps instruction is in the way of life,
But he who refuses correction goes astray.
Proverbs 10:17 (NKJV)

If I were to take all of Samson's flaws and problems, and key in on the one that got him into trouble more than any other, it would be this: he was unteachable. No matter what happened to him, for good or ill, he never seemed to grow any wiser. He kept going in his own wrong direction until his destructive end.

WHEN LEADERS LOSE THEIR TEACHABILITY

Samson is practically a prototype of a leader who disqualifies himself from leadership. He was so self-centered, so undisciplined, so arrogant, that he lost his teachability. And that loss can make even the most talented person ineffective as a leader.

WHAT HAPPENS WHEN LEADERS LOSE THEIR TEACHABILITY?

1. THEY LEAN ON THEIR OWN STRENGTH AND UNDERSTANDING

They don't seek guidance from God and others. Unteachable leaders are almost always out of touch with God and their people. Proverbs 3:5–6 declares,

> Trust in the LORD with all your heart,
>
> And lean not on your own understanding;
>
> In all your ways acknowledge Him,
>
> And He shall direct your paths. (NKJV)

Samson's life path went in the opposite direction.

Samson repeatedly used the brute force of his strength to cope with difficulties. Every time he faced a problem, he reacted with violence rather than deal with his character faults. When he was embarrassed at his wedding feast, he killed thirty men for their clothes (Judg. 14:19). When the men of Judah turned him over to the Philistines—which is the only record we have of his interaction with his people—he bludgeoned to death another one thousand Philistines (Judg. 15:15). When he was caught with a prostitute, he ripped apart the city gates of Gaza (Judg. 16:3).

Samson didn't take the advice of his parents, we have no record of his taking advice from his people, and he didn't look to God for guidance. Worse than that, Samson never acknowledged God as the source of his strength. Even though the Scripture states clearly that the Spirit of the LORD was his source of strength, he took all the credit for himself. He went from a man of anointing to a man of arrogance.

2. THEY FAIL TO LEARN FROM THEIR MISTAKES

A person's life goes either uphill or downhill, depending on whether he fails forward or backward. Look at Samson's life, and you see a record of no improvement. His is a downward spiral.

For leaders to learn from their mistakes, they must be . . .

- *big enough to admit mistakes.* It all starts here. Samson blamed everyone else for his problems. He never once admitted his sin and humbled himself before God.

- *smart enough to profit from them.* It's one thing to know you're wrong. It's another to figure out why you made a mistake. But without this step, a person is doomed to repeat mistakes.

⁓

> Knowing why you erred is essential to correcting mistakes, but if you can't implement the necessary changes in your life, you won't be able to improve yourself and your situation.

- *strong enough to correct them.* Knowing why you erred is essential to correcting mistakes, but if you can't *implement* the necessary changes in your life, you won't be able to improve yourself and your situation. And that takes strength—not Samson's kind, but strength of character.

Nothing is truly a mistake unless you don't learn from it. Leaders must be learners if they want to keep leading.

3. THEY REACT INSTEAD OF LEAD

Good leaders are proactive. But unteachable people spend almost all of their time reacting. Look at Samson's track record of reactions:

EVENT	REACTION
He sees the daughter of Timnah.	He asks for her in marriage.
The guests guess his riddle.	He kills thirty for their clothes.
His wife is given to his best man.	He burns the Philistines' fields.
The Philistines burn Timnah's house.	He attacks them "hip and thigh with a great slaughter."
The men of Judah hand him over to the Philistines.	He kills one thousand Philistines with the jawbone of an ass.
The Philistines lie in wait to kill him.	He tears down the city gates and carries them off.
He is captured, blinded, and enslaved.	He takes revenge by collapsing the Philistines' temple.

God had a plan for Samson's life, perhaps to use him to deliver His people from the Philistines (Judg. 13:5). But that purpose was never carried out. Instead, Samson reacted himself right into his death—and his people were still under the oppression of the Philistines.

4. THEY ARE EASILY DEFEATED

Unteachable people are always defeated eventually. Even great talent (like Samson's) can take a person only so far. In the end, Delilah deceived Samson, and that was the end of his leadership. Ironically when he most relied on his own strength and understanding, he was defeated, and along with defeat came the most damaging results. As G. K. Chesterton stated, "Anything done in our own strength will fail miserably or succeed even more miserably."

> "Anything done in our own strength will fail miserably or succeed even more miserably."
> —G. K. CHESTERTON

Samson's defeat began with a character flaw. That character flaw, left unrepaired because of an unteachable spirit, led to moral erosion and unchecked sin in his life. And that brought on his destruction. If during the course of his life he had ever humbly connected with God or sought the guidance and accountability of the people, who knows what might have happened differently.

❧

TODAY'S QUESTION FOR REFLECTION:
How well are you connected to God and your people?

Day 4

*The consequences of sin are always great for both
the leader and the people.*

> The path of the just is like the shining sun,
> That shines ever brighter unto the perfect day.
> The way of the wicked is like darkness;
> They do not know what makes them stumble . . .
> Ponder the path of your feet,
> And let all your ways be established.
> Do not turn to the right or the left;
> Remove your foot from evil.
>
> Proverbs 4:18–19, 26–27 (NKJV)

No leader can embrace sin and continue leading the people effectively. In my experience of more than thirty years as a pastor, I've watched many anointed leaders entangle themselves in sin and disqualify themselves from leading. Often they step over the line thinking, *This is a special case. God understands my special circumstances. I can do this.* But it always turns out the same. As Gary Richmond remarked in *A View from the Zoo*, "Sin too often comes dressed in adorable guise, and as we play with it, how easy it is to say, 'It will be different with me.' The results are predictable." The leader's credibility disintegrates, he loses trust with the people, and his leadership is finished.

WHAT SIN WILL ALWAYS DO

Sin always takes a terrible toll. And no matter who the leaders are or what circumstances they face, sin always has the same results:

1. SIN ALWAYS TAKES YOU FARTHER THAN YOU WANTED TO GO

All Samson wanted was a wife. He chose a Philistine woman, which was a sin, but he probably thought, *I'll step across the line this one time. I'll be over it only a second, I'll come right back, and that will be it. What will it hurt? She pleases me, and she's the one I want.*

But it didn't end that way. Once he stepped over, he found himself in sin again and again. He hosted a feast with lots of drinking, even though as a Nazirite he wasn't supposed to touch even grape juice. When he realized where he was headed, he could have stopped and said, "No. I made a mistake. I need to get back to my people." But that's not what he did.

Instead, he tried to impress his thirty male companions with a riddle so that he could trick them into giving him expensive gifts of clothing. When his wife got him to reveal the secret of the riddle, he was in even deeper. To pay his debt, he killed thirty men for their clothes. And we know that he was aware that he had done wrong because before his next vengeful act, he said, "*This* time I shall be blameless regarding the Philistines if I harm them!" (Judg. 15:3 NKJV, emphasis added). By the end of his wedding, Samson was already up to his neck in trouble.

2. SIN ALWAYS KEEPS YOU LONGER THAN YOU WANTED TO STAY

Samson might have intended to go only briefly over the line of sin, but he ended up taking the whole journey—ultimately leading to his destruction. After the first time Delilah tried to deceive him and learn the secret of his strength, a wiser man would have gone home and stayed away from her. But not Samson. He just couldn't resist, so he stayed. And he was there until Delilah "pestered him daily with her words and pressed him, so that his soul was vexed to death, [and] he told her all his heart" (Judg. 16:16–17 NKJV).

Sin often possesses an enticing appearance and gives promises of fulfillment. But it never delivers on any of the promises it makes. And that causes people to stay in sin or to keep going back to it for more. They keep hoping that the next time it will deliver on the promises; it never does.

3. SIN ALWAYS COSTS YOU MORE THAN YOU WERE WILLING TO PAY

No matter what leaders believe sin will cost them, the price is *always* higher. That's part of the subtlety of sin. Not only does the sinner always want more, but sin always demands more in payment—and the person doesn't recognize it until it's too late.

> No matter what leaders believe sin will cost them, the price is always higher.

Observe what happened to Samson after he told Delilah the secret of his strength:

> Then she lulled him to sleep on her knees, and called for a man and had him shave off the seven locks of his head. Then she began to torment him, and his strength left him. And she said, "The Philistines are upon you, Samson!" So he awoke from his sleep, and said, "I will go out as before, at other times, and shake myself free!" But he did not know that the LORD had departed from him. Then the Philistines took him and put out his eyes, and brought him down to Gaza. They bound him with bronze fetters, and he became a grinder in the prison. (Judg. 16:19–21 NKJV)

Samson thought he was still safe, that he could still go free "as before," but he was caught. His sin cost him everything—his leadership, his sight, and ultimately his life.

Samson's life, once filled with such promise and potential, got mired in sin. That led to his destruction. But it did more than that. God's people remained in bondage to the Philistines. And the Israelites wouldn't completely free themselves from their enemy's oppression until the reign of King David, nearly a hundred years later. No leader can embrace sin and fulfill his leadership calling at the same time.

TODAY'S QUESTION FOR REFLECTION:
What sin is undermining your leadership?

Day 5

Bringing the Law to Life

TAKING IT IN

Review the four thoughts related to the Law of Solid Ground:

1. Trust is formed by a leader's character and credibility.

2. There are always signs when a leader is not on solid ground.

3. When a leader is out of touch with God and his people, he loses his teachability.

4. The consequences of sin are always great for both the leader and the people.

Of all the laws of leadership, the Law of Solid Ground may be the most critical. Violation of this law often causes the most damage to a person's leadership ability. And it requires the greatest amount of time for recovery—if recovery is even possible.

SORTING IT OUT

If you're not sure where you stand when it comes to understanding and applying the Law of Solid Ground, visit the Web site www.injoy.com/21 Minutes to take a free twenty-five-question assessment quiz that will help you measure your ability.

PRAYING IT THROUGH

Use the following words to begin your time of prayer:

Dear God, Jesus taught us to pray, "Lead us not into temptation," and that is my request to You now. Protect me from the desire to sin, which would dishonor You and discredit me. And forgive me of the sins I have already committed. Help me to build trust with my people and to lead them with integrity and a servant's heart. Amen.

LIVING IT OUT

When the Law of Solid Ground is evident in a leader's life—and he demonstrates competence, orchestrates community, and incarnates character—the longer he leads, the better it gets. Take some time to identify the major phases of your life and reflect on whether your leadership has gotten stronger or weaker with each phase.

If you have seen a decline in your influence, then figure out why. Ask God to give you insight and wisdom. Once you have identified the source of the problem, plan how to address it. If you're not sure how, enlist the help of a trusted friend.

PASSING IT ON

Which one leadership concept, insight, or practice that you've learned this week will you pass on to another leader in the next two days?

Week 7

THE LAW OF RESPECT

PEOPLE NATURALLY FOLLOW LEADERS STRONGER THAN THEMSELVES

People don't follow others by accident. They follow individuals whose leadership they respect . . . The less skilled follow the more highly skilled and gifted. Occasionally, a strong leader may choose to follow someone weaker than himself. But when that happens, it's for a reason . . . The stronger leader may do it out of respect for the person's office or past accomplishments. Or he may be following the chain of command. In general, though, followers are attracted to people who are better leaders than themselves . . .

The more leadership ability a person has, the more quickly he recognizes leadership—or its lack—in others . . . When people get together for the first time as a group, take a look at what happens. As they start interacting, the leaders in the group immediately take charge. They think in terms of the direction they desire to go and whom they want to take with them. At first, people may make tentative moves in several different directions, but after the people get to know one another, it doesn't take long for them to recognize the strongest leaders and to follow them.

FROM "THE LAW OF RESPECT" IN *The 21 Irrefutable Laws of Leadership*

Day 1

Deborah
and the
Law of Respect

LEADERSHIP THOUGHT FOR TODAY:
When a leader gains respect, leading becomes easier.

Read
Judges 4:1–24; 5:1–9; 31

❧

> When leaders have influence, people begin to follow them. When they have respect, people keep following them.

We don't really know a lot about Deborah. The scriptural account of her leadership is very brief. However, even though her story may be short, we know her influence was great. And that was no small feat in her day. Men in her culture did not readily follow women, and few women were allowed to achieve leadership positions. But Deborah rose to the most influential position in Israel. And she had more than influence over the people of Israel; she had their respect. When leaders have influence, people begin to follow them. When they have *respect*, people *keep* following them. That's the power of the Law of Respect.

ONE LEADER'S JOURNEY

The story of Deborah contains the journey of any successful leader. I found that out as I entered the ministry in 1969. When I took my first pastorate in

Hillham, Indiana, I was twenty-two years old, and I found myself leading a congregation of people whose average age was twice my own.

One of my main responsibilities in that first church was counseling people. And during a session early in my pastorate, I sat across from a couple in their fifties who told me, "Pastor, you're a nice person, and we know you've been to school to be a preacher. But you're so young. We just don't think we can talk to you about our problems."

I spent a total of three years in Hillham. It took me about six months to gain significant influence with people in the church. But in time, I began to have influence not only with the members of the congregation, but also with other people in the community and with the leaders in the church.

Over the course of my twenty-six-year career as a senior pastor of churches, I learned a lot about influence, but it took me until the end of my career in my third and final church, Skyline in San Diego, to really understand what respect is all about. After fourteen years there, I had earned the respect of the people in my congregation, including its best leaders. Bob Taylor, the wonderful businessman who founded Taylor Guitars and who served as the leader of my board of elders, shared with me these words that I think sum up the idea of respect very effectively:

> If I were in the military, I'd call you Sir.
> If I were in the court, I'd call you Your Honor.
> If I were your apprentice, I'd call you Master.
> If I were on your team, I'd call you Coach.
> If I were an orphan, I'd call you Father.
> If I were a student, I'd call you a Teacher.
> As a layman, I've called you Pastor.
> To all of us you will always be a Leader!

LEARNING FROM THE LIFE OF DEBORAH

Those words could easily have been ascribed to Deborah because she was all those things to her people. She had the respect of everyone. Even Israel's greatest military ruler, Barak, followed her. He had so much respect for her that he wanted her by his side as they went into battle.

She was honored as a prophetess and respected as a leader. And she restored prosperity to the people for forty years because of her leadership. The people expressed their esteem for her by giving her the highest compliment they could imagine: they called her a "mother" to the people of Israel (Judg. 5:7).

❧

TODAY'S QUESTION FOR REFLECTION:
Is it becoming easier or more difficult to get people to follow you?

Day 2

LEADERSHIP THOUGHT FOR TODAY:
Respect is a matter of leadership—not position, title, or gender.

> My heart is with the rulers of Israel
> Who offered themselves willingly with the people.
> Bless the LORD!
>
> Judges 5:9 (NKJV), from the Song of Deborah

How did a woman gain the respect of a male-dominated culture like that of Israel around 1100 B.C.? How did she come to be the greatest leader of her generation, one who brought rest to her people for forty years? She did it the same way any man or woman would go about doing it today.

HOW DEBORAH GAINED RESPECT

Take a look at the process a leader goes through. I've outlined it based on the word *R-E-S-P-E-C-T*.

RESPECT YOURSELF AND THOSE YOU WORK WITH

Gaining the respect of others always begins with having respect for yourself. It's clear that Deborah was a person of respect. People from all of Israel came to her to settle their disputes. And when she summoned Barak, he came to her, and she made him commander of an army, showing that she was quick to empower others in the area of their gifts. If you desire to win the respect of others, first demonstrate a healthy respect for them and for yourself.

> Gaining the respect of others always begins with having respect for yourself.

Exceed the Expectations of Others

Few people would have expected Deborah to change the way the Israelites lived, yet that's what she did. She raised the standard of living for the common person and returned the nation to peace. Scripture notes,

> Village life ceased, it ceased in Israel,
> Until I, Deborah, arose,
> Arose a mother in Israel. (Judg. 5:7 NKJV)

Leaders who earn the respect of others always exceed their expectations. They go the extra mile, they fight to achieve victory, and they take others with them.

Stand Firm on Your Convictions

Imagine what it must have taken for Deborah, a woman from the southern part of the nation, to call Barak, a powerful man from one of the northern tribes, into her presence and command him to fight the Canaanite army to the north. That took a tremendous amount of courage, which comes from conviction.

When Barak revealed his doubts about the campaign and asked Deborah to accompany him, she didn't back down or waver in her belief that God had called them to fight their enemies. She agreed to go, and she told him that the glory he would have received for the battle would instead go to a woman.

Followers respect a leader who demonstrates conviction. The greatest leaders possess the vision to reach their destination, and they believe they will get there. And they act on that conviction. Followers can sense that, and it is one of the reasons they are willing to join with a leader and take the journey.

Possess Uncommon Security and Maturity

Though Scripture says the land had rest for forty years, we don't really know how old Deborah was or how long she served as Israel's judge, but we do know that she didn't try to take the credit for Israel's victory. Deborah sang, "My heart is with the rulers of Israel who offered themselves willingly with the people" (Judg. 5:9 NKJV). Then she recounted all the people who participated in the victory—even mentioning the command of Barak, despite her admonition to him that a woman, Jael, would have the honor of killing the Canaanite general, Sisera.

Leaders whom the people respect don't grab all the credit of a victory for themselves. They give as much as they can to the people. And doing that requires maturity and security.

> Leaders cannot help people experience success unless they have themselves been successful.

EXPERIENCE PERSONAL SUCCESS

Leaders cannot help people experience success unless they have been successful. Deborah was already a success (as a prophetess and a judge) before she asked the people to fight.

CONTRIBUTE TO THE SUCCESS OF OTHERS

When she did call the people to battle, Deborah did it right. She gave them a commander. She gave them the resources they needed—ten thousand men! And she gave them the word of the Lord that they would win. And they did. Under her guidance, "the hand of the children of Israel grew stronger and stronger against Jabin king of Canaan, until they had destroyed Jabin king of Canaan" (Judg. 4:24 NKJV).

THINK AHEAD OF OTHERS

Just as Nehemiah did, Deborah practiced the Law of Navigation. She gave Barak the battle plan, telling him how to attack. She supplied him with troops. She accompanied him to Mount Tabor, where the battle would be fought. She even told him when to engage in battle. The result was overwhelming victory. How could the people not respect a leader of such strategy and vision?

Weak leaders believe that their position or title *deserves* respect. Strong leaders know that they must earn it. Deborah

> Weak leaders believe that their position or title deserves respect. Strong leaders know that they must earn it.

understood that, gained the respect of her people, and stands out as one of the most remarkable leaders recorded in the Bible.

≫

TODAY'S QUESTION FOR REFLECTION:
What are you relying on for your respect?

Day 3

Make it your ambition to lead a quiet life . . . so that your daily life may win
the respect of outsiders and so that you will not be dependent on anybody.

1 Thessalonians 4:11–12 (NIV)

There are many kinds of respect. There is the respect you show another person because you have good manners and because you desire to love your neighbor as yourself. There is the respect you have for people because they have achieved a level of effectiveness in their work, family life, or other area of endeavor. And then there is leadership respect, the kind you have for world-class leaders who have spent their lives taking people to another level—the kind of respect you have for Mother Teresa, Billy Graham, or Martin Luther King Jr.

For years I've used and taught a leadership tool that puts that kind of respect into perspective. It's called the Five Levels of Leadership. Allow me to teach it to you.

THE FIVE LEVELS OF LEADERSHIP

1. POSITION

The lowest level of leadership for any person is based on a title or job description. If people follow a leader only because he is named boss or team leader, then he is a positional leader. People follow only because they *have* to (or think they do). The best way to test whether you are a positional leader is to ask people to follow beyond the boundaries of your stated authority. If they won't, you're on level 1.

All leadership begins on the position level. That's where Deborah began—as a prophetess. But leadership that stays on this level for long

THE FIVE LEVELS OF LEADERSHIP

5. Personhood

Respect
People follow because of who you are and what you represent.

NOTE: Only leaders who have spent years developing leaders and growing organizations achieve this level.

4. People Development

Reproduction
People follow because of what you've done for them.

NOTE: This is where long-range growth occurs. Commitment to developing leaders ensures ongoing growth of individuals and the organization. Strive to stay on this level.

3. Production

Results
People follow because of what you've done for the organization (group, church, or company).

NOTE: It is at this level that most feel successful. They like you and what you are doing. Because of momentum, problems are often easily solved with little effort.

2. Permission

Relationships
People follow because they want to.

NOTE: People begin following you beyond your stated authority. It is at this level that work begins to be fun. However, staying too long on this level without moving up to the production level causes highly motivated people to become restless.

1. Position

Rights
People follow because they have to.

NOTE: On this level, your influence will not extend beyond the boundaries of your job description. The longer you stay on this level, the higher the turnover will be in your organization, and the lower the morale.

becomes weaker, not stronger. A leader who wants others to follow him simply because he is "the boss" soon loses the respect of his people.

2. PERMISSION

The next level of leadership is based on the relationships of a leader with his people. As followers grow to like and trust a leader, they begin to follow because they *want* to. That was the case for Deborah. Because the people respected her, she became a judge. And because Scripture says people came to her, we know she had their permission to influence them.

When you have people's permission to lead, the whole leadership process becomes more enjoyable for everyone. But positive relationships alone aren't strong enough to create lasting leadership. To begin reaping the rewards of positive leadership, you have to go to the next level.

3. PRODUCTION

At the production level, influence is cemented and respect is increased because of what the leader and the people accomplish together. People begin to follow because of what the leader has done for the team or organization. Deborah's success as a judge was beneficial for all of the people.

Everyone loves results. People especially enjoy results when they take part in their creation. On the production level, the leader and followers begin to experience success together. If you reach this level, you and your team can achieve many of your goals. But to experience life-changing impact and lasting success, you have to make the leap to the next level.

4. PEOPLE DEVELOPMENT

The highest calling of any leader is to help people develop to reach their potential. The very best leaders help other *leaders* reach their potential. That's what Deborah did. She helped Barak achieve his God-given purpose.

> A leader who moves up to the people development level changes his focus. He goes from inspiring and leading followers to developing and leading other leaders.

And because she did that, the rulers of Machir (Judg. 5:14) and the princes of Issachar (Judg. 5:15) were successful, thousands of men became instruments in God's hands, and hundreds of thousands of people enjoyed the fruit of her leadership.

A leader who moves up to the people development level changes his focus. He goes from inspiring and leading followers to developing and leading other leaders. When you become a people developer, you strive to reproduce your leadership in others and help people reach their potential. The time you spend with people is an investment. As a result, they respect you not only for what you've done for the team, but also for what you've done for them personally.

5. PERSONHOOD

The fifth and highest level of leadership is personhood. It is the true respect level. A leader who spends his life developing people and organizations makes such an incredible impact for so long that people follow him because of who he is and what he represents. He is the best of the best. We don't have a long record of Deborah's accomplishments, but I believe that her being recorded as a "mother of Israel" indicates that she achieved personhood.

As a leader, you can't aspire to reach level 5. If you reach that level, it will be due to God's grace and time. The best you can try to do is to work your way up through the first four levels with as many individuals as you can with the purpose of adding value to their lives. Do that your whole life, and the rest will take care of itself.

TODAY'S QUESTION FOR REFLECTION:
What level are you on with your people?

Day 4

The highest compliment to a leader: other leaders follow.

Deborah said to Barak, "Up! For this is the day in which the Lord has delivered Sisera into your hand. Has not the Lord gone out before you?" So Barak went down from Mount Tabor with ten thousand men following him. And the Lord routed Sisera and all his chariots and all his army.

Judges 4:14–15 (NKJV)

When I started my career in leadership, my burning desire was to be liked by others. During my first two years of ministry, nearly everything I did was motivated by my goal to please people and win them over to me personally.

But then God dealt with me on that issue. I began visiting a man in the hospital who was the brother of a woman in my church. Each day for a week we'd chat about the Cincinnati Reds or some other unimportant topic. He was a nice guy, and I enjoyed talking to him. I think he really liked me.

Then one day a few hours after I had visited him, I got the call that he had died. And I realized that he had gone to the grave without ever hearing me share my faith. I was devastated. I had cared more about his opinion of me than about the condition of his soul.

For months I wrestled with the memory of my indifference to that man. It was one of the lowest points of my life. It truly broke me, and God was able to deal with me and turn my heart toward Him.

That incident changed my life forever. I decided that I would dedicate myself to what was truly important. Just as it had for Deborah, God's mission became my mission. And I dedicated the remainder of my life to building God's kingdom, not my reputation.

It has been nearly three decades since I made that decision. And during that time God has made it clear to me that my particular mission isn't to be raised up by others; it's to raise up leaders for His kingdom's sake. And because I've aligned myself with God's priorities for me, life has been an incredible journey.

WHEN A LEADER FOLLOWS

I've discovered that any time a leader humbles himself before God and makes that kind of adjustment, the respect that other leaders have for him increases mightily. Recently a friend in ministry shared a letter with me from one of the leaders who work under him. It is a marvelous illustration of the kind of impact a leader can make when he develops leaders and earns the respect of his people. It said,

> I had to get this note to you to say thank you for the "sermon" you have modeled for me over the last few years.
>
> The one word description that comes to mind as I think of you today is the word *respect*. As I reflect on your leadership, I see a number of examples where you have won the respect of both our staff and congregation.
>
> First, I have watched you handle pastoral staff for years now with the utmost integrity. I saw you remove two staff members who needed to be let go—then take criticism from laypeople who disagreed with your decision. Although the two staff were displaying destructive attitudes or immoral behavior, you never defended your decision by hanging out their "dirty laundry." You listened, then asked for [the people] to simply trust you. Later, when it became obvious that you were right, everyone saw the wisdom of your decision. But you never said, "I told you so." Your actions defended themselves.
>
> Second, I have watched you love the unlovable as you led them. I marveled at how you continue to hug people who criticized you or stabbed you in the back. I remember your reading a seven-page letter accusing you of everything but murder—then, I watched you respond to them with kind words and loving grace the next Sunday in the church foyer. Almost always your love and character would win them over.
>
> Third, I am amazed at how quickly you size up situations and form strategies for how to solve problems. Rarely have I seen you discouraged by a problem. You are challenged by them, never flustered. And always you do

what is right even when it means making a tough call. In fact, today when I run into struggles, I will often ask myself: "Now what would Pastor do in this situation?" You have lived a life that allows you to say, "Follow me as I follow Christ."

Pastor, you know how I struggled with people pleasing when I first came to work with you. I wanted so much to be liked. After watching you— my desire now is to be respected. It is a higher calling. I have learned the difference between being liked as a person and followed as a leader. Thank you for incarnating the qualities I needed to see.

If you desire to invest your life in others and gain their respect as my friend did his young colleague, then you need to "model a sermon" for your people. Model a life of integrity, and people will follow you as they did Deborah. Live a life of character-filled leadership, and you will find yourself leading not just followers, but leaders.

TODAY'S QUESTION FOR REFLECTION:
Do other leaders follow you?

Day 5

Bringing the Law to Life

TAKING IT IN

Consider how respect impacts leadership:

1. When a leader gains respect, leading becomes easier.
2. Respect is a matter of leadership—not position, title, or gender.
3. Respect is the highest level of leadership.
4. The highest compliment to a leader: other leaders follow.

Have you made it a priority to give and gain respect? If someone asked a half dozen people closest to you to describe their thoughts about you, would respect be a recurring theme? How many people are following you outside your stated position of leadership?

SORTING IT OUT

If you're not sure where you stand when it comes to understanding and applying the Law of Respect, visit the Web site www.injoy.com/21 Minutes to take a free twenty-five-question assessment quiz that will help you measure your ability.

PRAYING IT THROUGH

Use the following words to begin your time of prayer:

Dear God, help me to have the right attitude toward the people within my influence. Make me a giver, not a taker. Help me to see the potential You have given each person, according to his gifts and talents, and give me the ability and the desire to help him reach his potential. Teach me to respect people on the deepest level so that I can lead them to the highest level, not for myself, but for them and for You. Amen.

LIVING IT OUT

The Law of Respect says that people naturally follow leaders who are stronger than themselves. That means you can't get people to follow you by applying pressure to them. Instead, you must apply it to yourself. Because you are already acquainted with the Law of Process, you should

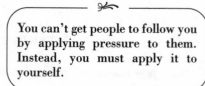

You can't get people to follow you by applying pressure to them. Instead, you must apply it to yourself.

be working intentionally to improve your leadership. The other thing you can do to improve your leadership is to focus on *how* you lead each person.

Follow this pattern with all the people you wish to lead (whether or not you have a position of authority over them):

- *Cultivate a positive relationship.* Extend yourself to them, initiating the relationship. Get to know them as individuals. Find common ground and develop rapport.

- *Help them be more productive.* Nothing boosts a relationship like a mutual win. Help them with encouragement, empowerment, resources—whatever it takes. You'll be helping yourself, them, and your organization.

- *Develop their potential.* It's one thing to help people for your sake. It's another to help them for their own sake. Help people to become the individuals God desires them to be, even if it doesn't benefit you personally.

This pattern takes time, but if you follow it, everyone wins, and you will earn the respect of the people whose lives you touch.

PASSING IT ON

Which one leadership concept, insight, or practice that you've learned this week will you pass on to another leader in the next two days?

Week 8

THE LAW OF INTUITION

LEADERS EVALUATE EVERYTHING WITH A LEADERSHIP BIAS

Leadership intuition is often the factor that separates the greatest leaders from the merely good ones . . . Some people are born with great leadership intuition. Others have to work hard to develop and hone it. But either way it evolves, the result is a combination of natural ability and learned skills. This informed intuition causes leadership issues to jump out. The best way to describe this bias is an ability to get a handle on intangible factors, understand them, and work with them to accomplish leadership goals . . .

Successful leaders . . . see every situation in terms of available resources: money, raw materials, technology and, most important, people . . . Intuitive leaders can sense what's happening among people and almost instantly know their hopes, fears, and concerns . . . [And] leaders have the ability to step back from what's happening at the moment and see not only where they and their people have gone, but also where they are headed in the future. It's as if they can smell change in the wind.

FROM "THE LAW OF INTUITION" IN *The 21 Irrefutable Laws of Leadership*

Day 1

Jethro
and the
Law of Intuition

Who you are is what you see.

Read
Exodus 18:1–27

When I teach the Law of Intuition at leadership conferences, often one of the attendees will come up to me during a break and say something like this: "John, you can talk all you want about intuition, but I'm just not intuitive."

When a person tells me that, I know that he is really trying to communicate that he feels he's not intuitive when it comes to leadership. And that may be true because not everyone possesses strong

> *Everyone* is intuitive in his or her area of natural giftedness.

leadership intuition. But all people possess intuition. *Everyone* is intuitive in his area of natural giftedness.

INTUITION FLOWS FROM YOUR GIFTING

Let me give you an example. Occasionally my wife, Margaret, is asked to speak at a conference. And I always dread it. Not because she can't speak. She's quite good. I dread the question she always asks me a few days before the speaking date: "How should I start?"

That question doesn't have a simple answer. When I want to communicate to a group of people, a hundred different factors may come into play to determine how I will begin: the size of the room, the number of people present, their background, their mood, how long they've been sitting, who spoke before me, what he or she said, the lighting, what kind of food they've been served, and so forth. I decide how to start based on my intuition because speaking is an area where I have God-given gifts.

Margaret, on the other hand, has different gifts. Never in my life have I known anyone else with her eye for color and style. In the morning when I walk into my closet, I'm a basket case. I have no idea what shirt to put with a pair of pants or which tie goes with what suit. On the days that I get up early and pick out my clothes by myself, I'll return home and walk into the kitchen, and Margaret will be absolutely mortified.

"Oh, John, you didn't wear *that* out, did you?" she'll ask. Then she'll gasp, "Who saw you?"

Most mornings I'll stand in my closet staring blankly, and Margaret will finally stick her head in and say, "Need help?" In three seconds she'll pull together an outfit that's dashing. At the end of the day, I'll put the whole outfit on the same hanger to save it for another time. Then a couple of weeks later, I'll put it on proudly, and when Margaret sees me, she'll say, "You're not going to wear *that* again, are you?" I just can't win.

MOSES AND JETHRO—LEARNED VERSUS GIFTED LEADERSHIP

If you think about your gifts, I think you'll be able to affirm what I'm saying. If your gift is mercy, then you can sense when someone needs comfort and know how to give it. If service is your gift, then you instinctively know when and how to help people in need. And if you are naturally gifted at leadership, then you see everything with a leadership bias.

When Jethro saw how Moses was leading the people, it must have gotten his attention like a slap in the face. The Scripture says that the two men met, Moses told Jethro about the things that God had done for the Hebrews, and Jethro rejoiced and sacrificed a burnt offering to honor God. But then *the next day*, Jethro watched as Moses tried to do everything by himself, and he immediately told his son-in-law, "The thing that you do is not good" (Ex. 18:17 NKJV).

Jethro instantly saw the problem, knew how it would affect the leader and his people, sensed the source of the problem, and knew how to fix it. As far as leadership is concerned, it was a clean sweep—he didn't miss a thing.

Moses was a good leader, but he wasn't a natural leader. When he met with Jethro, he hadn't been leading the children of Israel long. (The children of Israel had *just* left Egypt.) But over the course of the years in the desert, Moses' leadership improved, and so did his intuition.

Jethro, on the other hand, was a natural. How do we know that? We know because he looked at a leadership situation unlike anything he could have seen before—leading more than a *million* disgruntled, displaced people—and he knew exactly how to handle it. That's intuition in action. Who he was determined what he saw. Jethro was a leader, so he saw everything with a leadership bias.

❧

TODAY'S QUESTION FOR REFLECTION:
How is your view of life colored by your top two gifts or talents?

Day 2

Good judgment proves that you are wise,
and if you speak kindly, you can teach others.
Good sense is a fountain that gives life,
but fools are punished by their foolishness.

Proverbs 16:21–22 (CEV)

Of all the laws of leadership, the Law of Intuition is the most difficult one to teach. If you look in *Webster's New Universal Unabridged Dictionary*, you'll find that *intuition* is defined as the "direct perception of truth, fact, etc., independent of any reasoning process; immediate apprehension" or "a keen and quick insight." When I talk about intuition, I don't mean something that excludes thinking. But when it comes to intuition, the thinking occurs so quickly that you can't easily put your finger on the process.

The best analogy for helping you understand intuition is reading. Intuitive leaders are readers. If you think of intuition that way, you can learn to be more intuitive.

JETHRO, THE READING LEADER

Let's consider how Jethro handled the situation with Moses. Like all intuitive leaders, Jethro was a reader of . . .

1. SITUATIONS

An intuitive leader sees a situation and is able to size it up very quickly. That was certainly the case for Jethro. He watched Moses in action for a day and immediately reacted. Scripture describes what happened:

When Moses' father-in-law saw all that he did for the people, he said, "What is this thing that you are doing for the people? Why do you alone sit, and all the people stand before you from morning until evening? . . . The thing that you do is not good." (Ex. 18:14, 17 NKJV)

Jethro didn't have to hire a consultant, form a committee, or do extensive research. He knew instantly that there was a leadership problem. All leaders may not settle on a solution as quickly as Jethro did, but when they rely on their intuition, they become aware that a situation needs their attention.

2. TRENDS

An intuitive leader sees what's happening in the present, and he understands where an organization is headed in the future if it stays on its current course. Jethro could see that Moses was headed for trouble. He told his son-in-law, "Both you and these people who are with you will surely wear yourselves out. For this thing is too much for you; you are not able to perform it by yourself" (Ex. 18:18 NKJV).

Maybe Moses was performing the task of settling disputes effectively; maybe not. But even if he was able to get by with his current system of doing everything, he would not be able to sustain it. And as the population grew, the situation would worsen. Jethro knew that if Moses didn't change, disaster was inevitable.

3. RESOURCES

An intuitive leader knows how to resource his vision. He doesn't take anything for granted, and he maximizes whatever is at hand to achieve his goals. Jethro realized that the children of Israel's greatest assets were Moses' heart, God's favor, and the people themselves. He directed Moses to seek God's counsel, to teach the people God's statutes and laws, and to empower the people to share the burden. Jethro's plan would utilize everything of value the people possessed.

4. PEOPLE

Perhaps the greatest ability of an intuitive leader is his skill with people. That separates someone who can understand what it takes to lead from the person who can actually do it. Jethro understood people and leadership well enough to know how to empower Moses' leadership, even though he had no personal experience with the people who had escaped Egypt. Jethro knew that leadership had to be based on ability, not position, and he instinctively understood that the right people were there to lead thousands, hundreds, fifties, and tens. They just had to be put into place.

5. HIMSELF

An intuitive leader reads himself. He understands his strengths, his weaknesses, and his individual calling. Jethro was capable of doing that with himself. First, he read and understood the leadership problem Moses faced. Second, he must have realized that he was not the man to do the job of leading the Hebrews. He understood that was Moses' calling. So he read and evaluated Moses' leadership ability and planned accordingly.

Look at any leader whose intuition is sharp, and you will see an ability to read a leadership situation. When Nehemiah looked at the wall in Jerusalem, he knew what to do. When Joseph understood Pharaoh's dream, he knew how to prepare for the famine. Intuition, whether it's natural or has been developed intentionally, helps a good leader to become a great leader.

TODAY'S QUESTION FOR REFLECTION:
Do others see leadership issues before you do?

Day 3

A leader of good judgment gives stability;
an exploiting leader leaves a trail of waste.
Proverbs 29:4 (*The Message*)

Because leaders see the world with a leadership bias, they are capable of making an immediate impact on their people and organizations. And that makes it possible for them to add value to others' lives.

When Jethro stepped into Moses' life and helped him improve his leadership, his efforts made a huge difference not only for Moses, but also for all the children of Israel. He told Moses, "If you do this thing, and God so commands you, then you will be able to endure, and all this people will also go to their place in peace" (Ex. 18:23 NKJV).

PROVIDING WHAT OTHERS CAN'T

Take a look at the following five characteristics of leaders who use their intuition and how these characteristics help them to provide things for their people that others can't:

1. THEY SEE DIFFERENTLY—THEY PROVIDE CORRECTION

Just about anyone can see problems, but leaders know how to correct the problems. Because leaders view a situation in terms of the leadership dynamics, they are able to help an organization make critical adjustments.

It's clear that Moses saw the problems of the people. He told Jethro, "When they have a difficulty, they come to me, and I judge between one and another; and I make known the statutes of God and His laws" (Ex. 18:16 NKJV). Moses saw only the human needs; Jethro saw the leadership needs.

He corrected Moses' inclination to do everything himself instead of lead others.

2. THEY SEE GLOBALLY—THEY PROVIDE DIRECTION

As I mentioned yesterday, Jethro could see that Moses was headed for trouble if he continued in the way he was currently working. Good leaders always keep the big picture in mind. That's why they have the ability to look farther ahead than their followers.

Jethro knew instinctively that the long-term goal of the people was to "go to their place in peace" (Ex. 18:23 NKJV). He knew that a solution to Moses' predicament had to help everyone go in that direction.

3. THEY SEE CLEARLY—THEY PROVIDE STRUCTURE

Leadership is about getting people to follow. That's why this is my favorite leadership proverb: "He who thinketh he leadeth but hath no one following only taketh a walk." But good leaders do more than motivate people to follow in the moment. They provide structure that allows leadership to flourish.

When Jethro suggested that Moses create a system where men would be "rulers of thousands, rulers of hundreds, rulers of fifties, and rulers of tens" (Ex. 18:21 NKJV), he was suggesting a structure that would encourage good leadership,

> Good leaders do more than motivate people to follow in the moment. They provide structure that allows leadership to flourish.

not inhibit it. Leaders would be allowed to work, contribute, and flourish according to their ability. More gifted leaders would impact large numbers of people, and less gifted leaders would not be in over their heads.

4. THEY SEE RELATIONALLY—THEY PROVIDE SUPPORT

Leaders always take into account the relationships of the people they impact. Jethro knew that Moses and the leaders he appointed would be in a position to support one another. Each leader would solve the problems he could at his own level. That would help everyone to keep from burning out, including Moses. And Moses would hear the toughest cases that no one else could solve, which would support the leaders as well as the people they cared for.

5. THEY SEE EXPECTANTLY—THEY PROVIDE CONFIDENCE

With intuition comes confidence. Leaders who have developed their intuitive abilities and learned to rely on them bring a sense of accomplishment to their leadership. They become sure of themselves, and that confidence in themselves instills confidence in others.

Moses trusted Jethro's advice. Scripture tells us, "Moses heeded the voice of his father-in-law and did all that he had said . . . Then Moses let his father-in-law depart, and he went his way to his own land" (Ex. 18:24, 27 NKJV). Jethro stayed just long enough for Moses to implement his suggestion, then he moved on, confident that everything would work out as planned.

Jethro gained nothing from helping Moses become a leader. He wasn't rewarded. He didn't receive property. No songs were written about his leadership. His entire story occupies one short chapter in the Bible. The insight he shared from intuition was a gift he gave freely to add value to the lives of the Hebrew people. That's what great leaders do.

TODAY'S QUESTION FOR REFLECTION:
Do you use your insight to add value to others?

Day 4

A discerning man keeps wisdom in view,
but a fool's eyes wander to the ends of the earth.
Proverbs 17:24 (NIV)

All this talk about intuition has probably had one of two effects on you: (1) if you are a natural leader, you have felt encouraged because you have seen yourself in the leadership of Jethro; or (2) if you are not a natural leader, you have felt discouraged because you have realized that your leadership intuition is much weaker than you would like it to be.

If you identify with Jethro, that's great. Keep sharpening and using your intuition, especially with the purpose of adding value to others. But if you're in the second situation, please allow me to encourage you with this thought: you may be like Moses. Unlike his father-in-law, he wasn't a natural leader, yet he ended up being one of the greatest leaders in the Bible.

COMPETING WITH THE BEST

How can any leader, no matter how talented, compete with the best leaders? Let me give you the answer with an illustration I share at leadership conferences. I can compete with *and beat* the fastest sprinters in the world in the one-hundred-yard dash. Now, you may find that claim remarkable since I am over fifty years old and have never been fast. What's my secret? A fifty-yard head start. Give me fifty yards, and I'll beat the world record holder.

Possessing intuition is exactly like having a head start in a sprint. That's what intuition does for any leader: it gives him or her a head start. Jethro gave Moses a head start by sharing his intuition. It caused Moses to change his way of thinking and his way of working. To become a better leader, Moses did the following:

1. HE BECAME A MAN OF PRAYER

Jethro's first piece of advice to Moses was to "stand before God for the people, so that you may bring the difficulties to God" (Ex. 18:19 NKJV). Moses might have started praying for the benefit of the people, but he grew to be a great man of prayer—the greatest in the Bible.

2. HE COMMUNICATED PERSONALLY WITH THE PEOPLE

When God first recruited Moses as a leader, he was afraid to talk to the people. In fact, God allowed him to speak through Aaron. But good leaders don't abdicate the responsibility to communicate. When Moses began speaking for himself, he became closer to the people, and his leadership ability reached a new level.

3. HE LAID OUT THE VISION

Jethro instructed Moses to "teach [the people] the statutes and the laws, and show them the way in which they must walk and the work they must do" (Ex. 18:20 NKJV). When Moses shared God's ways with the people, he was sharing the vision for a whole new way of living. And he was also sharing the responsibility with the people.

4. HE SELECTED AND TRAINED LEADERS

The whole key to the success of Jethro's plan was the appointment of additional leaders. The Scripture states that "Moses chose able men out of all Israel, and made them heads over the people: rulers of thousands, rulers of hundreds, rulers of fifties, and rulers of tens" (Ex. 18:25 NKJV). That was no simple task. Exodus 12:37 records that 600,000 men left Egypt. Finding the leaders, teaching them, and placing them at the right level would have required tremendous leadership on the part of Moses.

5. HE RELEASED THEM TO LEAD

The final change in Moses' approach to leadership was his willingness to stop doing it all by himself. After Moses appointed the leaders, "they judged the people at all times; the hard cases they brought to Moses, but they judged every small case themselves" (Ex. 18:26 NKJV). From that time on, Moses empowered his people to do the work of leadership, and he did *only* what they could not do. That's good leadership.

Learning to become a better leader—a more intuitive leader—is a process. It takes time and trials. But anyone can do it. By the end of Moses' life, he knew intuitively that the people needed another leader to guide them after he died. And when

> ❧
>
> **Moses empowered his people to do the work of leadership, and he did only what they could not do. That's good leadership.**

he asked God to provide one, He gave the people Joshua, a man who had been learning leadership from Moses for more than forty years.

❧

TODAY'S QUESTION FOR REFLECTION:
What are you doing to increase your leadership intuition?

Day 5

Bringing the Law to Life

TAKING IT IN

One test of leadership intuition is whether you see things coming before others do or are continually blindsided by people, situations, and problems. If others in your organization are accurately sensing things ahead of you (especially people under your leadership), then you need to work on your intuition. And remember:

1. Who you are is what you see.

2. Intuitive leaders are readers.

3. A leader's intuition can add value to others.

4. Your leadership intuition can be increased.

SORTING IT OUT

If you're not sure where you stand when it comes to understanding and applying the Law of Intuition, visit the Web site www.injoy.com/21 Minutes to take a free twenty-five-question assessment quiz that will help you measure your ability.

PRAYING IT THROUGH

Use the following words to begin your time of prayer:

Dear God, the psalmist prayed, "Teach me good judgment and knowledge, for I believe Your commandments." I make that same request. Help me to increase my leadership ability and hone my intuition. And may I exercise good judgment for the benefit of the people You've placed in my care. Amen.

LIVING IT OUT

If you desire to gain the head start that leadership intuition provides, then take the following steps:

- *Learn all you can about leadership.* Intuition must be built upon a base of understanding. Study leadership. In particular, read biographies of noteworthy intuitive leaders.

- *Observe an intuitive leader.* The day Moses heeded the advice of Jethro, his leadership started going up to a new level. You need to spend time with intuitive leaders to learn how they think. Watch them, and ask questions about why they made certain leadership decisions.

- *Practice what you learn.* You cannot develop intuition only by studying leadership. It comes only with experience. As you learn new leadership principles, put them into practice.

- *Learn from your mistakes to improve.* Everyone fails. Every leader makes mistakes. Improved leadership comes not just from trying and failing. It comes from trying, failing, and learning from the experiences.

PASSING IT ON

Which one leadership concept, insight, or practice that you've learned this week will you pass on to another leader in the next two days?

Week 9

THE LAW OF MAGNETISM

WHO YOU ARE IS WHO YOU ATTRACT

Effective leaders are always on the lookout for good people. I think each of us carries around a mental list of what kind of people we would like in our organization . . . Believe it or not, whom you get is not determined by what you *want*. It's determined by who you are . . . In most situations, you draw people to you who possess the same qualities you do . . .

It is possible for a leader to go out and recruit people unlike himself . . . but it's crucial to recognize that people who are different will not naturally be attracted to [him] . . . The people who are drawn to you probably have more similarities than differences . . . Their quality does not depend on a hiring process, a human resources department, or even what you consider to be the quality of your area's applicant pool. It depends on you . . . If you think the people you attract could be better, then it's time for you to improve yourself.

FROM "THE LAW OF MAGNETISM" IN *The 21 Irrefutable Laws of Leadership*

Day 1

Elijah
and the
Law of Magnetism

LEADERSHIP THOUGHT FOR TODAY:
Leaders attract not whom they want but who they are.

Read
1 Kings 16:29–17:24; 18:20–46; 19:11–21;
2 Kings 1:1–2:25; 4:1–37

People either loved or hated him. King Ahab called him "O troubler of Israel" and "O my enemy." Ahab's wife, Jezebel, wanted him dead. But the people who loved God flocked to this man and sought his leadership. I'm talking about Elijah, the leader considered by some to be the most famous and most dramatic of all the prophets of ancient Israel.

Elijah's leadership was characterized by fire. He possessed a fiery passion for God and the truth. And his most memorable action as a leader occurred when he confronted the false prophets of Baal on Mount Carmel and called down fire from God to consume the sacrifice he offered. How appropriate it is that his time on earth ended with his being swept up in a chariot of fire sent by God to carry him to heaven.

Elijah's life was also characterized by magnetism. When he humiliated Baal's prophets, he won over the people. But he did more than that. He attracted people who were like himself. Groups of prophets followed him, including his chief protégé, Elisha, who ultimately asked for a "double portion" of Elijah's spirit. As a result, Elisha carried the torch after Elijah was gone by continuing the same kind of fiery leadership—and with even greater results than those of his predecessor.

THE TRUTH OF ATTRACTION

What made Elijah draw like-minded people to him? The answer is found in the Law of Magnetism. Who you are is who you attract. Here are some truths about magnetism and how it impacts leadership:

1. EVERY LEADER HAS A MEASURE OF MAGNETISM

All leaders attract people. Highly charismatic ones often attract large numbers of people, but even modest leaders have a following. If they didn't, they wouldn't be leaders, would they? After all, leadership is influence.

2. A LEADER'S MAGNETISM MAY IMPACT OTHERS INTELLECTUALLY, EMOTIONALLY, OR VOLITIONALLY

Not all leaders affect people in the same way, nor do they use the same means of influencing others. The greatest leaders connect on multiple levels: with followers' minds, hearts, and wills.

That was the case for Elijah. His magnetism affected people on every level. A perfect example is his defeat of the false prophets of Baal. He connected with the people first by calling down fire from heaven. Even confirmed skeptics in the crowd received proof that God was real. But that alone was not enough. To give his message more emotional impact, Elijah drenched his sacrifice in gallons of water. As a result, they declared, "The LORD, He is God!" (1 Kings 18:39 NKJV). Elijah's connection on a volitional level can be seen in his cry, "Seize the prophets of Baal!" (1 Kings 18:40 NKJV), which the people did in order to execute them.

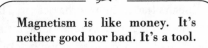

Magnetism is like money. It's neither good nor bad. It's a tool.

3. MAGNETISM IS NEITHER GOOD NOR BAD IN ITSELF— IT DEPENDS ON WHAT A LEADER DOES WITH IT

Charismatic leaders come in all shapes and sizes. There are Adolf Hitlers and Mother Teresas, Ahabs and Elijahs. Magnetism is like money. It's neither good nor bad. It's a tool. Elijah used his ability to attract like-minded people in order to fulfill his mission and extend his influence beyond his leadership and time on earth.

4. WHILE ALL LEADERS DRAW SIMILAR FOLLOWERS, SECURE LEADERS DRAW BOTH SIMILAR AND COMPLEMENTARY FOLLOWERS

Your natural tendency as a leader will always be to attract people similar to yourself: similar in values, age, and attitude, among other things. That was true of Elijah. His leadership attracted people who loved God and who were gifted in prophecy. But secure leaders—ones who acknowledge and accept their weaknesses as well as their strengths—also attract people who complement their ministry.

For example, secure, big-picture leaders attract detail people. And strategic leaders attract relationally talented people. When a leader is not threatened by people who shine in areas where he is weak, he is able to attract and retain these people.

5. A LEADER'S MAGNETISM IS NOT STATIC

A leader's magnetism can be cultivated, shaped, and matured. Like every other quality found in good leaders, magnetism can be developed. The ability to cast a vision and connect with people can be improved. Before Elijah drew crowds, he labored in obscurity helping a widow and her son. We don't know anything about his early life, but we do know God provided him with time to cultivate a vision for his life, to make his purpose clear, and to give him confidence. And all those things increased his level of magnetism.

If you will look at the people you have been attracting as a leader, you will find out a lot about yourself. What you observe may please you. But if it doesn't—if you aren't getting the kind or the number of followers you'd like—there's good news. You need not be stuck where you are. You can grow and change in this area of your leadership.

> If you will look at the people you have been attracting as a leader, you will find out a lot about yourself.

TODAY'S QUESTION FOR REFLECTION:
What kind of people are drawn to you?

Day 2

LEADERSHIP THOUGHT FOR TODAY:
People like those they are like.

He who walks with wise men will be wise,
But the companion of fools will be destroyed.
Proverbs 13:20 (NKJV)

You're probably familiar with the old joke that spouses who have been married for a really long time start to look like each other. Or this one: all dogs look and act like their owners. I think the reason people perpetuate these sayings is that they instinctively know that there is a degree of truth in them. We come together with others because of mutual attraction.

That was true of Elijah and Elisha. Theirs is a story of mutual attraction. Certainly Elijah was first drawn to Elisha because God directed him to anoint Elisha in his place. But Elijah didn't move on after he anointed him, as Samuel did with David. He continued to let his protégé work and travel with him. And for his part, Elisha showed his attraction to Elijah in his willingness to become his servant and follow him everywhere he went.

IT'S MORE THAN MERE CHEMISTRY

Mutual attraction is more than chemistry. It has a foundation that comes from many things. Here are four:

1. MUTUAL VISION

Followers do not naturally line up with a leader whose vision they don't respect. Both Elijah and Elisha possessed a vision to serve God for the sake of the people of

> **Followers do not naturally line up with a leader whose vision they don't respect.**

Israel. When Elisha had the opportunity to share Elijah's work, he turned away from his old life of farming and adopted Elijah's vision of leadership as his own. And to prove his dedication, he "took a yoke of oxen [the tools of his previous trade] and slaughtered them and boiled their flesh, using the oxen's equipment" (1 Kings 19:21 NKJV). For Elisha, there would be no turning back.

2. MUTUAL EXPECTATIONS

The natural result of mutual vision is mutual expectations. Both Elijah and Elisha expected to do great things for God. Elisha expected to receive a double portion of the anointing that was on Elijah. And when he received it, his expectations of great leadership were fulfilled.

3. MUTUAL CONTRIBUTION

People follow leaders because they believe that leaders can take them where they want to go. For their part, leaders enlist followers because they understand that followers help them to realize the vision. Together they contribute something to fulfill each other's expectations.

For his part, Elijah was the leader and mentor, giving Elisha the opportunity to remain close to him and learn how to be a godly leader. And when Elisha was ready, Elijah passed his mantle to his follower. Elisha's part of the arrangement required him to humble himself, follow the older prophet, and learn. The arrangement made both of them better leaders.

4. MUTUAL COMMITMENT

Without a strong commitment to each other, leaders and followers cannot achieve their mutual goals. As Elijah came to the end of his time of leadership, Elisha renewed his commitment to his mentor. Three times when Elijah offered to release his protégé, Elisha responded by saying, "As the LORD lives, and as your soul lives, I will not leave!" He was determined to be with his master to the very end.

Elijah's commitment to Elisha was equally strong, and it culminated in the offer to do whatever he could for his servant—extending to the offer of a double portion of his spirit.

As you evaluate your ability to attract people, think about what you have to offer them. Is the attraction mutual? If you're not trying to connect with people and lead them for mutual advantage, then something is missing from your leadership.

✌

TODAY'S QUESTION FOR REFLECTION:
What kind of people are you drawn to?

Day 3

Leadership is who you are before it's what you do.

Live right, and you will eat from the life-giving tree.
And if you act wisely, others will follow.

Proverbs 11:30 (CEV)

I believe that most people tend to think of leadership only in terms of action. But leadership is so much more than that. Leadership is not just something you do; it's something you are. And that's one reason that good leaders have such strong magnetism. People are attracted to *who they are.* (I'll talk more about that in the Law of Buy-In.)

All effective leadership results from who a leader is. That's where everything begins. But that idea is different from the way most people approach leadership. Most people focus on their goals, devoting their time and energy to making them happen. All leaders desire results,

> Leadership is not just something you do; it's something you are. And that's one reason that good leaders have such strong magnetism. People are attracted to *who they are.*

but *being* must precede *doing.* What you are able to do as a leader comes as the result of who you are. To achieve higher goals, you must *be* a more effective leader. To attract better people, you must *be* a better person. To achieve greater results, you must *be* a person of great character.

INCARNATIONAL LEADERSHIP

This whole concept is something I call *incarnational leadership.* The idea is that you must first *be* the leader you are capable of becoming before you are able to achieve the results you desire.

The following table illustrates that who you *are* determines what you *do*. And what you *do* determines the results you get.

WHO I AM	WHAT I DO	RESULT
Characterful	Do right	Credibility
Relational	Care	Love
Encouraging	Believe in people	High morale
Sensitive	Embrace flexibility	Openness for renewal
Visionary	Set goals	Direction
Teachable	Apply what I learn	Growth
Charismatic	Motivate	Inspiration
Humble	Rely on God	Power
Convictional	Remain steadfast	Commitment
Selfless	Focus on others	Outreach
Confident	Make decisions	Security
Spirit-filled	Witness	Fruit

Everything flows from the person you are. Leaders get into trouble when they put their desire for results before their willingness to develop themselves in areas of competence and character.

A common problem occurs when a leader's real identity and the

> Leaders get into trouble when they put their desire for results before their willingness to develop themselves in areas of competence and character.

results he desires don't match up. Given enough time, if there is a difference between what a leader says he wants to do and who he really is, the people will discern it. And that discovery will repel them. On the other hand, a leader who displays consistency of character, competence, and purpose makes a powerful statement to the people around him—and he draws people to him.

You see that kind of consistency in the life of Elijah. No matter what God asked Elijah to do, he did it—whether it was denouncing the king's actions, facing an angry mob of false prophets, traveling into the desert without provisions, or anointing a successor. Who he was, what he did, and the results he achieved all lined up. And that consistency drew people to him like a magnet.

IT'S NOT THE GOAL THAT MAKES THE LEADER

When I teach leadership, I often tell people that I could never teach a goal-setting seminar. I say that not because I haven't reached goals, but because if I had lived my life only according to goals, I would have set my sights too low. God has been very kind to me. He has taken me places that I never would have put on my agenda, and He has helped me accomplish things that I never would have dreamed possible. He has always prompted me to obey Him, cultivate my character, and develop the potential He gave me. And that has yielded results greater than I could have hoped for.

If you desire to do great things with your life, then seek to become a better person and a better leader. Nothing great can be achieved alone. Any task worth doing requires the help of others. And if you want to attract good people, you've got to become a better person. If you're willing to do that, then you can leave the results to God.

❧

TODAY'S QUESTION FOR REFLECTION:
Do you focus on what you've done or who you are becoming?

Day 4

Effective leadership begins with being yourself.

He who earnestly seeks good finds favor,
But trouble will come to him who seeks evil.
Proverbs 11:27 (NKJV)

Now that I've encouraged you to grow to your potential and become the best person you can be, I want to give you a crucial piece of advice: be yourself. As you desire to improve and grow, you will naturally look for role models to help you. That's a good thing. After all, Elisha had Elijah as his role model, and he became a remarkable leader. But you must learn to become the person *you* were created to be and not try to become like someone else.

LEADERS KNOW

That may sound like simplistic advice, but it's important. Good leaders understand themselves: their strengths and weakness, talents and skills, enthusiasms and blind spots. For Elijah to challenge the prophets of Baal and put himself on the line, he needed to know himself, know his God, and know where he stood with Him. Otherwise, he would have gotten himself into terrible trouble. He would have failed as a leader and paid with his life.

How well do you know yourself? Is that something you've ever thought about before? In truth, all people have to deal with four layers of understanding when it comes to their image of themselves. Take a look at the following diagram, and you'll see what I mean.

WHO ARE YOU REALLY?

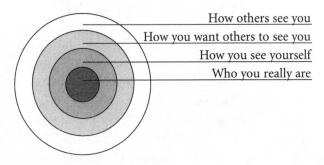

How others see you

How you want others to see you

How you see yourself

Who you really are

1. HOW OTHERS SEE YOU

The outermost layer is the image that others have of you. For better or worse, people have opinions about you—as a person, as a leader, as a parent or child. They see you in a particular light. That image is derived partly from you, but it is also filtered through the values and baggage of others.

For example, think about how others perceived Elijah. Ahab and Jezebel saw him as an enemy. On the other hand, the company of prophets from Bethel saw him as a great prophet and teacher. Elisha, who was closest to Elijah, saw him as his leader, master, and mentor.

2. HOW YOU WANT OTHERS TO SEE YOU

Not everyone is content to simply let other people think what they want about him. Some people spend a lot of time worrying about what others think, and some devote tremendous amounts of time, energy, and money to hiding who they are so that people will have higher opinions of them. Political leaders, entertainers, and professional athletes are notorious for having this focus, and they hire image consultants, PR firms, and spin doctors to handle it.

My experience has been that the weaker or more insecure a leader is, the more he tries to get others to perceive that he is different from the way he really is. There is no trace of image cultivation in the record of Elijah's leadership. He didn't worry about such things.

> The weaker or more insecure a leader is, the more he tries to get others to perceive that he is different from the way he really is.

3. How You See Yourself

Every person has an image of himself in his mind. For some people, self-awareness comes naturally, and their image of themselves is quite accurate. For others, nothing is farther from the truth than who they think they are.

Accurate self-knowledge takes time and intentional effort. It requires growing, exploring, and taking risks. And even a good leader who understands himself pretty well sometimes needs an adjustment in his self-perception. When Elijah escaped from Jezebel into the desert, he perceived himself to be the only person who loved God. He said, "I alone am left; and they seek to take my life" (1 Kings 19:14 NKJV). But God straightened him out, informing him that there were seven thousand others who had remained loyal to God. After that, Elijah's overblown sense of self-importance was diminished, and he was once again able to serve God effectively.

4. Who You Really Are

You may come close to perceiving who you truly are, but you will never see yourself as accurately and completely as God does. The psalmist declared,

> For You formed my inward parts;
> You covered me in my mother's womb.
> I will praise You, for I am fearfully and wonderfully made;
> Marvelous are Your works,
> And that my soul knows very well.
> My frame was not hidden from You,
> When I was made in secret,
> And skillfully wrought in the lowest parts of the earth.
> Your eyes saw my substance, being yet unformed.
> And in Your book they all were written,
> The days fashioned for me,
> When as yet there were none of them. (Ps. 139:13–16 NKJV)

Each of us should seek to discover how God has made us. And we must seek to accept both our assets and our deficits, and then grow to reach our potential. That process helps us to become the best leaders we can be. (And it equips us to help others with the process too.) If we do that, our image of ourselves will align with our real identity, and people will discover us to be who we are—genuine but flawed people doing the best we can. That gains us respect with others who are like-minded and draws them to our leadership.

❧

TODAY'S QUESTION FOR REFLECTION:
How well do my perception of myself, others' perception of me, and my true identity match up?

Day 5

Bringing the Law to Life

TAKING IT IN

What kind of people are you attracting to your organization? Are they people of strong character? Are they highly competent in their areas of expertise? Are they positive people? Do they have a strong sense of work ethic? Are they top-notch leaders? As you consider these questions, remember these truths about the Law of Magnetism:

1. Leaders attract not whom they want but who they are.
2. People like those they are like.
3. Leadership is who you are before it's what you do.
4. Effective leadership begins with being yourself.

Any discontentment with the people under your leadership is a message to you that you need to change.

SORTING IT OUT

If you're not sure where you stand when it comes to understanding and applying the Law of Magnetism, visit the Web site www.injoy.com/21 Minutes to take a free twenty-five-question assessment quiz that will help you measure your ability.

PRAYING IT THROUGH

Use the following words to begin your time of prayer:

Dear God, the apostle Peter understood what it meant to grow to become some-one You could use in leadership. I want to echo the words he wrote in 2 Peter 1:5–9:

> *For this very reason, giving all diligence, add to [my] faith virtue, to virtue knowledge, to knowledge self-control, to self-control persever-ance, to perseverance godliness, to godliness brotherly kindness, and to brotherly kindness love. For if these things are [mine] and abound, [I] will be neither barren nor unfruitful in the knowledge of our Lord Jesus Christ. For he who lacks these things is shortsighted, even to blindness, and has forgotten that he was cleansed from his old sins.*

Lord, show me who I truly am, and make me into the person You desire me to be so that I may effectively lead others to make a difference. Amen.

LIVING IT OUT

Becoming a powerfully magnetic leader doesn't happen overnight. Think about the top three qualities you desire people you attract to possess. Then think about the people who are drawn to you. If you aren't attracting the number and kind of people to your organization that you would like, then follow these guidelines:

1. KNOW WHO YOU ARE, AND ACCEPT THE TALENTS AND WEAKNESSES GOD GAVE YOU

Use a battery of tests such as DISC, Personality Plus, and Myers-Briggs to start off the journey of self-discovery. Study spiritual gifts. And talk to friends who will give you honest feedback on your strengths and weaknesses. Pray for God to guide you through the process.

2. BECOME MORE LIKE THE PERSON YOU DESIRE TO ATTRACT

Since you attract who you are, the way to get better people is to improve yourself. Focus on building strengths of talent and improving weaknesses of character.

3. DEVELOP A STRONG SENSE OF ACCEPTANCE AND SECURITY

Once you become effective at attracting good people like yourself, the next big leap in leadership is to attract complementary support people. Accept that you have little talent in some critical areas, and allow others to shine in those areas. Then support and reward them for their work. If you can do that with sincerity, you will find yourself and your team going to a whole new level.

PASSING IT ON

Which one leadership concept, insight, or practice that you've learned this week will you pass on to another leader in the next two days?

Week 10

THE LAW OF CONNECTION

LEADERS TOUCH A HEART BEFORE THEY ASK FOR A HAND

There's an old saying: To lead yourself, use your head; to lead others, use your heart . . . [Effective leaders know that] you can't move people to action unless you first move them with emotion . . .

Connecting with people isn't something that needs to happen only when a leader is communicating to groups of people. It needs to happen with individuals. The stronger the relationship and connection between individuals, the more likely the follower will want to help the leader . . . Some leaders have problems because they believe that connecting is the responsibility of followers . . . But successful leaders . . . are always initiators. They take the first step with others and then make the effort to continue building relationships . . .

When a leader has done the work to connect with his people, you can see it in the way the organization functions. Among employees there are incredible loyalty and a strong work ethic. The vision of the leader becomes the aspiration of the people. The impact is incredible.

FROM "THE LAW OF CONNECTION" IN *The 21 Irrefutable Laws of Leadership*

Day 1

Rehoboam
and the
Law of Connection

LEADERSHIP THOUGHT FOR TODAY:
*All great leaders have one thing in common:
they connect with people.*

Read
1 Kings 11:41–43; 12:1–33; 14:21–31

Great leaders learn that to be effective, they have to continually put their people first. That's especially true of new leaders who want to gain the confidence and support of their people. But it's also true of veteran leaders who desire to lead their people into new territory. The truth is that connecting with people is not an option for a leader. If you *do not* take the time to connect with your people, you *will not* be able to lead them effectively. A leader is not really *the* leader until he has connected with his people.

When I was the senior pastor of Skyline Church in San Diego, California, I was required to meet with the board of directors from my denomination each year for the purpose of answering one question: "Is there someone else who can better lead this church?" That's not an easy question to have to answer year after year. And it would be especially difficult for a leader who hadn't connected with his people. I know pastors who got bushwhacked at those meetings because church members had run to the board of directors with complaints. But I had no problem with the meetings. I felt I was leading the church the way God asked me to, and I felt confident that the people in my church would approach me with their complaints because I had taken the time to connect with them.

A QUESTION EVERY LEADER MUST ANSWER

Rehoboam never learned the Law of Connection. His life is a vivid example of how it's impossible for a leader to connect with people while pursuing selfish ends. Rehoboam was power hungry and was more concerned about flexing his political muscle than connecting with his people. Even when his people promised they would follow him forever if he lightened the burden on them, he refused their offer and pursued his agenda. As a result, he sealed his fate as an ineffective leader.

It's difficult to connect with people while pursuing your selfish agenda. By nature, connecting is a giving experience. If you desire to connect with others, check your motives according to the following guidelines:

> It's difficult to connect with people while pursuing your selfish agenda. By nature, connecting is a giving experience.

1. GET BEYOND YOURSELF

Dr. Albert Schweitzer asserted, "Whatever you have received more than others—in health, in talents, in ability, in success . . . all this you must not take to yourself as a matter of course. In gratitude for good fortune, you must render some sacrifice of your own life for another life." People who fail to get beyond themselves are usually selfish, insecure, or both. Clearly Rehoboam never got beyond himself. His motives were self-serving from the start, and he was caught up in the limelight of his position. He thought his bullying would produce more respect, but it produced only contempt. To connect with people, remain other-minded, and remember that leadership is a privilege.

2. GROW BEYOND YOURSELF

Mahatma Gandhi once remarked, "The difference between what we do and what we are capable of doing would suffice to solve most of the world's problems." If Rehoboam had gleaned from the experience of the elders, he probably would have realized how little he knew about leading Israel. But he was cocky and unteachable. He missed a great opportunity for growth, and he destroyed the nation. If you want to grow beyond yourself, you have to remain humble and teachable. That's the only way to tap into your potential and to connect with the people.

3. GIVE BEYOND YOURSELF

People with low self-esteem are almost always preoccupied with themselves. On the other hand, I once read a study done at the University of Michigan that revealed that people who volunteer their time on a regular basis heighten their overall zest for living and increase their life expectancy.

Rehoboam had no interest in what he could give. He was out to get whatever he could. Life's most urgent and persistent question for leaders is, "What are you doing for others?" To make an impact on your people, you must be a river, not a reservoir.

> Life's most urgent and persistent question for leaders is, "What are you doing for others?"

4. GO BEYOND YOURSELF

There's a Middle Eastern saying: "When you were born, you cried, and the world rejoiced. May you live your life so that when you die, the world will cry, and you will rejoice." The essence of going beyond yourself is having a connection with others that is so far-reaching that you make a difference in the lives of people whom you have never met. Scripture indicates that the only legacy left by Rehoboam was war. He had the distinction of being the king who destroyed the nation God had chosen as His own.

In contrast, leaders who genuinely touch the lives of their people over a sustained period of time can make an impact beyond themselves. When connecting with people is continually a priority in your life, going beyond yourself is almost inevitable.

The ability to connect is a quality you see in *every* great leader. No matter how much leadership talent or skill you possess, if you want to be a better leader, you must learn to connect with people effectively—not just for your own benefit, but for the benefit of your people. Do it, and it will raise your level of leadership dramatically. Do it well, and people will follow you anywhere.

TODAY'S QUESTION FOR REFLECTION:
How readily do you connect with people?

Day 2

Connecting with the people is the leader's responsibility.

My dear, dear friends! I love you so much. I do want the very best for you. You make me feel such joy, fill me with such pride. Don't waver. Stay on track, steady in God.

Philippians 4:1 (*The Message*)

As I mentioned in my book *Becoming a Person of Influence*, a leader who connects with people is a lot like a locomotive connecting to train cars. When I was a kid, I used to go to the GE yard not far from my home in Circleville, Ohio, and watch the locomotives. Never did the cars pull forward and connect to the locomotive. The locomotive always backed up until it hooked up with the cars. The same is true of leaders. Great leaders don't expect their people to move forward and latch on to them. Instead, they reach out to people, no matter where they are, and work to make a connection.

WHEN YOU CONNECT WITH PEOPLE . . .

Connecting with people isn't complicated, but it takes a lot of effort. I've noted some connection principles here. Observe how Rehoboam violated them:

1. WHEN YOU MOVE YOUR PEOPLE WITH EMOTION FIRST, THEY ARE MORE WILLING TO TAKE ACTION

Rehoboam had a cold and crusty heart. Even when King Solomon's elders wisely advised that the people would serve Rehoboam forever if he would lighten their workload, he turned a deaf ear. Because he never showed any concern for the physical or emotional welfare of his people, they sought another leader who would listen to them.

When you are open to your people's needs, they will be open to your vision. When you take action to meet their needs, they will take action to fulfill your vision. One of the wisest investments a leader can make is in discerning and meeting

> One of the wisest investments a leader can make is in discerning and meeting the needs of people.

the needs of people. That way when the time comes to move them to action, you will have a positive history to draw upon.

2. WHEN YOU GIVE FIRST, YOUR PEOPLE WILL GIVE IN RETURN

The elders had it right when they advised Rehoboam to serve his people. According to Scripture, Rehoboam had multiple opportunities to give to his people. But giving was not on his agenda. His desire was to be served, but his greed worked against him.

A paradox of leadership is that you get more by giving more. When you give of your time, talent, and possessions to others, you receive them multiplied. And when you're willing to make sacrifices for an organization, it gives back even more.

3. WHEN YOU CONNECT WITH INDIVIDUALS, SOON YOU WILL GAIN THE ATTENTION OF CROWDS

Rehoboam was an impersonal leader. Too arrogant to walk among his people, he tried to lead Israel from behind the palace walls. He thought his title released him from the responsibility of connecting with individuals.

The nature of leadership is that it often requires speaking before groups of people. But effective leaders understand that true connection doesn't happen with the masses—it happens one-on-one (even when speaking to a large crowd). People are glad to team up with a leader they know and respect.

4. WHEN YOU REACH OUT TO YOUR PEOPLE, THEY WILL REACH BACK TOWARD YOU

The initial confrontation between Rehoboam and his people took place because the people came to him. Although there was a big problem within the kingdom—the people were on the verge of revolting—Rehoboam was so out of touch that he failed to initiate any communication with the people. When it became clear that his actions (or lack thereof) were the cause of his people's displeasure, he pointed a finger at the people instead of trying to rectify the situation. Rehoboam was a *reactive* leader rather than a *proactive* one—and his reactions were negative at that. As a result, the kingdom ripped apart.

Whether you have just taken over a leadership position or are well established in your organization, being connected to your people is vital to your success as a leader. Remember that the telltale sign of a great leader is not what he has accomplished on his own, but what he has been able to accomplish through people. That comes only as the result of connection.

TODAY'S QUESTION FOR REFLECTION:
Do you initiate connection with your people?

Day 3

Connection starts with the heart.

Without counsel, plans go awry,
But in the multitude of counselors they are established.
Proverbs 15:22 (NKJV)

Too many leaders underestimate the importance of connection. They believe that people will follow them because they're supposed to. Although that may work initially, it won't sustain your leadership. In other words, being the leader may give you a small advantage by initially being given the benefit of the doubt. But you can't depend on that for lasting influence. In time, if you don't earn your right to be followed by connecting *with* your people, it will be increasingly difficult to accomplish anything of value *through* your people.

To earn the right to be followed, you have to touch people's hearts. That requires more than being a manager or a boss or a supervisor. It requires you to be their friend, their teacher, and their coach. You see, your people are smart—their minds won't embrace what their hearts can't explain. If you haven't taken the time to show your people that you genuinely care for their well-being, you won't be very successful in leading them, even if your motives are pure. But when people see that they matter to you as individuals, and that their concerns make a difference in what you do and don't do, they will listen to what you say.

CHANGES REHOBOAM COULD HAVE MADE TO CONNECT

Initially Rehoboam had several opportunities to connect to the hearts of his people. On more than one occasion, his people stated how he could win their hearts. And if he had listened, he would have had their hands in everything he wanted to accomplish. Instead, he tried to force them to follow him without any connection, and his kingdom fell apart.

Maybe you've read up to this point and realized that you've made the mistake of asking for a hand from your people before you connected to their hearts. Rehoboam could have made four changes to connect to the hearts of his people. Do any of them apply to you?

1. INSTEAD OF LECTURING, LISTEN

Rehoboam failed to listen—first to the people, then to the elders who gave him the right advice. He cared more about hearing his voice than that of his people.

If you struggle with doing too much talking and not enough listening, you may be missing opportunities to connect. Next time you're in a meeting, make a conscious effort to allow others to speak first. If you can, designate one meeting where you will do nothing but listen to the hearts of your people.

2. INSTEAD OF PROJECTING IMAGE, PROJECT INTEGRITY

Needless to say, Rehoboam cared very little about integrity. He was more concerned with asserting his newfound authority over the people so they wouldn't perceive him as a weak leader. And he was willing to do whatever it took to make sure the people knew *he* was in charge.

I've always maintained that anyone who has to tell people he's the leader isn't really the leader. Do you have to explain to some people that you are in charge? If you do, you may need to back up and spend some time building a trustworthy relationship with them first.

3. INSTEAD OF DEMANDING CONTROL, DEMONSTRATE COMPASSION

There's no doubt that Rehoboam was a control freak. From the moment he was crowned king, he ruled the people with an unmerciful hand.

If you've established a healthy connection with your people, there is no need to parade your control over them. Take a look at how you handle your people's mistakes. Do you hang the mistake over their heads and treat them like failures? Or do you take the time to show them how to improve and give them a second chance to succeed?

4. INSTEAD OF GLARING AT OTHERS, GAZE THROUGH THEIR EYES

If Rehoboam had looked through the eyes of his people, he would have seen their hardships and their genuine desire to serve him. And he would have observed an opportunity to win the loyalty of an entire nation.

Are your people excited about the work your organization is doing? Have you taken time to ask them? What do they think about your leadership? Always take time to put yourself in their shoes. Their insight can be a valuable tool for determining what direction you should lead them.

Every leader faces the prospect of making changes to improve the connection with his people. The way that leaders deal with change says a lot about their effectiveness. Ineffective leaders, like Rehoboam, often fear change at all costs and never break free of the status quo. The result: momentum eventually comes to a halt, and leadership becomes stagnant. On the other hand, effective leaders are teachable—their eyes and ears are always open to learn more, and they embrace change as a catalyst for growth and improvement. When it comes to developing productive relationships, flexibility is essential.

TODAY'S QUESTION FOR REFLECTION:
*What changes are you willing to make to improve
your ability to connect?*

Day 4

He who refreshes others will himself be refreshed.
Proverbs 11:25 (NIV)

Connection isn't something that just happens once you establish a relationship with a person. It requires more than saying hello in the halls or sending a Christmas form letter to everyone in your organization. It requires an investment in another's life. But unlike an investment that you make in a bank, your connection with others won't grow by making one deposit. For a productive connection, you must make regular deposits in others' lives.

The truth is that the work of connecting is never finished. True connection is an ongoing effort. But all great leaders know that no job is more important than their continual investment in people.

> The truth is that the work of connecting is never finished. True connection is an ongoing effort.

HOW TO CONTINUALLY CONNECT WITH PEOPLE

The following is a list of seven actions that I believe every leader needs to carry out on a continual basis. You can use it as a checklist for connecting with someone new or as a daily reminder for preserving and strengthening current connections.

1. CONNECT WITH YOURSELF

Do you know your strengths and weaknesses? Understand yourself before trying to understand others. A positive self-image helps others feel secure with you.

2. SHARE WITH OPENNESS AND SINCERITY

Are you willing to be vulnerable with others? Vulnerability is an equalizer and will immediately help others relate to you on their level.

3. LIVE YOUR MESSAGE

Are you doing what you're asking others to do? Make sure your actions are always consistent with your words. Integrity promotes trust.

4. KNOW YOUR AUDIENCE

Do you understand the needs of your people? When you know what your people need, you can focus your actions on meeting those needs.

5. COMMUNICATE ON OTHERS' LEVEL

How do you come across when you talk to your people? If you're condescending, your people will come to resent you. But when you talk to them as friends, they will come to respect you.

6. BELIEVE TOTALLY IN YOUR PEOPLE

Do you believe in the ability of your people to succeed? As a leader, you have the job of setting your people up for success. That requires you to demonstrate your trust in them.

7. OFFER DIRECTION AND HOPE

Are you inspiring to your people? In every form of communication, whether words or actions, you should be a positive encouragement to your people.

The ability to connect with people is essential if you want strong, successful leadership. Years ago, I determined what things were most important for me to invest in each day to succeed as a leader. I came up with these things:

- Creativity
- Connecting
- Networking
- Communicating

If you notice, three out of the four items have to do with connecting. I spend 75 percent of every day connecting with people. I do that because I've learned—as I believe every leader should—that the more time you contribute to establishing and strengthening your connection with people, the more opportunities you will have to lead.

❦

TODAY'S QUESTION FOR REFLECTION:
In what areas do you need to improve your connection with others?

Day 5

Bringing the Law to Life

TAKING IT IN

Review the following leadership thoughts related to the Law of Connection:

1. All great leaders have one thing in common: they connect with people.

2. Connecting with the people is the leader's responsibility.

3. Connection starts with the heart.

4. Connection requires intentional effort.

How are you doing when it comes to connecting with others? As the leader, have you taken the responsibility for connecting with your people? Or do you sit back and wait for them to initiate? Are you a natural people person? If you are, you may be leaning too heavily on your charisma instead of intentional connection. If you're not a people person, you may need to start with your heart and give others a chance to get to know you better.

SORTING IT OUT

If you're not sure where you stand when it comes to understanding and applying the Law of Connection, visit the Web site www.injoy.com/21 Minutes to take a free twenty-five-question assessment quiz that will help you measure your ability.

PRAYING IT THROUGH

Use the following words to begin your time of prayer:

Dear God, I want to make a significant impact in people's lives. Give me a heart that is genuinely concerned for other people. Help me to build honest, strong relationships, and show me opportunities where I can give of myself to better others. Amen.

LIVING IT OUT

Is there a key person in your life with whom you have had trouble connecting? Based on what you've read in this chapter, what has been the main source of your inability to connect? What one action can you take this week to promote connection with that person?

PASSING IT ON

Which one leadership concept, insight, or practice that you've learned this week will you pass on to another leader in the next two days?

Week 11

THE LAW OF THE INNER CIRCLE

A Leader's Potential Is Determined by Those Closest to Him

There are no Lone Ranger leaders. Think about it: If you're alone, you're not *leading* anybody, are you?

Leadership expert Warren Bennis was right when he maintained, "The leader finds greatness in the group, and he or she helps the members find it in themselves." Think of any highly effective leader, and you will find someone who surrounded himself with a strong inner circle . . .

Hire the best staff you can find, develop them as much as you can, and hand off everything you possibly can to them . . . When you have the right staff, potential skyrockets . . .

You see, every leader's potential is determined by the people closest to him. If those people are strong, then the leader can make a huge impact. If they are weak, he can't.

From "The Law of the Inner Circle" in *The 21 Irrefutable Laws of Leadership*

Day 1

David
and the
Law of the Inner Circle

LEADERSHIP THOUGHT FOR TODAY:
Teamwork makes the dream work.

Read
2 Samuel 8:1–8, 15–18; 10:6–14; 23:8–38;
1 Chronicles 12:1–40

What made David a great man? That's easy to answer: his heart for God. What made him a great leader? That's harder to answer. David had a lot of things going for him: talent, humility, courage, vision. But I assert that second only to his desire to love and serve God was David's ability to surround himself with strong people and team up with them to achieve greatness. Like the potential of any other strong leader, David's potential was determined by those closest to him. That's the power of the Law of the Inner Circle.

David was a man of many talents, and he was able to accomplish many things on his own. He was a skillful musician. He was a prolific songwriter. And he was a courageous warrior, as displayed by his single-handed defeat of Goliath. But David's destiny was for greater accomplishments than those he could do only on his own. He was to have influence over an entire nation. And his leadership would affect generations of people beyond his own lifetime. As you examine his life, you will see that his noteworthy accomplishments were made possible by the circle of people around him.

HIS CIRCLE STARTED WITH ONE

When David was on the run and Saul was determined to kill him, his future looked bleak. He was hated and hunted. But everything changed for David on the day his inner circle grew by one: Jonathan. Perhaps that relationship taught David the Law of the Inner Circle. From that moment on, David's success rose and fell in direct proportion to the quality of people he had around him.

David didn't wait until he held a leadership position to begin building his inner circle. Long before he ascended the throne of Israel, while he was

> David didn't wait until he held a leadership position to begin building his inner circle.

being hunted by Saul, David began drawing people to himself. First Samuel 22:1–2 gives this account of what happened after he fled from Saul: "When his brothers and all his father's house heard it, they went down there to him. And everyone who was in distress, everyone who was in debt, and everyone who was discontented gathered to him. So he became captain over them. And there were about four hundred men with him" (NKJV).

Ironically, David's next inner circle members were his father and brothers—the people who had dismissed and ignored him when Samuel sought to anoint a new king from the house of Jesse. David's other followers were misfits: the distressed, debt-ridden, and discontented. Yet David transformed the people who came to him into a winning team. That early group of men helped him stay out of the reach of Saul, assisted him in saving the city of Keilah (1 Sam. 23), and fought alongside him in many victories including those over the Geshurites, Girzites, and Amalekites (1 Sam. 27:8). Those men made up the core group that would remain with David during the worst of times.

FROM MISFITS TO MIGHTY MEN

As David gained experience and grew in his leadership, he continued to attract stronger and stronger people. And he also molded those who came to him into great warriors and leaders. Scripture speaks of David's mighty men, a group like no other in all the Bible. The men were strong when they came to David, but he made them even stronger. He mentored, inspired, and elevated them to become as good as or better than he was. David, a giant killer as a youth, developed and led them to become giant killers. Four other men—Abishai, Sibbechai, Elhanan, and Jonathan (son of Shimea)—became warriors who killed giants while serving David.

BUILDING A KINGDOM

By the time David ascended the throne of Judah, he had developed a strong inner circle. By the time he became king of all Israel, he was ready to build a powerful nation. He got to work immediately subduing his enemies. He and his men conquered the territories around them, beginning with the weakest: the Philistines. Then they continued counterclockwise to defeat Moab, Zobah, and Syria. They made Israel secure.

Then David developed some structure to keep his kingdom stable. He required the nations he conquered to serve him and pay tribute. And he placed garrisons in their territory to ensure his nation's security. Once he had that structure in place, he was able to turn his attention to setting up his administration with an emphasis on justice (2 Sam. 8:15).

It has been said that a good executive never puts off till tomorrow what he can have someone else do today. David had no trouble delegating to his leaders. Scripture contains several lists of people who

> It has been said that a good executive never puts off to tomorrow what he can have someone else do today.

were part of David's inner circle. Three separate times the names of the men who served him in his administration are recorded (2 Sam. 8:16–18; 20:23–26; 1 Chron. 18:14–17). And twice David's mighty men are listed by name (2 Sam. 23:8–39; 1 Chron. 11:10–47).

Thanks to David's strong leadership and the help of his inner circle, the king was able to accomplish many incredible feats during his reign:

- He consolidated and unified the kingdom of Israel.

- He conquered the Hebrews' enemies and made Israel stronger than it had ever been before.

- He established a lasting administration to dispense justice.

- He conquered the city of Jerusalem and made it the nation's capital.

- He brought the ark of the covenant to the city and reestablished worship.

- He established his dynasty and passed the crown to his son Solomon.

David was an incredible leader and team builder, but in many ways he was an ordinary person—with flaws, problems, and failures. Thanks to his inner circle, he became a remarkable king and ruler.

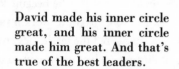

> David made his inner circle great, and his inner circle made him great. And that's true of the best leaders.

He made his inner circle great, and his inner circle made him great. And that's true of the best leaders.

❦

TODAY'S QUESTION FOR REFLECTION:
Will your current team fulfill your dream?

Day 2

A team is more than just a group of people.

Now these were the men who came to David at Ziklag while he was still a fugitive from Saul the son of Kish; and they were among the mighty men, helpers in the war, armed with bows, using both the right hand and the left in hurling stones and shooting arrows with the bow . . . Some Gadites joined David at the stronghold in the wilderness, mighty men of valor, men trained for battle, who could handle shield and spear, whose faces were like the faces of lions, and were as swift as gazelles on the mountains . . . captains of the army; the least was over a hundred, and the greatest was over a thousand . . . They put to flight all those in the valleys, to the east and to the west . . . Then the Spirit came upon Amasai, chief of the captains, and he said:

> "We are yours, O David;
> We are on your side, O son of Jesse!
> Peace, peace to you,
> And peace to your helpers!
> For your God helps you."

So David received them, and made them captains of the troop . . . For at that time they came to David day by day to help him, until it was a great army, like the army of God.

1 Chronicles 12:1–2, 8, 14–15, 18, 22 (NKJV)

With a strong inner circle, David was able to conquer his enemies and build Israel into a strong nation unlike any the Hebrews had ever known before. As he ascended the throne of Israel, David's circle of followers turned into a huge army. By the time warriors from all the tribes came to him, he had more than 230,000 warriors following him! But the size of the team (or army) isn't what makes a leader great. It's the core of the team—the leader's inner circle. And David built a remarkable inner circle.

THE GROWTH OF DAVID'S INNER CIRCLE

Examine the way that David pulled together the core people who made him great:

1. HE STARTED BUILDING A STRONG INNER CIRCLE BEFORE HE NEEDED IT

As I mentioned before, David began building his team long before he was crowned king. First Samuel 22 describes how warriors were drawn to David even from the time he was a fugitive. But the passage in 1 Chronicles that describes how the people came to him is much more specific. It emphasizes how many of them were leaders. For example, the eleven men listed from Gad were "captains of the army; the least was over a hundred, and the greatest was over a thousand" (1 Chron 12:14 NKJV). He didn't attract just anyone. He attracted strong leaders.

2. HE ATTRACTED PEOPLE WITH VARIED GIFTS

Scripture also captures the diversity of abilities possessed by the people David attracted, first at Ziklag before he became king, then at Hebron after he ascended the throne. Listed are experienced warriors with a variety of skills (ambidextrous bowmen, slingers, and spearmen), many mighty men of valor, and hundreds of captains. With these men's help, David would be ready for anything.

3. HE ENGENDERED LOYALTY

Throughout David's life, his followers displayed incredible loyalty. Before David was king, when he stated that he was thirsty for a drink from the well in Bethlehem, three of his men risked their lives to get him some of that water. Decades later when David's son Absalom committed treason against him and it looked as though David might be defeated, his closest men stayed with him. Ittai the Gittite spoke for all of them when he said, "As the LORD lives, and as my lord the king lives, surely in whatever place my lord the king shall be, whether in death or life, even there also your servant will be" (2 Sam. 15:21 NKJV). The people closest to David always seemed willing to put their lives on the line for him.

4. HE DELEGATED RESPONSIBILITY BASED ON ABILITY

David continually gave authority to people. He designated Joab as commander of the army after he led the charge that conquered Jerusalem. When seasoned captains came to him, he empowered them to continue in that capacity. And he was equally secure in giving others civil authority in his administration (1 Chron. 18:14–17).

Delegating authority is always a risky thing for a leader to do. It can cause problems, particularly mistakes in judgment or the abuse of power. That was the case when Joab decided to take matters into his own hands and kill Abner (2 Sam. 3:22–30). But great leaders risk delegation in order to reach the highest level of leadership. Unlike his predecessor, Saul, David didn't try to do it all himself, and as a result, he was able to do things no leader before him had done.

A group of people doesn't become a team without leadership, and a strong inner circle doesn't form itself. It takes a leader to do it. David was a team-building leader. Are you?

TODAY'S QUESTION FOR REFLECTION:
How are you building a team?

Day 3

The qualities inside the leader determine who is inside the circle.

Do not be misled: "Bad company corrupts good character."
1 Corinthians 15:33 (NIV)

Highly talented people surrounded David. (That makes sense since *he* was highly talented—that's the Law of Magnetism.) But David's inner circle didn't have value just because of what they could do. They had value because of who they were.

As you think about forming an inner circle, I want to encourage you to consider people's inner qualities before looking at their skills or abilities. That is sometimes difficult because we often tend to focus on productivity and results. But remember this, what's on the inside really matters.

> David's inner circle didn't have value just because of what they could do. They had value because of who they were.

INNER-CIRCLE QUALITIES

The following qualities spell out the words *inner circle*. If the people you depend on as a leader possess most of these qualities, they will be an incredible asset to you.

INFLUENTIAL

Everything begins with influence. If you desire to extend your reach, you must attract and lead other leaders, not just followers. That's what David did. In the list of warriors who came to David recorded in 1 Chronicles 12:23–37, more than twelve hundred leaders are mentioned.

NETWORKING

What people know isn't the only thing that matters. *Who* they know is also important. More than once when David was hiding from Saul, he was able to escape from the angry king because people who cared about him warned him.

NURTURING

People who care about each other take care of each other. Your inner circle should prop you up. Certainly Jonathan is the best example of a nurturer in David's life. He loved David unconditionally, encouraged him, and guarded his life.

EMPOWERING

The people in your inner circle shouldn't hold you back. They should spur you on. They should enable you to achieve more than you could alone. David's mighty men were incredibly empowering.

RESOURCEFUL

Inner-circle members should always add value. David encouraged resourcefulness among his people, and he often benefited from it. For example, when David desired to conquer Jerusalem, he offered to make the man who led the charge chief and captain over his army (2 Sam. 5:6–10). That is how Joab became chief of the army.

CHARACTER-DRIVEN

Without a doubt, character is the greatest of all qualities needed in an inner-circle member. People of weak character in David's inner circle, such as his son Absalom, cost him dearly. But people of strong character, such as Nathan the prophet, often helped to steer David out of trouble. Nathan never cringed in fear when his king did wrong. Instead, he spoke out. And for that David was grateful. David knew that repentance opened the door for restoration to God.

INTUITIVE

As I explained in the Law of Intuition, every person is naturally intuitive in his area of gifting. But that doesn't mean that all people use their intuition.

As you seek people for your inner circle, rely on people who have learned to trust their instincts.

RESPONSIBLE

The people closest to you should never leave you hanging. If you ask them to carry the ball for the team, they must be able—and willing—to follow through. David's companions were outstanding in this area. They made his cause their own.

COMPETENT

You can't get anything done if your people aren't capable of doing their jobs. Not everyone has to be a world-class performer—although high achievers are good to have on the team—but all of your inner-circle people must perform with excellence. The skill of David's people is one element that made him great.

LOYAL

As I've already mentioned, David's people were loyal even unto death. Loyalty alone does not make people candidates for your inner circle. But lack of loyalty definitely disqualifies them. Don't keep anyone close to you whom you cannot trust.

> Loyalty alone does not make people candidates for your inner circle. But lack of loyalty definitely disqualifies them. Don't keep anyone close to you whom you cannot trust.

ENERGETIC

Rounding out the list is high energy. Not every high achiever possesses boundless energy, but many do. Energy covers a multitude of mistakes because it helps a person to keep coming back, failure after failure. And tenacity is valuable to the team. Without tenacity, David and his men never would have survived in the wilderness nor would they have made the nation secure from its enemies.

When God desires a leader to do something of value, He provides the people needed to get the job done. That was true for David, and it will be true for you. All you need to do is look around.

TODAY'S QUESTION FOR REFLECTION:
Who on your team possesses inner-circle qualities?

Day 4

Teammates complete one another—not compete with one another.

A city without wise leaders will end up in ruin;
a city with many wise leaders will be kept safe.

Proverbs 11:14 (CEV)

Hall of Fame Coach John Wooden of UCLA once observed, "The main ingredient of stardom is the rest of the team." If anyone would know about that, it would be Wooden, the ultimate team-building coach. His

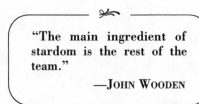

"**The main ingredient of stardom is the rest of the team.**"
—JOHN WOODEN

basketball teams won a remarkable ten national championships during his career.

The writer of Ecclesiastes, who was most likely Solomon, expressed a similar thought:

Two are better than one,
Because they have a good reward for their labor.
For if they fall, one will lift up his companion.
But woe to him who is alone when he falls,
For he has no one to help him up . . .
Though one may be overpowered by another,
two can withstand him.
And a threefold cord is not quickly broken. (4:9–10, 12 NKJV)

It's possible that Solomon learned this principle by observing his father, for David was a man who relied on others. Here are some of the responsibilities fulfilled by many of David's followers:

- Prophet: Nathan

- Priests: Zadok and Abimelech

- Recorder: Jehoshaphat

- Scribe: Shavsha

- Commander of the army: Joab

- Commander of the Cherethites and Pelethites: Benaiah

- Revenue overseer: Adoram

- Chief ministers: David's sons and later Ira

And that list doesn't include David's mighty men!

WHO'S ON YOUR LIST?

It's easy to understand the Law of the Inner Circle based on David's life. But it may be difficult to apply it to your life based on David's list of associates. For example, you probably won't need an army commander to work under your leadership. So please allow me to help you translate the principle to your life.

For years, I've been privileged to have wonderful people around me who have taken me to a higher level of leadership. In fact, when I turned forty, I made it my highest priority to start building a team of good people because I realized that I couldn't possibly go any farther on my own. I had no more time in the day.

Then several years ago, I taught a lesson on the idea of the inner circle, and I created a list of the kinds of people who help me, according to the way that they add value to my life. I'd like to share that list with you, and suggest that you start forming a similar circle of companions:

- *Intercessor.* You need someone to pray for you. Without God's favor and blessing, you can do nothing of value.

- *Listener.* Everyone needs a friendly ear—to confide in, vent to, and bounce ideas off.

- *Encourager.* Even people with great attitudes sometimes get discouraged. Encouragement is like oxygen to the soul.

- *Creator.* Creative people stretch your mind, challenge your direction, increase your vision, and multiply your gifts.

- *Discerner.* No matter how good you are, you will always miss some details when making decisions. Partner with people who will see what you don't.

- *Giver.* Your life should be focused on giving to others. But to keep giving, you will also need to have your "tank" filled. Connect with someone who loves you unconditionally.

- *Defender.* Everyone wants people in his corner. But sometimes you need more. On the days when you're too weary to fight your own battles, having someone who will step in the ring for you is a real blessing.

- *Implementer.* Of all the individuals in my inner circle, implementers are my type of people. Why are implementers so important? Marshall McLuhan's observation says it all: "After all has been said and done, more will have been *said* than *done*." Implementers are what I call door closers.

- *Celebrator.* When you accomplish your goals, don't just move on. Take a moment to celebrate. Do it with the people who helped you win, and enlist the assistance of someone who *really* knows how to throw a party.

- *Resourcer.* Every year I speak to 250,000 people and write at least one book. That requires lots of thinking and gathering of material. I'm grateful to the people willing to help me with these activities.

- *Sponsor.* You can't pick your sponsor; he has to pick you. Pray for God to put someone in your life who will believe in you and use his influence to help you along.

- *Thinker.* Some people are talented at solving problems. Everybody needs someone who can do that.

- *Networker.* It has been said you are five people away from contacting anyone in the world. Find a good networker and you're only two away.

- *Mentor.* No matter how advanced you are in your leadership, others ahead of you can help you along the way.

- *Protégé.* If you have leadership ability, you've not been given it to hoard for yourself. Find the right person to pour your life into.

Whew! That's a long list, but I couldn't do without the people who fulfill these roles in my life. Some people, such as my wife, Margaret, fulfill multiple functions. She is a listener, discerner, celebrator, and

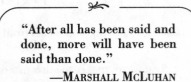

"After all has been said and done, more will have been said than done."
—MARSHALL MCLUHAN

resourcer for me—besides being my best friend. Take some time to figure out what you need to make you a better leader.

TODAY'S QUESTION FOR REFLECTION:
Does your inner circle make you more complete?

Day 5

Bringing the Law to Life

TAKING IT IN

Review the following statements from the Law of the Inner Circle:

1. Teamwork makes the dream work.

2. A team is more than just a group of people.

3. The qualities inside the leader determine who is inside the circle.

4. Teammates complete one another—not compete with one another.

How much value have you been putting on your team? Have you cultivated a strong team focus? Or have you tended to be more of a one-person show? If you're not sharing your vision, your responsibility, and your authority, then it's only a matter of time before you hit a huge wall in your leadership.

SORTING IT OUT

If you're not sure where you stand when it comes to understanding and applying the Law of the Inner Circle, visit the Web site www.injoy.com/21 Minutes to take a free twenty-five-question assessment quiz that will help you measure your ability.

PRAYING IT THROUGH

Use the following words to begin your time of prayer:

Dear God, teach me to think in terms of leading a winning team. Bring me the people You desire me to have as my teammates. Bring me a great inner circle of people. And empower me to be an inner-circle contributor for another leader. Amen.

LIVING IT OUT

David's people continually worked together as a team. A good example of their teamwork can be seen in their battle against the Syrians and Ammonites recorded in 2 Samuel 10. When Joab, the army's commander, faced enemies on both sides, he divided the forces between himself and Abishai his brother, and he said, "If the Syrians are too strong for me, then you shall help me; but if the people of Ammon are too strong for you, then I will come and help you" (v. 11 NKJV). That kind of teamwork made David's the most successful military regime in Israel's history.

What goal are you currently trying to achieve alone that you can approach from more of a team mind-set? Reevaluate your working method, and start building a team to accomplish the task. Then use your experience with these teammates to begin working on building your inner circle.

PASSING IT ON

Which one leadership concept, insight, or practice that you've learned this week will you pass on to another leader in the next two days?

Week 12

THE LAW OF EMPOWERMENT

ONLY SECURE LEADERS GIVE POWER TO OTHERS

Only empowered people can reach their potential. When a leader can't or won't empower others, he creates barriers within the organization that people cannot overcome. If the barriers remain long enough, then the people give up, or they move to another organization where they can maximize their potential . . .

If you want to be successful as a leader, you have to be an empowerer. Theodore Roosevelt realized that "the best executive is one who has the sense enough to pick good men to do what he wants done, and the self-restraint enough to keep from meddling with them while they do it." . . .

Only secure leaders are able to give themselves away . . . The truth is that the only way to make yourself indispensable is to make yourself dispensable. In other words, if you are able to continually empower others and help them develop so that they become capable of taking over your job, you will become so valuable to the organization that you become indispensable.

FROM "THE LAW OF EMPOWERMENT" IN *The 21 Irrefutable Laws of Leadership*

Day 1

Barnabas
and the
Law of Empowerment

LEADERSHIP THOUGHT FOR TODAY:
There are no limits to success when we do not limit people.

Read
Acts 9:1–31; 11:19–30; 12:25–13:52

A tremendous thrill of being a leader is seeing people succeed. But there's something even better than that—being part of other people's success. When that happens, their success literally becomes your success. Nothing is more fulfilling for a leader.

When I consider someone in the Bible who empowered others, I first think of Barnabas. Of all the leaders in Scripture, he seemed to be a master at taking people to another level. Even the name by which he was called was given to him in acknowledgment of that gift. His real name was Joseph (or Joses), but everyone called him Barnabas, which means "Son of Encouragement" (Acts 4:36).

UNEXPECTED MESSAGE

Encouragement can be incredibly empowering. I was reminded of that when I received a letter from a young couple named Dan and Dana Denton. I first met them in the fall of 1998 at a leadership conference I taught in San Jose, California. At the time, they were leading a church they had planted two years earlier that had grown to more than one hundred members, and they had come to the conference with ten of their key leaders.

Just before lunch on the first day of the conference, I asked all the pastors to stand so that they could be recognized for their hard work. From the platform, I could see that Dan and Dana looked discouraged. So I walked down to where they were standing and put my arms around them. I asked God to bless their efforts. And I told their group that I saw great potential in them because I could see they had a genuine desire to be godly leaders. At the time I didn't know their situation, but I wanted very much to plant seeds of encouragement in their lives.

A few weeks later I received a letter from them. In it they said that they had arrived at the conference with enthusiasm, but their excitement soon turned to discouragement. Dan wrote that when I began to teach, it was as if I had been reading their mail and watching them lead their people. They quickly became acquainted with some of the reasons they were having difficulty in their church. And they realized that if they continued in the same way they had been going, they would be on the verge of a church split. Their letter touched my heart, and all I could do was pray that God would meet their needs.

NEVER UNDERESTIMATE THE POWER OF AN ENCOURAGING WORD

In March 2000 in Los Angeles, I got the opportunity to see Dan and Dana again, this time with eighteen of their leaders. And again I had the chance to pray with them, but this time they didn't seem discouraged. About a month later, I received another letter from them. Here is what they wrote:

> When we got to the conference, we wanted to see you. Again, you remembered us. Again, you hugged us. This time you looked at a new group and said, "These guys are special." . . . You invested yourself in us. You gave us credibility and love. The team saw it and it has changed how this church sees us. God used you to form a core of leaders that now sees my wife and me as leaders who have stature and value and credibility . . . We could have pastored here for twenty years and never gotten the credibility you gave us in those few short minutes.

Dan and Dana give me way too much credit. All I did was practice something that my dad taught me as a teenager: walking slowly through the crowd. All that means is loving people, putting them ahead of my agenda, and helping them and others see the potential God has put in them.

That's the essence of what Barnabas did in the lives of other leaders. He put his agenda on the back burner and helped people go to a higher level in their leadership. He was so secure as a person that he didn't mind when someone else passed him up and became a better leader than he was.

> Every leader is either a lifter or a limiter of people. If you limit people, you limit not only them but also yourself. But if you lift them up, then there's no telling how far they—or you—can go.

Every leader is either a lifter or a limiter of people. If you limit people, you limit not only them but also yourself. But if you lift them up, then there's no telling how far they—or you—can go.

TODAY'S QUESTION FOR REFLECTION:
Do you lift or limit your people?

Day 2

LEADERSHIP THOUGHT FOR TODAY:
Empowering leaders lift people to a higher level.

And when Saul had come to Jerusalem, he tried to join the disciples; but they were all afraid of him, and did not believe that he was a disciple. But Barnabas took him and brought him to the apostles. And he declared to them how he had seen the Lord on the road, and that He had spoken to him, and how he had preached boldly at Damascus in the name of Jesus.

Acts 9:26–27 (NKJV)

A leader's plate can get overloaded very quickly. And in the midst of much busyness, it's not difficult to forget about people. But effective leaders know that when they short-change their people, their leadership breaks down. And they also

> To make an impact, you must add value to your people because the only way for you to truly succeed is to help others.

shortchange themselves. You see, to make an impact, you must add value to your people because the only way for you to truly succeed is to help others.

CAN I GET A LIFT?

Barnabas was definitely a lifter of people. It seems as though he let no opportunity escape him to add value to others. And his greatest single contribution in terms of empowerment can be seen in his interaction with Paul.

1. HE BELIEVED IN PAUL BEFORE ANYONE ELSE DID

It's easy to give an opinion about a controversial person or subject after other leaders have given their support. It's something else to step up and speak before *anyone* else does. That's what Barnabas did. He didn't wait until the apostles endorsed Paul before believing in him. In fact, he believed in Paul while Peter and the others feared him.

To be an encouraging leader, you have to be willing to take chances on people. You have to look for the potential in them and encourage them to believe in themselves. And that can be risky

> To be an encouraging leader, you have to be willing to take chances on people.

because you may choose to support people who don't come through. But if they do, the payoff can be huge. You may be responsible for inspiring a new leader to achieve things he never thought possible. And leaders never forget the first person who believed in them.

2. HE ENDORSED PAUL'S LEADERSHIP TO OTHER LEADERS

In describing Barnabas's actions, Scripture states, "Barnabas took him and brought him to the apostles. And he declared to them how he had seen the Lord on the road, and that He had spoken to him, and how he had preached boldly at Damascus in the name of Jesus" (Acts 9:27 NKJV).

I can just imagine how things might have gone in Jerusalem in those days. Paul arrived in the city, and word reached the apostles that Paul was claiming to be a supporter of Christ. They must have thought it was a trick. He was the same man who had stood by and approved the stoning of Stephen, the first Christian martyr.

Barnabas must have shown up at one of the apostles' gatherings with Paul in tow. I can imagine an uncomfortable silence falling over the gathering as people realized who Barnabas's companion was. And then Barnabas shared Paul's story. Paul didn't have to say a word. All the believers knew Barnabas. They knew his reputation, his integrity. That was all it took. Scripture records, "So he was with them at Jerusalem, coming in and going out" (Acts 9:28 NKJV). Paul was accepted.

One of the best things you can do as an empowering leader is to sing your people's praises to others. When they're doing a good job, tell everyone. Be especially intentional about praising them to their friends and families. But also bring them before other leaders. Help them to make a connection on the strength of your credibility.

3. HE EMPOWERED PAUL TO REACH HIS POTENTIAL

Barnabas's connection to Paul didn't end in Jerusalem. After Barnabas's endorsement enabled Paul to move freely throughout Jerusalem teaching people and debating the truth of Scripture, it

> One of the best things you can do as an empowering leader is to sing your people's praises to others.

wasn't long before Paul became an enemy of nonbelievers. The apostles wisely sent him back to Tarsus for his own safety. But later when Barnabas was assigned to help the church in Antioch, he took the opportunity to find Paul and make him his companion.

That action empowered Paul to take his first "assignment" as a leader, and it led to Paul's partnership with Barnabas as a missionary—the role for which God had destined him.

To be an empowering leader, you must do more than believe in emerging leaders. You need to take steps to help them *become* the leaders they have the potential to be. You must invest in them if you want to empower them to become their best.

Empowering people takes a personal investment. It requires energy and time. But it's worth the price. If you do it right, you will have the privilege of seeing someone move up to a higher level. And as an added bonus, you create power in your organization when you empower others.

TODAY'S QUESTION FOR REFLECTION:
Whom are you committed to empowering?

Day 3

LEADERSHIP THOUGHT FOR TODAY:
Leaders live a life of empowerment.

Let us consider how we may spur one another on toward love and good deeds . . . Let us encourage one another.

Hebrews 10:24–25 (NIV)

Empowering leaders never stop looking for opportunities to lift people to a higher level. They thrive on seeing others reach their potential, and they seize every opportunity to add value to others' lives. For them, empowerment isn't an event; it's a lifestyle.

BARNABAS'S MINISTRY OF EMPOWERMENT

Although Barnabas's most famous protégé was Paul, he empowered a lot of others as well. A pattern of empowerment was evident in his life.

1. HE ENCOURAGED PEOPLE WITH NEEDS

The first mention of Barnabas in Scripture describes an event that was characteristic of his true nature—giving. Read Acts 4:36–37: "And Joses, who was also named Barnabas by the apostles (which is translated Son of Encouragement), a Levite of the country of Cyprus, having land, sold it, and brought the money and laid it at the apostles' feet" (NKJV). When his fellow disciples had a need, Barnabas was quick to meet it.

2. HE EMPOWERED PEOPLE WHEN THEY EXPERIENCED SUCCESS

When Barnabas encountered people who were doing well, he encouraged them and empowered them to do even better. Scripture describes his actions when he arrived at the church in Antioch: "When he came and had seen the grace of God, he was glad, and encouraged them all that with purpose of heart they should continue with the Lord. For he was a good man, full of the Holy Spirit and of faith. And a great many people were added to the Lord" (Acts 11:23–24 NKJV).

3. HE EMPOWERED PEOPLE WHEN THEY FAILED

Most leaders approach people in one of two ways:

1. They test peoples's worthiness, then empower them.

2. They empower people first, then discover their worth.

The second method of dealing with people is the way empowerers work. That's the way Barnabas worked with people. Even when someone let him down, such as

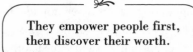

> They empower people first, then discover their worth.

John Mark, who deserted Barnabas and Paul in Pamphylia, he still believed in him. If Paul had prevailed, John Mark wouldn't have received a second chance. But Barnabas still believed in John Mark, he gave him a second chance, and before all was said and done, Paul believed in him too (2 Tim. 4:11).

If you can keep believing in people, no matter how difficult a time they're having, then you will really be able to make a difference in their lives.

4. HE EMPOWERED LEADERS TO LEAD

An important task Barnabas completed in the new churches was the appointment of leaders to help the people: "When they had appointed elders in every church, and prayed with fasting, they commended them to the Lord in whom they had believed" (Acts 14:23 NKJV).

Nothing empowers an organization like an infusion of leadership. When you empower leaders, you help those individuals, you also help everyone whom they are able to touch in the organization.

No matter where Barnabas went or what his responsibilities were, he encouraged people along the way. Even when he returned to Antioch after making a circle through Lystra, Iconium, and Derbe, he couldn't help encouraging the people and empowering them to persevere. Scripture records that he was "strengthening the souls of the disciples, exhorting them to continue in the faith, and saying, We must through many tribulations enter the kingdom of God'" (Acts 14:22 NKJV).

Encouragement empowers people and builds momentum. If you can learn to believe in people and live a lifestyle of encouragement, you will help others achieve more, and people will always welcome your leadership.

❧

TODAY'S QUESTION FOR REFLECTION:
Is empowering others a natural and continual lifestyle for you?

Day 4

Then Barnabas departed for Tarsus to seek Saul. And when he had found him, he brought him to Antioch. So it was that for a whole year they assembled with the church and taught a great many people. And the disciples were first called Christians in Antioch.

Acts 11:25–26 (NKJV)

As Barnabas traveled and took emerging leaders under his wing, he seemed to create an environment of empowerment everywhere he went. Great leaders do that. They not only know how to pass skills on to others to help them succeed, they also create an atmosphere where achievement seems to come naturally to everyone.

SUCCESS IN THE AIR

Recently, I came across a study by a University of Southern California professor, Gretchen Spreitzer, in a book entitled *Deep Change: Discovering the Leader Within,* by Robert E. Quinn. Spreitzer studied managers at a Fortune 500 company and found four conditions that gave an organization an environment of empowerment:

1. A CLEAR BUT CHALLENGING VISION

Spreitzer discovered that people feel most empowered when they have a clear understanding of their leader's vision. I believe that was the case for the people who worked with Barnabas. From the day that he and Paul were called in the church of Antioch (Acts 13:2), he had a strong sense of purpose. And he communicated that purpose to others. He told the Jews who rejected him at Antioch in Pisidia:

Behold, we turn to the Gentiles. For so the Lord has commanded us:
"I have set you as a light to the Gentiles,
That you should be for salvation to the ends of the earth." (Acts 13:46–47
NKJV)

Leaders who don't possess a clear vision and communicate it well always have a difficult time empowering others, because their people can't determine what their goals are or how to serve the organization.

> Leaders who don't possess a clear vision and communicate it well always have a difficult time empowering others.

2. AN ATMOSPHERE OF TEAMWORK

Spreitzer reported that empowered people also feel a sense of participation, flexibility, and creativity among fellow workers who work together as a team. Barnabas certainly demonstrated that he valued teamwork. He shared his authority with Paul without hesitation. He happily appointed elders in every church to share in leading the team. And he always brought people such as John Mark with him to be a part of his ministry. An atmosphere of teamwork makes everyone feel valued and appreciated.

3. CLEARLY DEFINED ROLES

The third factor Spreitzer found in an empowering environment was clearly defined roles. When people know what their responsibilities are and what authority they possess, they are likely to work with confidence and demonstrate creativity within their area.

It appears that as soon as Barnabas and Paul began to work together as a team following their calling in Antioch, Barnabas encouraged Paul to take the role of communicator. From that time on when Luke recorded their speech in Acts, he attributed the words to Paul or to "Paul and Barnabas."

If you want your people to excel, then let them know where and how you want them to contribute. And if you encourage them in their areas of gifting, they will truly be empowered.

4. A SUPPORTIVE SENSE OF SECURITY

Finally, Spreitzer's study indicated that people in an empowered environment have a strong sense of security in their relationships and feel that they can trust and be trusted by others.

We know that Barnabas was a secure leader because he readily gave his power away. As Paul became a stronger leader and eclipsed him, he didn't seem to mind a bit. The only hint of conflict between the two men occurred when Paul wanted to prevent Barnabas from empowering John Mark, the man whom Paul no longer considered worthy of their development. If you are secure and can communicate a sense of security to your people, then your people are on solid ground and are set up to succeed.

Creating an empowering environment isn't overly complicated. So why don't more leaders create one? First, it takes work. Second, it is by its nature an unselfish act, because in that kind of environment, the benefits exist for the people, not the leader. And finally, it takes security. Only secure leaders empower others. As people become empowered, they become more powerful. Weak leaders are threatened by that. Strong ones revel in it.

TODAY'S QUESTION FOR REFLECTION:
How are you creating an environment of empowerment?

Day 5

Bringing the Law to Life

TAKING IT IN

When you work with people, do you find yourself hoarding power or giving it away? Are the people under your leadership growing in strength and ability, or do they seem to be on a plateau? When a leader in your area becomes particularly strong, does he usually stay or move on? Remember, the keys to the Law of Empowerment are these:

1. There are no limits to success when we do not limit people.

2. Empowering leaders lift people to a higher level.

3. Leaders live a life of empowerment.

4. Leaders create an environment of empowerment.

If you are willing to share your power, you help others and yourself.

SORTING IT OUT

If you're not sure where you stand when it comes to understanding and applying the Law of Empowerment, visit the Web site www.injoy.com/ 21 Minutes to take a free twenty-five-question assessment quiz that will help you measure your ability.

PRAYING IT THROUGH

Use the following words to begin your time of prayer:

Dear God, I want to be used as an instrument of empowerment in the lives of people. Please help me to continually sense Your love for me so that I can be

secure in my relationships with others. And give me a discerning eye for others'
needs, so that I may serve them as Barnabas did the people in his life. Amen.

LIVING IT OUT

Think about the one person in your life who has been your main empowerer.
Take a moment to write that person a note expressing your appreciation for
what he or she has done for you.

Now think of someone in your life whom you want to empower. What
one thing can you do today to help him or her feel encouraged, loved, and
empowered? Do it.

PASSING IT ON

Which one leadership concept, insight, or practice that you've learned this
week will you pass on to another leader in the next two days?

Week 13

THE LAW OF REPRODUCTION

It Takes a Leader to Raise Up a Leader

I've been taking time to conduct an informal poll to find out what prompted the men and women who attend [conferences] to become leaders. The results of the survey are as follows:

HOW THEY BECAME LEADERS

Natural Gifting	10 percent
Result of Crisis	5 percent
Influence of Another Leader	85 percent

It's true that a few people step into leadership because their organization experiences a crisis, and they are compelled to do something about it. Another small group is comprised of people with such great natural gifting and instincts that they are able to navigate their way into leadership on their own. But more than four out of five of all the leaders that you ever meet will have emerged as leaders because of the impact made on them by established leaders who mentored them . . .

It all starts at the top because . . . only leaders are capable of developing other leaders . . . Followers can't do it. Neither can institutional programs.

It takes one to know one, show one, and grow one . . . If a company has poor leaders, what little leadership it has will only get worse. If a company has strong leaders—and they are reproducing themselves—then the leadership just keeps getting better and better . . .

FROM "THE LAW OF REPRODUCTION" IN *The 21 Irrefutable Laws of Leadership*

Day 1

Moses and Joshua
and the
Law of Reproduction

LEADERSHIP THOUGHT FOR TODAY:
People teach what they know, but they reproduce what they are.

Read
Exodus 17:8–16; 3:7–11; Deuteronomy 31:1–8;
Numbers 27:12–23

Have you ever thought about what would have happened to Joshua if Moses hadn't mentored him as a leader? Have you ever thought about what would have happened to the children of Israel? Everything rises and falls on leadership. Any

> "When the country is in chaos, everybody has a plan to fix it—but it takes a leader of real understanding to straighten things out."
> —PROVERBS 28:2 (THE MESSAGE)

situation either improves or declines based on whether the leadership is good or bad. And if there is a leadership vacuum, the people really suffer. Think about what happened when Moses was absent from the Hebrews for forty days when he was meeting with God on Mount Sinai. They corrupted themselves by building and worshiping a golden calf! As it says in Proverbs,

> When the country is in chaos,
> everybody has a plan to fix it—

But it takes a leader of real understanding

to straighten things out. (28:2 *The Message*)

Joshua was a leader of real understanding. And he was able to straighten things out for the children of Israel. But he never would have been capable of that if it hadn't been for Moses. It took a leader of Moses' caliber—someone who was able to take the Hebrews out of Egypt—to mentor Joshua so that he could become a world-class leader capable of taking the people into the promised land.

IT TAKES ONE TO KNOW ONE, SHOW ONE, AND GROW ONE

Because of the influence of television, the Internet, and other media in our culture, I think we've lost sight of what it means to mentor people so that we can reproduce our leadership in others. We tend to want to do things quickly and from a distance. But that doesn't work. Not only does it take a leader to raise up a leader; it also takes time and proximity. If you examine the relationship between Moses and Joshua, you can see that dynamic at work.

People who try to reproduce themselves in others generally go about it in one of three ways:

LEVEL 1: IMPRESS

In our mass-market culture, many people have the goal of impressing others. That's particularly true in the entertainment industry. People go to a movie, and they walk away saying, "I really like that actor." They feel as though they know and like the person, but they are only embracing an image that may or may not be anything like the real person behind the role.

There's nothing wrong with wanting to make a good impression on followers. Good leaders want to do that. But leadership on the impression level is shallow and weak. Why? Because it doesn't require the follower to buy in to anything real. And no relationship is involved. The leader projects an image that the follower passively receives.

When the children of Israel heard that Moses had arrived in Egypt and that he was confronting Pharaoh on God's behalf, they must have been impressed. When God performed miracles through Moses, they probably got excited. But that alone didn't change their lives.

LEVEL 2: INFLUENCE

The next level of reproduction is influence, and that is where real mentoring begins because it requires a degree of buy-in on the part of the follower. He reacts to what the influencer is doing. For example, when a particular actress cuts her hair a certain way, thousands of television watchers do the same. When an athlete endorses a particular product, millions of people buy it. Or when a leader teaches using books, tapes, or other materials, people learn new skills.

Although the influence level is a major step forward in the process of reproduction, it can do only so much. The bond of a relationship is begun between the leader and the follower, but it is one-sided. There is no real interaction between the two. The follower receives information or inspiration, but little else.

In the case of the children of Israel, they truly began to be influenced by Moses when they started to react to his leadership and obey his instruction. As a result, they escaped Egypt and the oppression of slavery. Because they had the will to follow, their lives changed. But even then, Moses didn't make a personal impact on them. When it comes to people's lives, you can't make a real difference from a distance.

LEVEL 3: INVEST

The highest level of mentoring is investment, and the result is genuine *impact* on a follower's life. It requires close proximity. It requires a close relationship. And it requires mutual dedication.

The interaction between Moses and Joshua illustrates that kind of arrangement. Joshua accompanied Moses wherever he went. We know the two men were close because Moses changed his protégé's name from Hoshea to Joshua (another form of the name Jesus). And the duration of their relationship is a testament to their mutual dedication.

Of all the children of Israel, only Moses could have raised up a Joshua to become a great leader, for people reproduce who they are. Fortunately Moses had the will and the time to do it. And the Hebrews were finally able to enter the promised land.

TODAY'S QUESTION FOR REFLECTION:
If you reproduced yourself in another leader,
would you be pleased with the results?

Day 2

Reproducing leaders is a lifetime commitment.

A disciple is not above his teacher . . . It is enough for a disciple that he be like his teacher.

Matthew 10:24–25 (NKJV)

Where have all the leaders gone? Ours is a country that was once remarkable for the way it produced leaders. Recall our history. When the United States was birthed, the number of strong leaders present in our small population was remarkable: people such as George Washington, Thomas Jefferson, Benjamin Franklin, and Thomas Paine, just to name a few. But today, the number of quality leaders we have for our population seems disproportionately small. Why? Because we have a microwave mind-set.

People want instant everything. They want their food from the drive-through window handed to them in seconds. They order books on-line and have them shipped overnight so they won't need to leave the house to get them. They order movies on demand. People are impatient. But leaders aren't developed overnight. They can't be made in a microwave. They have to be simmered in a Crock-Pot.

> Leaders aren't developed overnight. They can't be made in a microwave. They have to be simmered in a Crock-Pot.

FORTY YEARS OF FAITHFULNESS

People are always in a hurry, but God never is. When God makes something special, He takes His time, whether it's an oak tree or a leader. If you observe the relationship between Moses and Joshua, you see a classic godly timetable.

Joshua was a leader eighty years in the making—half of which he spent with Moses in the desert. For four decades, the two men faithfully engaged in the leadership development process.

Think about what went into the mentoring process of Joshua:

1. MOSES WAS FAITHFUL TO JOSHUA

It all begins with the mentor. He must be committed to the process of raising up another leader. Here is how Moses showed his faithfulness to his protégé:

- *Moses gave Joshua experience and application.* Joshua's apprenticeship was not the transfer of information. It involved hands-on experience. Moses shared his life and his responsibilities with Joshua. When the Hebrews had to face the Amalekites in battle, Moses made Joshua the commander. When a spy was needed from the tribe of Ephraim, Joshua was sent. And when Moses needed a personal assistant, Joshua was given the job.

- *Moses gave Joshua encouragement and affirmation.* A leader can offer time and access to encourage the person being mentored. Moses gave both. He affirmed Joshua repeatedly by allowing him to accompany him where no one else could.

- *Moses gave Joshua power and authority.* When the time came, Moses laid his hands on Joshua and publicly commissioned him before the people. He gave Joshua his authority and power.

2. JOSHUA WAS FAITHFUL TO MOSES

As leaders, we are sometimes impatient in our desire for our protégés to rise up, take responsibility, and become impact players for the team. The only people more impatient for that process to occur are the protégés. And that desire sometimes causes them to try to leave the nest and fly on their own too soon.

That was not the case for Joshua. For forty years, he was loyal, faithful, and patient as he worked under Moses' guidance. He served Moses. Whatever Moses asked him to do, Joshua did wholeheartedly. And when Joshua thought the people were treating Moses disrespectfully, his strong love and loyalty for Moses shone through (Num. 11:24–30). He was the perfect recipient of Moses' mentoring.

3. BOTH WERE FAITHFUL TO GOD

Ultimately both Moses and Joshua were faithful to God. They fulfilled God's calling on their lives, which involved not only the deliverance of the children of Israel out of Egypt and into the promised land, but also their relationship with each other. Deuteronomy 34:9 states, "Now Joshua the son of Nun was full of the spirit of wisdom, for Moses had laid his hands on him; so the children of Israel heeded him, and did as the LORD had commanded Moses" (NKJV).

When God is involved and people are obedient, incredible things happen. A cycle of credibility is created that looks something like this:

But that whole process takes time. Reproducing leaders doesn't happen by itself, and it doesn't happen in a moment. It takes a lifetime.

❧

TODAY'S QUESTION FOR REFLECTION:
How committed are you to reproducing leaders?

Day 3

Reproducing leaders is a parenting process.

We were gentle among you, just as a nursing mother cherishes her own children . . . You are witnesses, and God also, how devoutly and justly and blamelessly we behaved ourselves among you who believe; as you know how we exhorted, and comforted, and charged every one of you, as a father does his own children, that you would walk worthy of God who calls you into His own kingdom and glory.

1 Thessalonians 2:7, 10–12 (NKJV)

The interaction of Moses and Joshua makes it evident that reproducing leaders is not a quick, simple process. It is a lot like parenting. It requires time, emotional investment, and sacrifice. But the good news is that if you choose an emerging leader with the right attitude, he can be as hungry and compliant as Joshua was.

THE NEEDS OF NEXT-GENERATION LEADERS

Moses undoubtedly tailored his mentoring to the needs of Joshua. That's important. If you are a parent and have more than one child, then you understand that you have to parent each child a little bit differently. Your children have different gifts, interests, talents, and needs. But certain aspects of the parenting process remain fairly constant.

As you embark on the leadership development process of the next generation of leaders, recognize that the emerging leaders you mentor will need certain things:

> Some things only emerging leaders themselves can provide. You cannot give them the right attitude or the will to learn and obey.

1. FROM THEMSELVES: CONVICTION, COURAGE, AND OBEDIENCE

Some things only emerging leaders themselves can provide. You cannot give them the right attitude or the will to learn and obey. When Joshua came to Moses, he had already demonstrated the conviction to follow God, the courage to fight for his beliefs, and the willingness to obey both God and his mentor. That made him a good candidate for further leadership development. As you look for people to mentor, seek those who possess qualities similar to those of Joshua.

2. FROM THEIR MENTOR: EQUIPPING

As the mentor, you bear the responsibility for providing emerging leaders with the things they cannot get on their own. My recommendation is that you equip them according to the following guidelines, based on the word *PARENT*:

- *Purpose.* Don't simply spend time with emerging leaders. Be strategic. Think of your interaction as an investment that is based on vision and is charged with purpose.

- *Assessment.* Give protégés honest feedback. If you don't let them know how they are doing, who will?

- *Relationships.* The relationships you build will be the glue that holds you and your protégés together during the mentoring process. The greater the challenges, the more solid the relationships need to be.

- *Encouragement.* Protégés will make mistakes and fail. You can count on that. Your positive words may be the only things of value they have during their most difficult times. Without encouragement, they may not have the will to persevere and keep moving forward.

- *Navigation.* The less experienced emerging leaders are, the more help they will need navigating through the obstacle course that is life—and the more help they will need learning how to make good leadership decisions.

- *Tools.* Protégés need skills and resources that only a more experienced person can provide.

Above all, as you equip your protégés, approach them as you would children you love: with patience, perspective, and a positive attitude.

3. FROM GOD: VISION

As you begin to invest in potential leaders, you will invite them to come alongside you and participate in the fulfillment of your vision. That is as it should be. But there will come a time as you release your protégés when they will need to have a vision of their own. That's not something you will be able to give them. You can't borrow vision. Each person must possess his own vision. Ask God to bless the people you mentor with a godly vision that will sustain them as they become leaders in their own right.

4. FROM THE PEOPLE: BUY-IN

Without the support and participation of the people, the individuals you mentor cannot make the difficult transition from protégé to leader. This concept is so important that we will look at it in greater depth when we examine the Law of Buy-In. But as far as it is in your power to do so, publicly invest your authority in your protégés when they are ready for the responsibility.

The development of emerging leaders is challenging and rewarding. Not everyone in whom you invest the time will become the leader he has the potential to become. But if you sharpen your mentoring skills and invest continually, God may bless you with a Joshua who will go to the highest level of leadership.

TODAY'S QUESTION FOR REFLECTION:
In which area of the "parenting" process do you most need to improve?

Day 4

LEADERSHIP THOUGHT FOR TODAY:
When leaders reproduce other leaders,
they touch the lives of people they will never meet.

The LORD was even angry with me because of you people, and he said, "Moses, I won't let you go into the land either. Instead, I will let Joshua your assistant lead Israel to conquer the land. So encourage him." Then the LORD spoke to you again: People of Israel, you said that your innocent young children would be taken prisoner in the battle for the land. But someday I will let them go into the land, and with my help they will conquer it and live there.

Deuteronomy 1:37–39 (CEV)

When Moses led the people out of Egypt and into the wilderness, he had no reason to believe that he would fail to realize his dream of living in the promised land. It was only natural for him to expect to be leading the way as the people crossed over the Jordan into the land of milk and honey.

But then the people rebelled. Their fear outweighed their faith after they heard the report of the spies, and they refused to take possession of the land that God had promised them. That added a forty-year delay to the fulfillment of Moses' expectations. Then one day at Kadesh, Moses lost his temper and disobeyed God, striking the rock to give the people water instead of speaking to it as God directed. And that was it. Moses had disqualified himself from making the final leg of the journey. God told Moses, "Because you did not believe Me, to hallow Me in the eyes of the children of Israel, therefore you shall not bring this assembly into the land which I have given them" (Num. 20:12 NKJV).

Fortunately all was not lost. Even before Moses learned the news that he would not enter Canaan, he had begun to do something that would ensure the fulfillment of God's promise to Abraham's descendants. The dream would live on, even if Moses wouldn't. You see, Moses had already taken Joshua under his wing and had begun to mentor him.

We don't know what prompted Moses to take on Joshua as his student. Maybe it was his heart. After all, Joshua remained obedient to God's call on the people. But then, so did Caleb, yet Moses didn't mentor him. Whatever the reason, this is clear: Joshua was a leader who was able to fulfill the calling of God because of the favor he received.

FAVOR COMES IN PHASES

Joshua received favor in phases:

PHASE 1—POTENTIAL: THE LEADER GIVES HIS APPRENTICE FAVOR

The whole reproduction process begins with the favor of the leader. The day that Moses took Joshua to be his assistant, the older man's favor was upon him. As mentors, we must be willing to give whatever we can to the potential leaders under our care. If we don't, we create a major roadblock to their growth and potential.

PHASE 2—PROGRESS: THE LEADER AND THE PEOPLE GIVE THE APPRENTICE FAVOR

Favor from the mentor alone is never enough to create effective leadership. Obviously, to be a leader, the protégé must have people to follow him. The process of transferring leadership from the leader to the apprentice can be aided by the investment of the mentor's authority in the protégé. That's what Moses did. And the people responded positively: "Now Joshua the son of Nun was full of the spirit of wisdom, for Moses had laid his hands on him; so the children of Israel heeded him, and did as the LORD had commanded Moses" (Deut. 34:9 NKJV). With the endorsement of both Moses and the people, Joshua was ready to move forward.

> The acid test for a new leader comes when his mentor is no longer in the picture.

PHASE 3—POWER: THE LEADER, THE PEOPLE, AND GOD GIVE THE APPRENTICE FAVOR

The acid test for a new leader comes when his mentor is no longer in the picture. He no longer has the benefit of the older leader's wisdom, nor does he enjoy the power of that person's authority. At that moment, the new leader either succeeds or fails.

The factor that really determines what will happen is whether God extends His favor to that leader. Up to the point of Moses' death, Moses and Joshua had done everything right. Yet in the moment that Joshua tried to move the children of Israel forward across the Jordan, they still could have turned on him. Once before they had failed to heed Joshua's advice. They were, after all, a stiff-necked people capable of self-defeating disobedience.

But God extended Joshua His favor. He made a promise to him: "No man shall be able to stand before you all the days of your life; as I was with Moses, so I will be with you. I will not leave you nor forsake you" (Josh. 1:5 NKJV).

Without God's favor and blessing, all the hard work in the world would not have been able to fulfill God's purpose for the people. As a leader, you cannot provide God's favor for your protégé, but you certainly can ask for it. And you can teach and encourage the people you mentor to ask for it too. That's critical because it makes the difference between a good work and a great work.

In the heat and chaos of demanding leadership, many people default to doing what brings only an immediate benefit. They don't think ahead, and they don't try to see things from God's perspective. But a great leader, like Moses, always invests in the next generation because he knows that if he doesn't help to reproduce himself, the next generation will be in trouble. He understands that by mentoring potential leaders today, he is leading beyond his lifetime.

TODAY'S QUESTION FOR REFLECTION:
Are you ready to begin thinking beyond your lifetime?

Day 5

Bringing the Law to Life

TAKING IT IN

Review the four thoughts related to the Law of Reproduction:

1. People teach what they know, but they reproduce what they are.

2. Reproducing leaders is a lifetime commitment.

3. Reproducing leaders is a parenting process.

4. When leaders reproduce other leaders, they touch the lives of people they will never meet.

What kind of perspective have you had when it comes to investing in the lives of others? Did you realize that only a leader can raise up another leader, and that if you aren't mentoring the leaders of tomorrow, your organization is headed for trouble?

SORTING IT OUT

If you're not sure where you stand when it comes to understanding and applying the Law of Reproduction, visit the Web site www.injoy.com/21 Minutes to take a free twenty-five-question assessment quiz that will help you measure your ability.

PRAYING IT THROUGH

Use the following words to begin your time of prayer:

Dear God, please give me Your perspective. Help me to see the work I do and the contribution I can make in terms that extend beyond my life span. And help me to see the potential leaders around me so that I can begin investing in them for Your sake. Amen.

LIVING IT OUT

Think about the people God has put in your life. Then make a list of the top five who have the potential to become good leaders. (Choose only people of your own gender so that there is no potential problem with moral issues.) Pray about them, and then observe them. Pay attention to their attitudes. Look for conviction, courage, and obedience. You may need to do some low-intensity mentoring or teaching with them to identify the potential Joshua in the bunch. Once you have identified a protégé, then dedicate yourself to mentoring that person to reach his potential. Start passing on what you've learned.

PASSING IT ON

Which one leadership concept, insight, or practice that you've learned this week will you pass on to another leader in the next two days?

Week 14

THE LAW OF BUY-IN

PEOPLE BUY IN TO THE LEADER, THEN THE VISION

When I teach leadership seminars, I field a lot of questions about vision. Invariably someone will come up to me during a break, give me a brief description of an evolving vision, and ask me, "Do you think my people will buy in to my vision?" My response is always the same: "First tell me this. Do your people buy in to you?"

You see, many people who approach the area of vision in leadership have it all backward. They believe that if the cause is good enough, people will automatically buy in to it and follow. But that's not how leadership really works. People don't at first follow worthy causes. They follow worthy leaders who promote worthwhile causes. People buy in to the leader first, then the leader's vision . . . Every message that people receive is filtered through the messenger who delivers it . . . You cannot separate the leader from the cause he promotes . . . It's not an either/or proposition. The two always go together.

FROM "THE LAW OF BUY-IN" IN *The 21 Irrefutable Laws of Leadership*

Day 1

Gideon
and the
Law of Buy-In

LEADERSHIP THOUGHT FOR TODAY:
When people become confident in the leader,
they become confident in the vision.

Read
Judges 6:11–7:25

Gideon was an unlikely leader. He certainly didn't see himself as a leader. We can gain insight into his image of himself by observing his reaction to the angel's proclamation that he would be Israel's instrument of deliverance from the Midianites. After the angel spoke, Gideon responded, "O my Lord, how can I save Israel? Indeed my clan is the weakest in Manasseh, and I am the least in my father's house" (Judg. 6:15 NKJV).

Despite Gideon's doubts, God used him. The people rallied around Gideon—the youngest member of the puniest clan—and he became the leader of the most lopsided victory in the history of Israel.

WHICH COMES FIRST?

Which comes first: the vision or the gathering of the people? I assert that the answer depends on your perspective:

The leader finds the vision—then the people.
The people find the leader—then the vision.

If you see things from a follower's perspective, the people buy in to the leader, then the vision. That's the Law of Buy-In. But if you are the leader, you know that the vision comes first for you. Leaders embrace the vision first, and then they look for people to help them achieve it.

Vision can be a powerful thing. It's easy to see that the vision came first for Gideon, because his calling came straight from God. But you don't need an angel of the Lord to visit you in person in order to have a powerful vision.

THE POWER OF VISION

The vision has power because it provides leaders with . . .

1. AWARENESS—THE ABILITY TO SEE

Leaders have to see the vision first, otherwise they will never be able to help the people see it. Gideon understood what his role was to be before anyone else did.

2. ATTITUDE—THE FAITH TO BELIEVE

It's one thing to possess the vision of what could happen. It's another to *believe* that you can make it happen. Initially Gideon had a very difficult time believing that he could free his countrymen from the Midianites, but the angel helped him to overcome his doubt.

3. ACTION—THE COURAGE TO DO

If moving from seeing to believing is a big step, then finding the courage to act on your belief is even bigger. Gideon had such a hard time with this phase that he put out a fleece to test God—twice. Yet God was gracious and reassured Gideon, and he moved forward.

4. ACHIEVEMENT—THE HOPE TO ENDURE

Once a leader begins moving forward, his troubles have just begun. It takes perseverance to turn action into achievement. By the time Gideon faced huge obstacles, the people were firmly behind him.

The gift of the leader to the people is the vision. The gift of the people to the leader is the fulfillment of that vision. That's why God always puts the leader and the people together. But before the people are willing to follow and make the dream a reality, they have to buy in to the leader, and that requires good leadership.

❦

TODAY'S QUESTION FOR REFLECTION:
Would you follow you?

Day 2

LEADERSHIP THOUGHT FOR TODAY:
Buy-in is an ongoing process.

> Cast your bread upon the waters,
> For you will find it after many days.
> Ecclesiastes 11:1 (NKJV)

All leaders have vision. But all people who possess vision are not leaders. I've known a lot of would-be leaders who possessed vision but lacked the ability to get people to buy in to them. That's why the Law of Buy-in has such an impact. A compelling vision alone will not make someone a leader. Nor will a great vision automatically be fulfilled simply because it is compelling or valuable.

Once Gideon possessed the vision to deliver Israel from its enemies, he wasn't finished. He still needed to get the people to buy in to his leadership. That didn't happen in an instant. Although God ordained the vision, Gideon had to devote his time and actions to fulfilling the vision.

> **All leaders have vision. But all people who possess vision are not leaders. I've known a lot of would-be leaders who possessed vision but lacked the ability to get people to buy in to them.**

THE ANATOMY OF BUY-IN

As Gideon progressed from being an obscure member of a minor clan to a leader of the northern tribes, his influence grew in the way that ripples do when a pebble is dropped into quiet water. After buying in to the vision, Gideon . . .

1. **STARTED AT HOME (CHARACTER)**
   A good leader first proves himself to the people closest to him. Your fam-

ily and close friends know your character and can tell when your actions are in line with it.

Gideon started with ten servants from his household. With their help, he was able to destroy the altar of Baal, build a new altar to God, and offer the sacrifice requested by God. We don't know how difficult it was for his servants to buy in to his leadership, but we know they believed in him enough to take action.

2. WON A KEY INFLUENCER (CHARISMA)

According to Scripture, the men of the city of Ophrah were furious with Gideon's actions. When they discovered what he had done, they said to his father, Joash, "Bring out your son, that he may die, because he has torn down the altar of Baal, and because he has cut down the wooden image that was beside it" (Judg. 6:30 NKJV). In that moment, Gideon's life was in the balance. And without help, he might have met his end.

But in that moment, Gideon won over a powerful ally: his father. Though Gideon described his clan as the smallest of the tribe of Manasseh, his father obviously had strong influence among the people in his city. They listened when he stood up to them. He not only supported his son, but he also mocked Baal by renaming his son *Jerubbaal,* which roughly translates "let Baal plead for himself."

3. BROADENED HIS CIRCLE (CREDIBILITY)

After you win a core group of people and they buy in to your leadership, it's possible to broaden your circle of influence. When Gideon won the influence of Joash, he won over the entire city. The buy-in of his leadership had begun. And when he blew the trumpet to gather the Abiezrites (the people of his region), they came. Having won them, he extended the call beyond his borders and called on Asher, Zebulun, and Naphtali. And they all came! Even the people of Ephraim joined with him. Everyone was clearly sold on Gideon as a leader.

4. MOVED WHEN THE TIME AND INFLUENCE WERE RIGHT (CULMINATION)

The truth of the matter is that so many people bought in to Gideon's leadership so completely that God had to send a bunch of them home. He told Gideon, "The people who are with you are too many for Me to give the Midianites into their hands, lest Israel claim glory for itself against Me, saying, 'My own hand has saved me'" (Judg. 7:2 NKJV). The number of followers was reduced to three hundred, and they fought under Gideon's leadership. And God got the glory for their victory.

I found in my leadership experience that the buy-in process followed the same kind of pattern as it did for Gideon. It began when I became the senior pastor at Skyline Church in July 1981. I recognized before I accepted the position that I would have to eventually relocate the church to keep it growing. From day one, I had a vision for the church. In fact, my first sermon at Skyline contained the vision for moving the church. But I couldn't try to act on that vision before the people bought in to me as their leader. I worked hard, led with character, and did what I could to earn the respect of those closest to me.

Everything changed for me there during a morning service on Thanksgiving Day in 1982. At a point in a prayer time, Roy Conrad, who was the lay leader of the congregation, stood up and prayed. He began, "God, I thought no one would ever be able to replace Pastor Butcher. [Orval Butcher is the wonderful man of God who founded the church.] But today I just want to say thank You for bringing Pastor Maxwell to us." As he finished praying, one by one, people in the church stood. Soon the entire congregation was on its feet, and the people were clapping. In that moment, I thought, *Today I am their leader. Now I can start relocating the church.*

I will forever think of Roy Conrad with deep affection, for he was my Joash. I had been working steadily with the people closest to me for more than a year, but when Roy stood up for me, the core of the church followed his lead. And the buy-in continued to grow outward from there. The next year, we started the campaign to relocate the church.

Just because a person has vision and occupies a leadership position doesn't necessarily mean that the people will follow. Before they get on board, they have to buy in. And that doesn't happen in an instant. Buy-in is an ongoing process.

᎒᎒

TODAY'S QUESTION FOR REFLECTION:
Is your leadership as compelling as your vision?

Day 3

LEADERSHIP THOUGHT FOR TODAY:
*People get on board with a leader who'll take them
where they want to go.*

Then the children of Israel did evil in the sight of the LORD. So the LORD delivered them into the hand of Midian for seven years, and the hand of Midian prevailed against Israel. Because of the Midianites, the children of Israel made for themselves the dens, the caves, and the strongholds which are in the mountains. So it was, whenever Israel had sown, Midianites would come up; also Amalekites and the people of the East would come up against them. Then they would encamp against them and destroy the produce of the earth as far as Gaza, and leave no sustenance for Israel, neither sheep nor ox nor donkey . . . So Israel was greatly impoverished because of the Midianites, and the children of Israel cried out to the LORD.

Judges 6:1–4, 6 (NKJV)

How are you living your life? Are you on a mission, or are you just making it day to day? Are you striving to succeed and take others with you, or are you barely surviving? The answers to these questions have a major impact on whether people are buying in to you as a leader. People who float along, reacting to life instead of pursuing their mission, are rarely taken seriously as leaders.

When the angel of the Lord came to him, Gideon was simply trying to survive. He had no mission or grand vision. He was hiding out in a winepress, hoping that he could secretly thresh some grain before the Midianites descended like locusts, consuming everything in their path. If he had tried to lead the people while maintaining that directionless mind-set, people never would have bought in to him, he never would have gained a following, and he never would have accomplished the liberation of Israel. The people's unwillingness to participate wouldn't have stemmed from their unwillingness to free themselves from their enemies. It's just that people only get on board with a leader who they believe will take them where they want to go. And until Gideon had a vision for the future and a mission that would achieve that vision, he wasn't qualified to lead.

ON A MISSION FROM GOD

In the calling of Gideon, you can see a pattern that is fairly common for a person who receives a God-given vision and mission to fulfill. Here are the steps he took:

1. HE ASSUMED RESPONSIBILITY

A calling by God always begins with responsibility. I think people's natural tendency is to ask God to give the vision before they intend to act. But God wants us to take action first. When we see an immediate need that touches our hearts or we have a burden (as I explained in Day 2 of the Law of Navigation), God wants us to work to meet that need.

> Gideon's willingness to take responsibility opened the door for God to ask him to step up to a whole new level of responsibility—to leadership.

Gideon knew the need of his family, the need for food. And he was taking action to fulfill that need. He was threshing wheat in the winepress. Perhaps the reason the angel called him a mighty man of valor was that he was risking his life by defying the Midianites. Gideon's willingness to take responsibility opened the door for God to ask him to step up to a whole new level of responsibility—to leadership.

Overanalysis creates paralysis. God is under no obligation to explain His reasons for His actions. He is much more likely to reward our obedience with an explanation than He is to give an explanation to encourage our obedience. If you know God is asking you to do something, don't keep asking Him *why*.

If you lack vision, don't sit still waiting for it to hit you like a bolt of lightning. When you see a need that tugs at your heart, take action. Address the need, and if God desires to speak to you and call you to take the next step, He will.

❦

God is much more likely to reward our obedience with an explanation than He is to give an explanation to encourage our obedience.

---

2. HE ANTICIPATED RESULTS

When God asks us to move forward, there *will* be positive results. They may not be what we expect, but something good will happen. As God said in Isaiah 55:11,

> So shall My word be that goes forth from My mouth;
> It shall not return to Me void,
> But it shall accomplish what I please,
> And it shall prosper in the thing for which I sent it. (NKJV)

Gideon was given every reason to anticipate positive results. The angel of the Lord promised, "Surely I will be with you, and you shall defeat the Midianites as one man" (Judg. 6:16 NKJV). To receive a vision and accomplish your mission, you must believe that God is faithful. You must have faith that He will achieve results and fulfill His promises.

3. HE ACCEPTED RISKS

At some point, the only thing left to do is to act. That means accepting that risk is inevitable and taking the appropriate action. Moving forward almost always involves an act of faith.

Once Gideon had gained confirmation that God was calling him to act, he needed to follow through. And he did. He took his people to Mount Moreh in the shadow of the army of Midian. From there, God delivered Israel's enemies into Gideon's hands.

Gideon never would have discovered his destiny or grown to his potential if he hadn't listened to God and then acted. Nor would the people have experienced God's blessing. That's why it's so important for leaders to sense and seize their calling.

෫

TODAY'S QUESTION FOR REFLECTION:
Where are you going? Why would anyone want to go with you?

Day 4

LEADERSHIP THOUGHT FOR TODAY:
*The more attraction assets you possess,
the more attractive you become.*

The mark of a good leader is loyal followers;
leadership is nothing without a following.
Proverbs 14:28 (*The Message*)

What made people *want* to follow Gideon? What caused people to buy in to his leadership? For that matter, what causes *any* followers to buy in to their leader?

Our culture puts a lot of stock in the concept of IQ, a person's intelligence quotient. But I believe that when it comes to leading people, intelligence alone is overrated. More important than intellect is AQ—a person's *attraction quotient.*

Every person has some ability to attract others, based on his attraction assets. When I say that, I'm not talking about physical attractiveness. I mean qualities that are desirable in a leader. The greater the attraction assets a person possesses, the more likely people will want to follow that leader.

SEVEN ASSETS THAT FOLLOWERS DESIRE IN A LEADER

Many factors are involved when it comes to why followers buy in to the leadership of a person. Anyone who has studied leadership could probably list dozens. But it is possible to narrow the list. (Besides, as someone learning to become a better leader, you can't focus on thirty areas to improve at one time.)

Every follower is attracted to a leader who possesses these seven qualities:

1. CALLING
Few things are as compelling to followers as a clear calling in the life of a

leader. Someone who has received and accepted a calling usually possesses vision, passion, energy, and commitment. Gideon's calling was certain. And once he accepted his calling, it transformed him. Beforehand, he was a fearful man who doubted himself and asked for multiple signs to confirm his mission. Even as he began to take his first steps of obedience, he acted at night. But once he embraced the truth of his calling, he became passionate and bold. With 300 men, he attacked and overcame an army of 120,000 warriors (Judg. 8:10).

2. INSIGHT

People respect a leader who possesses keen insight, who has the wisdom to see the real issue in any situation, and who can see what's ahead. Scripture says that God gave Gideon insight into the weak hearts of the Midianites before he was to attack their camp. By the time Gideon called his men to battle, he understood that God had assured their victory.

3. CHARISMA

People are attracted to leaders who make them feel good about themselves. That, in a nutshell, is the secret of charisma. When Gideon invited the people of Ephraim to join in the pursuit of the dispersed Midianites, they reacted with anger. But Gideon was able to help them see the significance of their role, having captured and killed the princes of Midian.

4. TALENT

You don't need to look any farther than the entertainment industry to know that followers are highly attracted to people with talent. Actors and musicians are idolized for their natural gifts and talents. We don't know much about Gideon's natural abilities. But the angel called him a "mighty man of valor" (Judg. 6:12 NKJV) and instructed him to "go in this might of yours" (Judg. 6:14 NKJV). More than likely, some of Gideon's talents were physical strength and courage.

5. ABILITY

People love competence. They are naturally attracted to someone who can get things done. As I mentioned on Day 3 of the Law of Respect, production is the third level of leadership; people follow because of what the leader does for the team.

Gideon must have known that the people of Ephraim would be the most difficult people to get to buy in to his leadership. He started with the people closest to him with whom he had strong relationships. But he didn't attempt to get the Ephraimites on board with him until he had proved his ability. And even then, he had to work to get them to accept him as leader.

6. COMMUNICATION SKILLS

A leader who cannot communicate his calling and vision has difficulty getting the people to understand and buy in to his leadership. Whenever Gideon spoke to the people, they understood and eagerly followed—even when they might have been better off resisting his leadership. And that leads us to the seventh quality.

7. CHARACTER

It takes character to win over people's trust. The closer the leader is to the people, the greater the need for character. But it also takes character to keep the people going in the right direction. Gideon started out strong. He stood up when others wouldn't. He displayed courage in the face of incredible odds. But in the end, a flaw in his character betrayed him and the people. After his victories, Gideon created an idol and erected it in Ophrah: "All Israel played the harlot with it there. It became a snare to Gideon and to his house" (Judg. 8:27 NKJV).

Everyone possesses these seven qualities in various degrees. Some come naturally. Others must be fought for. But the number and degree to which a leader possesses them will determine what kind of people and how many people will follow him. The greater the diversity of assets, the greater the diversity of followers. The stronger the quality, the better the follower who is attracted to it. If you want to get people to buy in to you, work to increase your AQ.

TODAY'S QUESTION FOR REFLECTION:
How much effort are you giving to increasing your attraction assets?

Day 5

Bringing the Law to Life

TAKING IT IN

Are you the type of leader whom followers readily buy in to? Do you seem to have more people than you can handle trying to join your team or organization? Or are you continually trying to convince people to follow your lead? If your situation is more like the latter, review and embrace these four statements concerning the Law of Buy-In:

1. When people become confident in the leader, they become confident in the vision.

2. Buy-in is an ongoing process.

3. People get on board with a leader who'll take them where they want to go.

4. The more attraction assets you possess, the more attractive you become.

SORTING IT OUT

If you're not sure where you stand when it comes to understanding and applying the Law of Buy-In, visit the Web site www.injoy.com/21 Minutes to take a free twenty-five-question assessment quiz that will help you measure your ability.

PRAYING IT THROUGH

Use the following words to begin your time of prayer:

Dear God, grant me the courage to act on every leading You give me, and reveal to me the next steps of obedience You would have me take. My desire is to fulfill the vision You have for my life. Mold me into the kind of leader who can attract people I can help and take where You want them to go. Amen.

LIVING IT OUT

What is your AQ? Would you characterize yourself as having many assets that attract others? Note the seven qualities listed along with examples of leaders who possessed the qualities in abundance. Then judge yourself in each area. Rate yourself from 1 (low) to 10 (high):

ASSET	THE BEST BIBLICAL EXAMPLES	YOUR SCORE
1. Calling	David, Elijah, Peter	_____
2. Insight	Solomon, Samuel, Ezra	_____
3. Charisma	Barnabas, Apollos, John	_____
4. Talent	Samson, Elisha, Joseph	_____
5. Ability	Nehemiah, Paul, Titus	_____
6. Communication skills	Jeremiah, Amos, Isaiah	_____
7. Character	Moses, Daniel, Joshua	_____

Pick the quality for which you have the lowest score, and find a mentor to help you work to improve it. (For example, if your score for calling was low, follow the guidelines from Day 3 to correct that deficiency. If your character score was low, begin meeting with an accountability partner to work through issues related to that area of your life.)

PASSING IT ON

Which one leadership concept, insight, or practice that you've learned this week will you pass on to another leader in the next two days?

Week 15

THE LAW OF VICTORY

LEADERS FIND A WAY FOR THE TEAM TO WIN

Have you ever thought about what separates the leaders who achieve victory from those who suffer defeat? What does it take to be a winner? It's hard to put a finger on the quality that separates a winner from a loser. Every leadership situation is different. Every crisis has its own challenges. But I think that victorious leaders share an inability to accept defeat. The alternative to winning seems totally unacceptable to them, so they figure out what must be done to achieve victory, and then they go after it with everything at their disposal . . .

When the pressure is on, great leaders are at their best. Whatever is inside them comes to the surface . . . Leaders who practice the Law of Victory believe that anything less than success is unacceptable. And they have no Plan B. That keeps them fighting.

FROM "THE LAW OF VICTORY" IN *The 21 Irrefutable Laws of Leadership*

Day 1

Josiah
and the
Law of Victory

LEADERSHIP THOUGHT FOR TODAY:
Victory is preceded by a breakthrough.

Read
2 Chronicles 34:1–35:27

How does someone become a Michael Jordan? Or a Winston Churchill? Or a Wynton Marsalis? Or a Mother Teresa? How do you become so good at what you do that you refuse to do anything but succeed—no matter what circumstances you face? I believe the answer is that you first have a breakthrough.

WHERE IT ALL BEGINS

Of the four people I just mentioned, none lacked talent. And all four are examples of people who worked hard. But talent and a strong work ethic aren't enough to ensure victory. (Haven't you met a lot of talented, hardworking people who *never* win?) Breakthroughs make the difference—whether the person is leading or following, famous or obscure, powerful or weak.

I learned the power of breakthroughs while I was pastoring my first church. A woman in the church asked me to visit her ailing brother in the hospital. I was glad to do it, and I made his room one of my regular stops when I went to visit people every week. And I enjoyed the visits. We chatted about all kinds of things. Our favorite subject was the Cincinnati Reds, our favorite baseball team.

Then one day after making my rounds at the hospital, I called my wife, Margaret, to let her know I was headed home. And to my shock, she said the man had died. I couldn't believe it because I had seen him less than an hour before. That's when it hit me: I had never shared my faith with him. I realized that at that moment he might be in hell because he had the misfortune of having me as his pastor. I was devastated, and I started to cry.

A few days later, I officiated at his funeral, and I couldn't stop weeping. His sister thought I was crying because I loved him, but I knew that I had failed him—and God. For months I couldn't get over the pain of that failure. It ate away at me. Finally one night I couldn't take it anymore. At 3:00 A.M. I lay on the floor of our dining room wrestling with God. I discovered that I had made God my Savior, but not my Lord. And I knew I had to choose whether I was going to let Him break me and remake me into the man He wanted me to be. It was a breakthrough moment, and I eagerly gave myself to God anew.

My whole life changed after that. My priorities completely changed. I stopped worrying about winning over people and gave my all to pleasing God. My ministry turned around, I started sharing my faith, and the church began to grow. And the lives I touched were affected by God.

BREAKTHROUGH FOR GOD

As I look back on my life, I can identify seven major victories in my leadership, and I can trace every one of them to a personal breakthrough that preceded it. And if you look at the life of Josiah, you can see the same thing. When he sought God, he had a breakthrough that allowed a great victory. We read in Scripture, "He did what was right in the sight of the LORD, and walked in the ways of his father David; he did not turn aside to the right hand or to the left" (2 Chron. 34:2 NKJV). As a result, the nation was purged of idols, the Book of the Law was rediscovered, and the people returned to true worship of God. More than anything, Josiah wanted to win the heart of God. And he did. The Bible records that he was the most godly of all the kings of the Hebrews.

Just as victory was possible for Josiah, it's possible for you. But to achieve it, you can't focus only on winning. You need to lay the groundwork, and that means seeking a breakthrough.

TODAY'S QUESTION FOR REFLECTION:
Have you experienced a breakthrough that leads to victory?

Day 2

Victory is possible despite impossible circumstances.

Now before him [Josiah] there was no king like him, who turned to the LORD with all his heart, with all his soul, and with all his might, according to all the Law of Moses; nor after him did any arise like him.

2 Kings 23:25 (NKJV)

Most people secretly believe that winners achieve what they do because they have it easier than we do. They're lucky. They have more talent. They are born into the right family. In other words, their circumstances are better than ours. That's a cop-out! People who succeed often do so despite terrible odds and miserable circumstances. (If you doubt that, read the story of Dave Anderson or that of one of many other people in my book *Failing Forward*.)

UPHILL BATTLE

If ever a leader faced a deck stacked against him, it was Josiah. As he started his reign, everything seemed to be against him. He had to overcome several obstacles:

1. HIS AGE

Josiah was only eight years old when he became king. He was a child, even by the standards of the Hebrews who marked the passage from boyhood to manhood at age thirteen. He was five years younger than the age at which most boys *started* their apprenticeship for a trade. He had no influence and no experience.

2. A HORRIBLE FAMILY HERITAGE

Josiah's family had left Judah a legacy of pain. If you were to compile a list of the worst kings in the history of the Hebrews, Manasseh, Josiah's grandfather, would be right at the top of the list. Here is a description of his actions:

> He did evil in the sight of the LORD, according to the abominations of the nations whom the LORD had cast out before the children of Israel. For he rebuilt the high places . . . he raised up altars for Baal, and made a wooden image, as Ahab king of Israel had done; and he worshiped all the host of heaven and served them. He also built altars in the house of the LORD . . . And he built altars for all the host of heaven in the two courts of the house of the LORD. Also he made his son pass through the fire, practiced soothsaying, used witchcraft, and consulted spiritists and mediums. He did much evil in the sight of the LORD, to provoke Him to anger . . . And Manasseh seduced them to do more evil than the nations whom the LORD had destroyed before the children of Israel. (2 Kings 21:2–6, 9 NKJV)

Josiah's grandfather was more corrupt than the evil Canaanites God had driven from the promised land. And Josiah's father, Amon, followed Manasseh's example. Josiah had no godly heritage to draw upon.

3. THE ABSENCE OF A POSITIVE ROLE MODEL

Most good leaders are developed by following the lead of another strong leader. Josiah is a rare exception. Not only did the kings who preceded him fail to provide good modeling for him, but there appeared to be no other leaders present in Jerusalem who could guide and direct him. The prophet Jeremiah didn't begin his ministry until *fourteen years* after Josiah ascended the throne. By then, the young king had already swept the entire nation clean of idols and altars to false gods.

4. THE MISERABLE SPIRITUAL CONDITION OF THE COUNTRY

At the time Josiah became king, the temple in Jerusalem would have been a dramatic representation of where the people were spiritually. God's house was in ruins—and there was no desire or expectation to repair the damage. The people of his day had gone their own way. They wanted nothing to do with God, and as a result, they had never experienced His blessing or spiritual renewal.

NO MOUNTAIN TOO HIGH

Josiah let none of that stop him. His greatest desire was to dedicate himself wholeheartedly to God and win the people over to him as well. And he did it. He rid the nation of idols. He repaired God's temple and returned the ark to it. And in the process the Hebrews rediscovered the Book of the Law, which led to widespread renewal of their dedication to God. Josiah's leadership is summarized in 2 Chronicles 34:33:

> Josiah removed all the abominations from all the country that belonged to the children of Israel, and made all who were present in Israel diligently serve the LORD their God. All his days they did not depart from following the LORD God of their fathers. (NKJV)

It really doesn't matter what kind of circumstances leaders face or how many obstacles they must overcome. Victory is always possible. But first, leaders must be willing to face their greatest foe: themselves. That's the subject of tomorrow's lesson.

∾

TODAY'S QUESTION FOR REFLECTION:
In what impossible circumstances have you accepted defeat?

Day 3

Do you not know that those who run in a race all run, but one receives the prize? Run in such a way that you may obtain it. And everyone who competes for the prize is temperate in all things. Now they do it to obtain a perishable crown, but we for an imperishable crown. Therefore I run thus: not with uncertainty. Thus I fight: not as one who beats the air. But I discipline my body and bring it into subjection, lest, when I have preached to others, I myself should become disqualified.

1 Corinthians 9:24–27 (NKJV)

Everybody loves to win. There's nothing like a victory and the celebration that follows. We like receiving the winner's prize. It's a mark of achievement. But a danger of focusing on the prize is that we may come to think that victory is something that occurs *outside* us. It's not. Winning is an inside job. The trophy or medal is an acknowledgment of the inner victory. Paul's focus in the passage from 1 Corinthians is on the way we train and the way we run, not on the trophy.

The team that achieves victory is the one comprised of individuals who first win their internal battles. And the first person on any team who must face and win these internal battles is the leader—whether he happens to be a coach, parent, employer, pastor, team captain, or entrepreneur.

ACHIEVING A PERSONAL VICTORY

How does a leader go about seeking the first victory over self? What does it require? Consider what Josiah did and how he conquered himself first to gain some insight:

1. HE REMAINED OPEN AND TEACHABLE

Unteachable leaders never win. But leaders who are willing to learn and are open to change put themselves in a position to win their battles. Even people with a strong track record of past wins need to remain teachable if they want to keep winning. That was the secret of UCLA basketball coach John Wooden, as I explained in *The Success Journey*. After having won multiple NCAA championships, he was open to change and hungry to grow as a leader.

The same kind of openness and teachability can be seen in Josiah. We learn from Scripture that "in the eighth year of his reign, while he was still young, he began to seek the God of his father David" (2 Chron. 34:3 NKJV). As a sixteen-year-old, instead of trying to convince everyone that he already knew it all (as many teenagers do), he humbled himself. He departed from the ways of his arrogant father, and he sought God.

It takes teachability to win internal battles. If you desire to win the first battle—with yourself—then you need to possess that quality too.

2. HE REMOVED OBSTACLES CARRIED FORWARD FROM THE PAST

All leaders have to deal with baggage. It's inescapable. If a leader takes over an organization following another leader, he inherits problems. But leaders who found their own organizations bring personal baggage from the past into play. One way or another, a leader has to win battles involving past problems.

For Josiah, a major battle involved idol worship. Since the time of King Solomon, the worship of other gods had been a stumbling block to the Jews. Josiah realized that and decided to do something about it. He swept the country clean of idols. That took incredible courage. At only twenty years old, he was fighting against more than three hundred years of tradition and willful disobedience against God, not only by the people, but also by all the kings of Israel and Judah.

As you seek to achieve victory in your organization, you will face and overcome problems that were created in the past. They may be traditions to which the people cling, despite their ineffectiveness. They may be poor players on the team who need to be released. They may be errors in judgment made by you or predecessors. They may involve past sins that remained unrepented. Whatever they are, you must find the courage inside yourself to face and resolve them.

3. HE REALIZED WHAT HE NEEDED TO GIVE AND GAVE IT

Victory always carries a personal cost for leaders. They cannot remain outside the process and direct it. They have to be involved.

For Josiah, that meant repairing the temple and reinstating the Passover celebration. First, Josiah faithfully delivered the funds to the high priest, a practice that had evidently been neglected by the previous kings, considering the

> Victory always carries a personal cost for leaders. They cannot remain outside the process and direct it. They have to be involved.

run-down state of the temple. But that was not enough for Josiah. He wanted to honor and worship God, and he wanted God's people to do the same. So he led the Hebrews to keep the Passover with dedication and reverence, and he did it at great personal cost. From his possessions, he gave thirty thousand lambs and young goats and three thousand cattle to be sacrificed by the people:

> The children of Israel who were present kept the Passover at that time, and the Feast of Unleavened Bread for seven days. There had been no Passover kept in Israel like that since the days of Samuel the prophet; and none of the kings of Israel had kept such a Passover as Josiah kept. (2 Chron. 35:17–18 NKJV)

4. HE RECOGNIZED THE KEY TO VICTORY

Every leader is invested with the responsibility of finding the key to victory for his people. For Josiah, that key was repentance. After the Book of the Law was discovered and read, he genuinely repented for his own sins and those of the people. And he prompted his countrymen to follow his lead.

> Every leadership situation is different, but they all contain a key to victory. If you are the leader, you must find that key and turn it.

Every leadership situation is different, but they all contain a key to victory. If you are the leader, you must find that key and turn it.

5. HE RETAINED A PERSONAL COMMITMENT TO SUCCEED

The people will never be more committed than their leader. If people in an organization discover that their commitment is higher than their leader's, they will find another organization with another leader.

Josiah's personal commitment inspired the people to be faithful despite their evil desires and their history. Scripture recalls,

> Then the king stood in his place and made a covenant before the LORD, to follow the LORD, and to keep His commandments and His testimonies and His statutes with all his heart and all his soul, to perform the words of the covenant that were written in this book. (2 Chron. 34:31 NKJV)

The result of Josiah's faithfulness and dedication were faithfulness and dedication on the part of the people. The writer of Chronicles went on to say, "All his days [the people] did not depart from following the LORD God of their fathers" (2 Chron. 34:33 NKJV).

If you want your team to succeed, then you need to win some battles inside yourself. You cannot win unless you first win within. Do that, and you put yourself—and your team—in position for victory.

TODAY'S QUESTION FOR REFLECTION:
Are you taking responsibility for your victories?

Day 4

The people's victory follows the leader's breakthrough.

I am already being poured out as a drink offering, and the time of my departure is at hand. I have fought the good fight, I have finished the race, I have kept the faith . . . The Lord stood with me and strengthened me, so that the message might be preached fully through me, and that all the Gentiles might hear.

2 Timothy 4:6–7, 17 (NKJV)

If you have experienced significant breakthroughs in your life, and you're fighting the battles you should on the inside, then you are putting yourself in the best place to lead your team to victory. But that may not be enough. For the organization to go to the next level, your people may need to experience their own breakthroughs.

HELPING OTHERS BREAK THROUGH FOR VICTORY

As a leader, you can make an impact on your people when it comes to breakthroughs. Here's a good way to go about doing it:

1. UNDERSTAND BREAKTHROUGH TIMING

The issue of timing in leadership is so important that it has a leadership law all its own. But when it comes to creating a breakthrough for your people, recognize that there are three prime times for leading people to a breakthrough that can lead to victory. People are ripe for a change when . . .

- they hurt enough that they need a breakthrough.
- they learn enough that they want a breakthrough.

- they receive enough that they are able to break through.

As you work with the people in your organization, provide them with learning opportunities, give them resources and encouragement, and pay attention to where they are mentally, spiritually, and emotionally. Then when they're ready, give a little nudge to help them over the hump.

2. PRAY FOR A BREAKTHROUGH

When it comes to experiencing a breakthrough, it may not be worth doing if God's not in it. Besides, if God's not in it, you won't be able to make it happen anyway. The eminent evangelist John Wesley observed, "God does nothing but in answer to prayer."

The best thing you can do for your people is to pray for them. Intercede for them. Ask God for a breakthrough. Then ask God to help you do your part, to reveal to the people their part, and to fulfill His part.

3. BECOME A BREAKTHROUGH PERSON

People do what people see. If you live your life so that it shows what it means to be a breakthrough person, your people will value breakthroughs, and they will have a real-life role model to follow.

How do you become a breakthrough person? I have found that most breakthrough people exhibit these qualities:

- *Vulnerability.* They realize that they aren't perfect, they can't do it all, and they need God to make up the difference.

- *Humility.* They're not out to prove anything, and they don't care who gets the credit. They're glad to share the spotlight with others when they succeed.

- *Transparency.* They live their lives as open books. They share where they're coming up short as well as where God is working in their lives.

You cannot guarantee that you will experience a breakthrough. But you can control whether you possess these qualities.

4. FIND BREAKTHROUGH LEADERS

Having a few strong leaders around you who are capable of experiencing breakthroughs can make a huge difference in the lives of your people. When these people are on the team, breakthroughs for the organization are almost inevitable. It's like having a team of breakthrough catalysts working alongside you.

If you want to have a winning team, you've got to have winning players. The best way to do that is to create breakthroughs. And if you can become a breakthrough person who leads a team of breakthrough leaders who oversee and lead an organization filled with breakthrough people, then victory becomes inevitable.

❧

TODAY'S QUESTION FOR REFLECTION:
Are your people winning or losing?

Day 5

Bringing the Law to Life

TAKING IT IN

How are you doing when it comes to the Law of Victory? Like Josiah, do you find a way for your team to win? Remember these thoughts:

1. Victory is preceded by a breakthrough.
2. Victory is possible despite impossible circumstances.
3. A leader's first victory is over himself.
4. The people's victory follows the leader's breakthrough.

If you're not sure how to measure your breakthrough ability, consider this: victorious leaders are always raising (1) men and women; (2) morale; and (3) money. If these three areas are growing, then you're positioning yourself and your team for victory.

SORTING IT OUT

If you're not sure where you stand when it comes to understanding and applying the Law of Victory, visit the Web site www.injoy.com/21 Minutes to take a free twenty-five-question assessment quiz that will help you measure your ability.

PRAYING IT THROUGH

Use the following words to begin your time of prayer:

Dear God, the chronicler said that when the people of Ammon, Moab, and Mount Seir were about to attack the children of Israel, Jehoshaphat prayed, "If disaster comes upon us—sword, judgment, pestilence, or famine—we will stand before this temple and in Your presence (for Your name is in this temple), and cry out to You in our affliction, and You will hear and save." Only You, Lord, can bring victory to me and my people. I submit myself to You and ask that You partner with me according to Your will. Amen.

LIVING IT OUT

Talk to three friends or colleagues who know you well. (If you're really brave, talk to your spouse.) Ask them to rate you from 1 (low) to 10 (high) on the three qualities displayed by breakthrough people: vulnerability, humility, and transparency. Address weaknesses in the three areas by doing the following:

- *Vulnerability.* Make a point for at least a week to admit it every time you make a mistake and to apologize to the person or people involved.

- *Humility.* Determine to take no credit for successes accomplished by your team for a set amount of time—a week, a month, or the duration of a particular project.

- *Transparency.* Have lunch with a friend once a month for six months, and share where you are falling short of your goals and how God is working in your life. Also ask the person for advice, if appropriate.

PASSING IT ON

Which one leadership concept, insight, or practice that you've learned this week will you pass on to another leader in the next two days?

Week 16

THE LAW OF THE BIG MO

MOMENTUM IS A LEADER'S BEST FRIEND

It takes a leader to create momentum. Followers catch it. And managers are able to continue it once it has begun. But *creating* it requires someone who can motivate others, not who needs to be motivated. Harry Truman once said, "If you can't stand the heat, get out of the kitchen." But for leaders, that statement should be changed to read, "If you can't *make* some heat, get out of the kitchen."

All leaders face the challenge of creating change in an organization . . . Just as every sailor knows that you can't steer a ship that isn't moving forward, strong leaders understand that to change direction, you first have to create forward progress . . . When you have no momentum, even the simplest tasks can seem to be insurmountable problems. But when you have momentum on your side, the future looks bright, obstacles appear small, and trouble seems temporary . . . With enough momentum, nearly any kind of change is possible.

FROM "THE LAW OF THE BIG MO" IN *The 21 Irrefutable Laws of Leadership*

Day 1

Solomon
and the
Law of the Big Mo

LEADERSHIP THOUGHT FOR TODAY:
*Often the only difference between winning
and losing is momentum.*

Read
1 Kings 1:28–40; 3:1–28; 4:1, 20–34;
5:1–12; 9:15–19, 26

Have you ever experienced being on a roll? Some people call it being "in the zone." Everything goes right, every prospective customer says yes, and no matter what you try, you can't seem to miss. It's something you occasionally see in sports: a basketball player can't seem to miss a shot, a quarterback completes a dozen passes in a row, or a pitcher executes a perfect game in baseball.

If you've had an experience like that, then you know it's an awesome feeling. But have you ever experienced that kind of thing as a leader? If you **have**, I can tell you how you did it: momentum. When it comes to achievement, momentum is a leader's best friend. That's the Law of the Big Mo.

FOUR KINDS OF KINGS

The first four kings of Israel present a remarkable study in momentum that peaked with the reign of Solomon. You may never have thought about the Hebrews' first four leaders in that way before, but as you reflect on who they were and what they did, you will see what I mean. Here's how each stacked up when it came to momentum:

1. SAUL LACKED MOMENTUM

Two tasks for a leader are harder than any other he will ever have to perform. The first is getting a stalled (or backward-moving) organization to start moving forward. It's like getting a train moving. It takes tremendous energy. A train is so heavy and its inertia has such force that even the smallest things prevent it from moving forward. A block of wood under the wheels of a stationary locomotive will prevent it from moving forward at all.

The other difficult task for a leader is changing an organization's direction. With forward progress, it's difficult. Without forward progress, it's impossible.

When Saul was anointed king, his task was to take Israel in a new direction. For more than three hundred years, judges ruled the Hebrews. During half of that time, the Philistines were their adversaries and oppressors. As the new ruler of the nation, Saul was to create and consolidate a kingdom, overcome the Hebrews' oppressors, and dedicate himself to God so that he and the people could continue receiving His blessing.

Saul was not equal to the task. Because of his weak character, his selfishness, and his improper motives, he was incapable of creating momentum. Even when God blessed him and gave him victories, as He did at Jabesh Gilead (1 Sam. 11:1–11), Saul squandered the opportunity and sabotaged it with his disobedience. Creating a kingdom was a difficult task that required a great leader—a momentum maker. But in the end, Saul was nothing more than a momentum faker.

2. DAVID CREATED MOMENTUM

David, on the other hand, was a momentum maker. Even before he became king, he had a knack for creating momentum—beginning with his defeat of Goliath. When he was in exile, he spent the time building momentum: he capitalized on his victories, consolidated his army, and cultivated his character. By the time he ascended the throne, he was already a strong leader capable of moving the country in the direction it needed to go.

3. SOLOMON BUILT MOMENTUM

Although Solomon possessed both wealth and wisdom as he began his reign as king, his best friend was the momentum his father, David, had created during his reign. It was an incredible legacy: Israel had become known as a major military force, its ruler possessed the respect of other kings, and the people had seen a king who loved God and had a heart for justice. In addition, David had accumulated wealth and some of the materials for the building of the temple.

Solomon took a good kingdom, and he turned it into a great kingdom. He built an impressive administration that relied on the talents of twelve governors. He made numerous alliances with neighboring powers. He secured trade and shipping routes that made Israel the crossroads of the world. He engaged in an extensive building campaign that made a marvel of Jerusalem. His projects included the temple of the Lord, an elaborate new palace, the House of the Forests of Lebanon, the Hall of Pillars, the Hall of Judgment, and extensive defensive fortifications for the city. And he accumulated incredible wealth.

To sum up Solomon's reign, Scripture says of David's son, "King Solomon surpassed all the kings of the earth in riches and wisdom. And all the kings of the earth sought the presence of Solomon to hear his wisdom, which God had put in his heart" (2 Chron. 9:22–23 NKJV). Solomon took the momentum his father had given him and created the most powerful and prosperous nation in the world. No one had ever seen anything like it before, and no one would ever see anything like it again.

4. REHOBOAM STOPPED MOMENTUM

Everything that Solomon achieved over the course of his forty-year reign, his son Rehoboam destroyed in a matter of days. Solomon's projects had taken a toll on the people, and they desired relief. When Jeroboam and the other leaders of Israel came to Rehoboam, they said they would pledge their loyalty to him if only he would lighten their load. Upon Rehoboam's decision of how to handle that request rested the question of whether he would continue the momentum his father and grandfather created, or whether it would stop with him.

The men who had spent their lives in the presence of the wise Solomon recognized the opportunity that Rehoboam had. They advised, "If you will be a servant to these people today, and serve them, and answer them, and speak good words to them, then they will be your servants forever" (1 Kings 12:7 NKJV). But the pride of Solomon's son was boundless. He rejected the people's offer, and that was the end of the nation as Solomon had built it. Rehoboam became the greatest momentum breaker in the history of the Hebrews.

No matter where you are as a leader—whether you're starting an organization from scratch, building an organization that's already off the ground, or following a great leader—momentum can make or break your organization. Learn to use it to your advantage, and you can take your people *anywhere.*

TODAY'S QUESTION FOR REFLECTION:
How is momentum affecting your progress?

Day 2

Momentum is a good leader's gift.

Now the days of David drew near that he should die, and he charged Solomon his son, saying: "I go the way of all the earth; be strong, therefore, and prove yourself a man. And keep the charge of the LORD your God: to walk in His ways, to keep His statutes, His commandments, His judgments, and His testimonies, as it is written in the Law of Moses, that you may prosper in all that you do and wherever you turn; that the LORD may fulfill His word which He spoke concerning me, saying, 'If your sons take heed to their way, to walk before Me in truth with all their heart and with all their soul,' He said, 'you shall not lack a man on the throne of Israel.'"

1 Kings 2:1–4 (NKJV)

If you as a leader could ask for and receive any gift, what would you choose? Would you pick a few quality leaders to have on your team? Or would you prefer immense material resources? How about better facilities? Solomon picked wisdom, but he was able to choose that because of the luxury of momentum his father had already given him as a legacy. And that wisdom enabled him to have all the other things he needed as king, including greater momentum.

HOW SOLOMON BUILT MOMENTUM

The time of transition from one leader to another is the most critical time for continuing momentum. Rehoboam's story illustrates that. How was Solomon so successful in taking the reins from his father,

> The time of transition from one leader to another is the most critical time for continuing momentum.

David? Take a look at the following five things the young Solomon did that ensured a smooth transition:

1. HE STARTED WITH WHAT DAVID PROVIDED

Solomon's father gave him everything he needed to start his reign as king: a stable kingdom, resources, wise counsel, and his public endorsement. David made it clear to everyone in Israel that his choice for king was Solomon.

2. HE HUMBLY ASKED FOR LEADERSHIP WISDOM ABOVE ALL ELSE

It is believed that Solomon was about eighteen years old when he became king of Israel. Think about the people you know who are that age (or yourself back then), and consider what most of them would ask for, given the chance to have anything they wanted. Many eighteen-year-old boys today would choose a $100,000 sports car and the best stereo equipment on the market.

Solomon recognized that leadership would be difficult and that his greatest need was wisdom—an understanding heart to judge God's people. That request kept his motives pure and made it possible for him to avoid momentum breakers.

3. HE MADE WISE DECISIONS THAT WON HIM CREDIBILITY

Solomon made several deft decisions concerning enemies to the throne immediately after the death of David. He exiled one opponent, executed two others, and put a fourth under house arrest. But even more important, he cemented his credibility with the people. Scripture states that the wisdom he displayed in the matter of the two harlots and the baby had a profound impact on the people: "All Israel heard of the judgment which the king had rendered; and they feared the king" (1 Kings 3:28 NKJV).

4. HE MAINTAINED THE PEACE

Solomon's few bold moves against enemies within Israel maintained peace at home, thus preventing a bloody civil war, like the one his father experienced. But Solomon wisely took additional measures to keep other nations from threatening the country's progress. He used his wisdom to advise and entertain his own governors and the rulers of neighboring nations, and according to Scripture, "He had peace on every side all around him" (1 Kings 4:24 NKJV).

5. HE SURROUNDED HIMSELF WITH WISE ASSOCIATES

In the Law of the Inner Circle section, I wrote about the lists of David's key leaders contained in the Bible. The only king of Israel who can challenge him as the gatherer of a great inner circle is Solomon. A few men were trusted servants of David whom Solomon kept on in his administration. But the majority were not. In addition to Solomon's twelve competent governors, these people assisted him:

- Azariah: Priest

- Elihoreph and Ahijah: Scribes

- Jehoshaphat: Recorder

- Benaiah: Commander of the army

- Zadok and Abiathar: Priests

- Azariah: Overseer of officers

- Zabud: Priest and special adviser

- Ahishar: Head of the royal household

- Adoniram: Chief of the labor force

With a good handoff, wisdom, a great inner circle, and good decision making, how could Solomon lose? He had everything he needed, and because he made the most of it, he took himself, his people, and his nation to their potential.

TODAY'S QUESTION FOR REFLECTION:
Have you been given the gift of momentum? If you have,
what are you doing with it?

Day 3

Momentum does not sustain itself.

Well done, good and faithful servant; you were faithful over a few things, I will make you ruler over many things. Enter into the joy of your lord.

Matthew 25:21 (NKJV)

They say that one of the most difficult challenges for any sports team is back-to-back championships. Getting everything on a team to come together for a season is an incredible challenge. Making it happen two seasons in a row is close to impossible. Yet occasionally it happens. Recently the New York Yankees did it. So did the Denver Broncos. But more often, a team reaches the pinnacle and then fades back into the middle of the pack. Why? Because the players on the team think that once they've made it to the top, they can cruise to stay there. But that's not the way it works. Momentum never sustains itself.

If Solomon as king of Israel had believed that the momentum his father created would have been enough to sustain

> *Momentum never sustains itself.*

him for the forty years he was on the throne, he would have been in big trouble. His father gave him the momentum he needed to have a good start as king. There's no doubt about that. But to keep the momentum going (and to increase it), he had to make his own ongoing contribution.

WHAT IT TAKES TO SUSTAIN MOMENTUM

How does a winning team keep winning? What is the key that makes it possible for an organization to keep the momentum going? The answer is not *what* but *who:* the leader. It takes a leader to sustain momentum.

What is the key that makes it possible for an organization to keep the momentum going? The answer is not *what* but *who:* the leader. It takes a leader to sustain momentum.

A leader must deal with three critical issues to sustain momentum. To keep an organization going with positive momentum, a leader must possess . . .

1. A WILLINGNESS TO ACCEPT RESPONSIBILITY FOR THE ORGANIZATION'S MOMENTUM

Most leaders are happy to accept responsibility when an organization is succeeding. However, when the organization isn't doing so well, that can be another story. The truth is that no matter whether the momentum is positive, negative, or nonexistent, it is the leader's responsibility.

I've observed that leaders are most likely to excuse themselves from the responsibility of an organization's momentum when they first begin leading it. Because they are often facing issues that they didn't create, they tend to dismiss or ignore them. If the issues happen to be momentum killers, that's a problem.

But no matter what, the buck stops with the leader. My friend Olan Hendrix, CEO of the Leadership Resource Group, maintains that after you've been in charge of an organization for three years, every problem is your problem. The sooner a leader owns up to the responsibility of sustaining momentum, the sooner he will start doing something about it.

2. A WILLINGNESS TO DIRECT MOMENTUM INSTEAD OF LETTING IT DIRECT HIM

Momentum always has a direction. Most people in an organization are carried by that momentum and have little impact on it. But leaders cannot afford to *surf* momentum; they must *steer* it.

Before Solomon became the king of Israel, an outstanding military leader, David, had created the nation's momentum. David had established a stable administration, which

---

Momentum always has a direction.

---

enabled Israel to move from a judgeship to a kingdom. But first and foremost, David was a warrior. His greatest accomplishments were military. The greatest leaders under him were warriors. His mighty men were incredible.

Solomon, on the other hand, was not a warrior. And the things he desired to accomplish were not military in nature. He wanted to give most of his attention to trade and construction. That meant he had to change the direction of the nation's momentum. And he was able to do it through wise leadership, the selection of a talented group of leaders (his governors and court officials) who would assist him, and the communication of his vision for the nation to the people.

The momentum in an organization doesn't always go the way you want it to go. As a leader, you don't want to stop momentum, reset the direction, and then start it up again from a standstill because too much time and energy are needed. Instead, do everything you can to steer positive momentum where you want it to go; then you can continue to build on it.

3. A WILLINGNESS TO BE ENTHUSIASTIC AT ALL TIMES

The third key to sustaining positive momentum is remaining positive. Eleanor Doon says, "You cannot kindle a fire in any other heart until it is burning within your own."

For some personality types, remaining enthusiastic is easy. For others, it's not. Here are my secrets to keeping my leadership positive all the time. I truly believe . . .

> "You cannot kindle a fire in any other heart until it is burning within your own."
>
> —ELEANOR DOON

- *the work I'm doing is most important.* My vision, my mission, and my actions all line up. It's easy to stay excited when what you're doing really matters.

- *the people I'm sharing it with are the best.* I place a high value on everyone I work with. I expect the best of them, and they give their best. It's a win-win situation.

- *the results will be positive.* For the most part in life, you get what you expect. I always expect the best, and only occasionally am I suprised—but even then, I'm just as often surprised by better results as I am by worse results.

I have yet to meet a leader with a chronically negative attitude who was able to continually sustain positive momentum.

If you have leadership responsibility for an entire organization or for a small team of people, you can't ignore the impact of momentum. If you've got it, you and your people will be able to accomplish things you never thought possible. If you don't, the smallest tasks will seem difficult. As the leader, you have to make the choice to have it.

> I have yet to meet a leader with a chronically negative attitude who was able to continually sustain positive momentum.

TODAY'S QUESTION FOR REFLECTION:
Are you gaining or losing momentum?

Day 4

LEADERSHIP THOUGHT FOR TODAY:
While a good leader sustains momentum, a great leader increases it.

For whoever has, to him more will be given; but whoever does not have, even what he has will be taken away from him.

Mark 4:25 (NKJV)

Solomon took the nation of Israel to a place it had never been before. It became the most prosperous kingdom in the world. And as a result, it became a living demonstration of God's favor and glory to everyone who came into contact with it. The Queen of Sheba's remarks to Solomon sum up the idea well:

> It was a true report which I heard in my own land about your words and your wisdom. However I did not believe the words until I came and saw with my own eyes; and indeed the half was not told me. Your wisdom and prosperity exceed the fame of which I heard . . . Blessed be the LORD your God, who delighted in you, setting you on the throne of Israel! Because the LORD has loved Israel forever, therefore He made you king, to do justice and righteousness. (1 Kings 10:6–7, 9 NKJV)

HOW TO MOVE THE BIG MO

Like all great leaders, Solomon did more than sustain momentum; he increased it. What David started, his son took to its highest potential. If you desire to take your organization to a higher level by increasing the momentum rather than merely sustaining it, then follow these guidelines:

1. UNDERSTAND THE VALUE OF MOMENTUM
No organization—whether it's a nation, business, church, family, or

sports team—will reach its potential without continually increased momentum. The pull of the world is toward sin and entropy. Everything naturally runs downhill. If you're not working hard to move forward, then you're moving backward.

2. IDENTIFY THE MOTIVATING FACTORS IN YOUR ORGANIZATION

Every organization possesses potential momentum motivators for its people. Your job is to discover and encourage them. Certainly it starts with the vision of the leader. But it takes more than that. Leaders who create momentum tap into the passions of their people. You learn those only by getting out among your people and connecting with them.

3. REMOVE THE DEMOTIVATING FACTORS FROM YOUR ORGANIZATION

Just as every organization has motivating factors, it also has potential motivation busters. Sometimes people are the problem. Chronically negative people always lower morale and hurt momentum. So do people who continually put themselves ahead of the team. Other times momentum is hindered by values held in the organization, such as idealizing the past, which encourages people to hold to outdated traditions.

If you want to move your organization forward, do what Solomon did: clear the way for positive momentum. He removed people who would hurt his progress, and he never tried to recapture or repeat his father's accomplishments. He went his own way.

4. SCHEDULE TIMES FOR DIRECTION AND CELEBRATION

The leaders of the Old Testament knew how to celebrate. Every time God showed the people favor, their leader built an altar or a monument to honor God and remind the people of where they had been and where God intended to take them.

Solomon followed that same pattern. Once he became king, he determined to honor God. But instead of building an altar, he built an entire temple to commemorate God's goodness. And he took that opportunity to remind the people of their history and the future God desired for them so that they could make appropriate adjustments in their lives.

As you lead people, follow Solomon's example. Take time to let the people enjoy their achievements. Nothing builds morale like a celebration. As you celebrate, honor the men and women who made the victory possible. And use the opportunity to clarify and communicate your vision to the people so that the momentum that is created propels them in the right direction.

5. PRACTICE CHARACTER LEADERSHIP: DO WHAT'S RIGHT NO MATTER HOW YOU FEEL

The most important factor in the ongoing process of building momentum is character. If the leader discredits or disqualifies himself, then momentum stops building, and it can quickly come to a grinding halt. As the Law of Solid Ground states, "Trust is the foundation of leadership."

Solomon was an illustrious leader in nearly every respect—except the area of character. He allowed his passion for God to become clouded by his passion for women, and that led to widespread idolatry in Israel:

> King Solomon loved many foreign women, as well as the daughter of Pharaoh: women of the Moabites, Ammonites, Edomites, Sidonians, and Hittites—from the nations of whom the LORD had said to the children of Israel, "You shall not intermarry with them, nor they with you. Surely they will turn away your hearts after their gods." Solomon clung to these in love. And he had seven hundred wives, princesses, and three hundred concubines; and his wives turned away his heart. For it was so, when Solomon was old, that his wives turned his heart after other gods; and his heart was not loyal to the LORD his God, as was the heart of his father David ... Therefore the LORD said to Solomon, "Because you have done this, and have not kept My covenant and My statutes, which I have commanded you, I will surely tear the kingdom away from you and give it to your servant." (1 Kings 11:1–4, 11 NKJV)

WITHOUT CHARACTER, EVEN A GREAT LEADER CANNOT SUSTAIN MOMENTUM

If you desire to take your people and your organization to the highest level, you must learn to create momentum. It isn't easy, but nothing you can do as a leader compares with the impact it can make.

TODAY'S QUESTION FOR REFLECTION:
What are you currently doing to build momentum?

Day 5

Bringing the Law to Life

TAKING IT IN

Review the four thoughts related to the Law of the Big Mo:

1. Often the only difference between winning and losing is momentum.

2. Momentum is a good leader's gift.

3. Momentum does not sustain itself.

4. While a good leader sustains momentum, a great leader increases it.

Now think about teams or organizations you've led in the past. Do they have a history of winding down or gearing up? Has your goal been to preserve gains achieved by a predecessor? Or has your desire been to break new ground? Your answer should help you see whether you've been a momentum maker, momentum taker, or momentum faker.

SORTING IT OUT

If you're not sure where you stand when it comes to understanding and applying the Law of the Big Mo, visit the Web site www.injoy.com/21 Minutes to take a free twenty-five-question assessment quiz that will help you measure your ability.

PRAYING IT THROUGH

Use the following words to begin your time of prayer:

Dear God, help me to understand my current leadership situation. Show me whether my organization is moving forward or backward. Reveal the motivat-

ing and demotivating factors that are the keys to momentum building. And
please make me a change agent for positive growth for my team. Amen.

LIVING IT OUT

If you cannot readily name the positive and negative factors that inspire and deter motivation among your team members, then you don't know what will make or break momentum in your organization. Spend the next week connecting with people individually to find out what makes them tick. Then formulate a plan to capitalize on what you learned.

PASSING IT ON

Which one leadership concept, insight, or practice that you've learned this week will you pass on to another leader in the next two days?

Week 17

THE LAW OF PRIORITIES

LEADERS UNDERSTAND THAT ACTIVITY IS NOT NECESSARILY ACCOMPLISHMENT

Leaders never grow to a point where they no longer need to prioritize. It's something that good leaders keep doing, whether they're leading a small group, pastoring a church, running a small business, or leading a billion-dollar corporation . . . Stephen Covey remarked, "A leader is the one who climbs the tallest tree, surveys the entire situation, and yells, 'Wrong jungle!'"

The things that bring the greatest personal reward are the fire lighters in a leader's life. Nothing energizes a person the way passion does . . . Tim Redmond admitted, "There are many things that will catch my eye, but there are only a few things that will catch my heart." . . .

Take some time to reassess your leadership priorities . . . Are you spread out all over the place? Or are you focused on the few things that bring the highest reward? . . . The greatest success comes only when you focus your people on what really matters.

FROM "THE LAW OF PRIORITIES" IN *The 21 Irrefutable Laws of Leadership*

Day 1

Peter
and the
Law of Priorities

LEADERSHIP THOUGHT FOR TODAY:
Leaders put first things first.

Read
Mark 9:1–13; John 21:1–19;
Acts 1:1–2:47; 6:1–7

When it comes down to it, success is largely a matter of keeping the main thing the main thing. William Gladstone put it this way: "He is a wise man who wastes no energy on pursuits for which he is not fitted; and he is wiser still who from among the things he can do well, chooses and resolutely follows the best."

Successful people don't allow the unimportant things in their lives to become important. And conversely they don't allow the important things to become unimportant. They form a habit of spending their best resources on their best pursuits. In short, they order their activities so that they're always gravitating toward success.

UNDERSTANDING WHAT'S MOST IMPORTANT

When Peter was a young fisherman in Galilee, no one would have thought he was destined to become the passionate leader of the first Christian church. After all, he had almost no education and probably would have been happy to live the remainder of his life in obscurity. But God had something else in mind, and the moment Peter met Jesus, his priorities began to change.

Like many leaders, Peter had to learn how to put first things first. Scripture reveals a lot about the inconsistencies of his behavior and his many irrational decisions. But the more time Peter spent with Jesus, the more he learned the difference between mere activity and accomplishment.

For three years, Peter watched as Jesus' priorities were tested on a regular basis. And for three years, he saw Jesus consistently invest only in the things that would allow Him to fulfill His mission—despite all the demands on His attention. I believe that over time, Jesus' actions made a lasting impression on Peter. When Peter's time came to lead, his priorities were in order, and he led his people with utmost confidence.

GOD BLESSES RIGHT PRIORITIES

Every time Peter focused on the important, God blessed his actions. At pentecost, he waited for God to prepare the hearts of the people before speaking to them, and three thousand people caught his vision and were converted (Acts 2). Before the religious courts, he refused to quit preaching because he knew that listening to God was more important than listening to men (Acts 4:18–20). And when the Grecian Jews complained about their limited food supply, Peter delegated the task to seven capable men so that he and the other disciples could concentrate on their mission to preach.

Like Peter, great leaders sift through the many things that demand their time and discern not only what needs to be done first, but also what doesn't need to be done at all. That starts with a passion to excel. Peter was arguably the most animated character in Scripture. He was passionate about everything—even the wrong things at times. But Peter eventually learned where to focus his passion. He learned what needed to take precedence in his life. And when that happened, he was able to lead with effectiveness.

The same is true of every leader. When you focus your passion on what's most important,

> "If you really know what you want out of life, it's amazing how opportunities will come to enable you to carry them out."
>
> —JOHN M. GODDARD

your leadership climbs to new heights, and you're able to continually advance in the direction of success. John M. Goddard said, "If you really know what you want out of life, it's amazing how opportunities will come to enable you to carry them out."

❧

TODAY'S QUESTION FOR REFLECTION:
How do you decide what comes first?

Day 2

Act like people with good sense and not like fools . . . Make every minute count. Don't be stupid. Instead, find out what the Lord wants you to do.

Ephesians 5:15–17 (CEV)

Your mission is the foundation of your priorities. Once Peter understood that his mission was to spread Christianity—and nothing else—that became the foundation of his decisions. Everything he did supported the direction he was going. And yet he didn't have tunnel vision. Like all great leaders, he was able to see the whole picture first, then decide on what he needed to focus.

SHARPENING YOUR FOCUS BY EXPANDING YOUR VIEW

Maybe you're similar to the way Peter was at first—full of passion, but lacking direction. The good news is that you already have half of the equation. The bad news is that if you don't know where you're going, you'll end up spinning your wheels. Or worse, you could spend years going in the wrong direction altogether.

But when you're confident of where you should be headed, your priorities become clearer, and your actions take on significant meaning. The complete equation looks something like this:

Great Passion + Clear Mission = Focused Action

When the Grecian Jews came to Peter to voice their complaints, Peter recognized that by meeting their felt need, he could further his mission. But he also knew it wasn't a priority for him to do it personally. He understood that *his* job was to focus on the people's *real* need—to hear the truth of

God's Word. Instead of trying to do it all, he delegated the task to seven men that he knew were competent to follow through. As a result, both needs were met.

By examining Peter's situation more carefully, we can learn a lot about remaining focused on priorities while still seeing the big picture. Peter demonstrated that when a need arises, focused leaders . . .

1. DETERMINE THE VALIDITY OF THE NEED

Strong leaders are always the first to recognize when a course of action needs to be taken, and they quickly consider how to go about it. Peter knew that if the Grecian Jews' request wasn't met, the church could lose momentum. Rather than trying to meet the need by himself (as many leaders do), however, he determined that it wasn't his top priority and figured out another way to meet it.

How do you react when your people bring a genuine need before you? Do you stop what you're doing and immediately try to take care of it? Do you nod your head as if you're interested, then push it to the side and forget about it? Or, like Peter, do you step back, look at the big picture, and determine what action is appropriate according to your priorities?

2. LOOK FOR A LEADERSHIP OPPORTUNITY

Even when a valid need isn't *your* priority, it may provide a learning opportunity for one of your people. Peter quickly recognized that it was more important for him and the other disciples to continue teaching rather than hand out food. But he also recognized an opportunity to use the situation to develop some emerging leaders.

Are your people one of your top priorities? Before you put something on a back burner, evaluate whether it fits the responsibilities of one or more of your people. Remember that the most effective leaders have to focus only on a few things—they trust their people to do the rest.

3. DELEGATE THE TASK TO COMPETENT PEOPLE

Delegation is a basic tool of a leader. Used the right way, it can take your efficiency to a whole new level. Once Peter and the disciples determined that it wasn't their priority to personally meet the need at hand, they carefully chose a team of seven whom they deemed mature and capable to carry out the task for them.

Where delegation is concerned, it's always your responsibility to appoint the right people. There's nothing worse than having to revisit a need because the person you assigned to fulfill it wasn't competent. That decreases your efficiency, and it can eventually damage your credibility as a leader. Before you delegate a task, make sure you know your people's skills and abilities.

4. PUBLICLY CONFIRM AND COMMISSION THEIR PEOPLE

Peter and the disciples set their team up for success. They not only made sure the seven men were well suited to meet the need at hand, but also presented them to the people as worthy leaders. In doing so, they built trust and confidence in the men to succeed for the whole cause.

Is it more important to you to get things done or to get things done *right*? Many leaders are so driven that they hurriedly delegate a task just to be able to check it off their to-do list. They falsely perceive delegation as a way of decreasing distractions instead of increasing effectiveness. But great leaders understand that their effectiveness is a function of their people's success, and they make it a priority to help them succeed.

Like all effective leaders, Peter understood the difference between activity and accomplishment. He always viewed a need through the biggest lens first—his overall mission. Then he zoomed in on what needed to be done— first by him, then by others. As a result, Scripture says the number of Christians continually increased under his leadership.

❦

TODAY'S QUESTION FOR REFLECTION:
Are you focusing on the right things?

Day 3

Leaders invest their time in what produces the greatest return.

> Get your fields ready
> and plant your crops before starting a home.
> Proverbs 24:27 (CEV)

Missionary Amy Carmichael wisely noted, "We will have all eternity to celebrate the victories, but only a few hours before sunset to win them." Without the limitation of time, there might be no need to prioritize. But time limits you and forces you to make choices. The more time you spend on the wrong things, the less time you have to invest in what's right—and the longer it takes to succeed. But when you learn to spend your time wisely on the things that bring your organization the most fulfillment and success, you often end up with time to spare.

In short, being successful is not about how *hard* you work; it's about how *smart* you work. There's a story I often share at my conferences about a man who was told that if he worked his very hardest, he would become successful and rich. The hardest work

> "We will have all eternity to celebrate the victories, but only a few hours before sunset to win them."
>
> —AMY CARMICHAEL

he knew was digging holes, so he began digging huge holes in his backyard, each one bigger than the one before. But in the end, he didn't get rich; he got a backache. He spent a lot of time working hard, but the work had no purpose.

ORGANIZE OR AGONIZE

Generally speaking, there are five ways that people decide how to spend their time. Once Peter understood the right way to organize his time, he made a huge impact. Read through the following organizational styles, and determine which one best describes how you spend your time:

1. URGENT—*LOUD THINGS FIRST*

Peter could have easily fallen into the trap of attending to urgent needs first. When the Grecian Jews were voicing their complaints, he could have taken matters into his own hands to shut them up. But he knew it would have been a waste of his time. Instead, he sent others to take care of the matter for him and barely broke stride.

You've no doubt heard the saying: the squeaky wheel gets the grease. Well, that shouldn't always be the case in leadership. Over time, you will probably encounter a lot of "squeaky wheels" in the form of requests, suggestions, or complaints from the people in your organization. Some of them will be valid and merit spending some of your time on them. But often, oiling the squeaky wheels in your organization isn't the best use of your time. Though it's tempting—especially if you happen to be a people pleaser—you have to learn to discern which wheels really need grease, which ones can be greased by others, and which ones will squeak no matter what you do.

2. UNPLEASANT—*HARD THINGS FIRST*

When we were young, many of us were taught to do hard things first. It's the "dinner before dessert" mentality. There is some value in it, but just because something is hard doesn't mean it should be at the top of your to-do list.

If Peter had subscribed to this notion, he himself would have probably distributed the food to the widows. Of all that he was doing at that time, that might have seemed the most unpleasant. Scripture doesn't say how long it took to complete the task of distributing the food, but it probably ended up being a full-time job. If Peter had taken on that task, he would have missed out on many opportunities to teach and lead.

You need to be able to check your motives. If you have a strong work ethic, you may naturally want to get the harder things done first. But don't just start in on the hard stuff before determining the value of your actions. If doing something easier is a better use of your time, then do that before you tackle a difficult task.

3. UNFINISHED—*LAST THINGS FIRST*

If you're like most leaders, you work on a day-to-day schedule. And many times your to-do list is left partially undone at the end of the day. If you complete only eight of the ten items on your list, your tendency is to automatically place the remaining two items at the top of your list the following day. But that's not always the best use of your time. Chances are, if the two items were on the bottom of your list, they weren't top priorities in the first place. And they won't necessarily be top priorities the following day either.

What do you think Peter would have done if only half of the widows had received food initially? Even if the men that the disciples had assigned never completed the task, he would have almost certainly continued preaching to the people.

Before you spend time completing an unfinished task from the day before, evaluate it in comparison to the other things you need to accomplish. If finishing the task is still not a top priority, place it at the bottom of your list again, and work on it *after* you finish more important items.

4. UNFULFILLING—*DULL THINGS FIRST*

Of the five styles, this one is probably the most common. If you subscribe to this notion, your tendency is to do the dull, mindless things first, but these things are rarely the most important.

Because Peter was human, there were probably times in his life when he would have preferred to focus on where he would be getting his next meal or the best route for his next journey. But Jesus had taught him not to worry about those things. He was to focus on what was most important—sharing the gospel.

5. ULTIMATE—*FIRST THINGS FIRST*

Peter understood the concept of spending time only on what ultimately needed to be done. He didn't try to get more done in a day by doing easier or more appealing things. He stuck with the most important and left the rest to be done by others or not to be done at all.

Do you naturally spend time on the most important things first? Commit to follow Peter's example, and give your best time—now and every time—to your most important tasks.

Although it's admirable to be ambitious and hardworking, it's even more desirable to be *smart* working. You see, the key to becoming a more efficient leader isn't in checking off all the items on your to-do list each day. It's in forming the habit of prioritizing your time so that you're always doing what's most important. When you're able to do that, it won't be long before you begin to exceed your expectations as a leader.

❧

TODAY'S QUESTION FOR REFLECTION:
Are you investing your time wisely?

Day 4

For in fact the body is not one member but many. If the foot should say, "Because I am not a hand, I am not of the body," is it therefore not of the body? And if the ear should say, "Because I am not an eye, I am not of the body," is it therefore not of the body? If the whole body were an eye, where would be the hearing? If the body were hearing, where would be the smelling? But now God has set the members, each one of them, in the body just as He pleased. And if they were all one member, where would be the body be?

1 Corinthians 12:14–19 (NKJV)

Anyone who has spent any amount of time around me is familiar with the Pareto Principle. The concept states that the top 20 percent of your priorities give you an 80 percent return. I've found that most leaders agree that the 80/20 principle works well when it comes to prioritizing in the area of finances or time. They recognize the return it brings. Yet many leaders are reluctant to apply it to people.

PUTTING YOUR BEST PEOPLE FIRST

Peter, like Jesus, practiced the 80/20 principle with people. Everything Peter needed to learn about prioritizing people, he was able to learn from Jesus' example. When you study how Jesus spent time with people, you realize that He didn't invest an equal amount in everyone. Although He spent a lot of time

> Jesus didn't invest an equal amount of time in everyone. Although He spent a lot of time with the crowds, He spent the vast majority of His time with twelve men—the disciples.

with the crowds, He spent the vast majority of His time with twelve men—the disciples to whom He passed on His legacy. And if you look even closer, you notice that of the group of twelve, there were a select few with whom Jesus invested more time than the others—Peter, James, and John. They would later become the founding fathers of the first Christian movement. Jesus loved everyone, but He invested His time in the people who would lead others and invest in them.

There's no doubt in my mind that Jesus' method of prioritizing His time with people had a lasting effect on Peter. Early on, Peter instinctively sought to position people where they would most effectively carry out the mission. When he was confronted by the situation with the Grecian Jews, Peter's first inclination was to appoint competent people to meet the needs that he and the apostles couldn't. The apostles remained where their gifts were most useful, and new leaders were commissioned to utilize their talents.

FIND YOUR TOP 20 PERCENT

It's the leader's job to put the right people in the right places. Like a coach during tryouts, you must be able to discern who the key players are, then position them where their gifts will best advance the team toward victory.

To find your key players, evaluate each person according to the following criteria:

1. THE INFLUENCE TEST

Peter and the other apostles required that the seven men designated to feed the widows be selected from among the people of the community. This suggests that they were well known and had already established influence with others.

Any potential leaders with whom you intend to spend time must have a degree of influence with the rest of your people. Otherwise, they will have trouble leading others to carry out the tasks before them.

2. THE RELATIONSHIP TEST

Peter also required that the men selected be "brethren." The implication is that each leader had maintained good relationships with the majority of the people.

As you select leaders, determine how candidates relate to the rest of your people. Are they on good terms with everyone? Do others consider them friendly and positive? The people with the most potential will be relationally strong.

3. THE CREDIBILITY TEST

Another requirement of the seven men was that they be of "good reputation." That's very important. As you seek potential leaders, determine whether they are respected by your people. Do others come to them with their problems? Your potential leaders must have established a foundation of trust with others in order to lead them well.

4. THE SPIRITUAL TEST

The seven men were required to have strong values. Peter knew that if the potential leaders didn't share the same spiritual convictions as the apostles, they couldn't effectively act on their behalf. Or worse, they might act in a manner contrary to their beliefs and lead others astray.

The same should be true of the people you select. Their values must be similar to yours. A potential leader who obeys God is in a much better position to succeed than one who ignores God's will for his life.

5. THE ADMINISTRATIVE TEST

One quality that qualified the seven men to serve was an ability to discern what was best for the people. Scripture isn't explicit, but it seems from the passage that the seven were given very little direction about how the food should be distributed to the needy widows. They had to work that out on their own.

Do your potential leaders have a track record of making wise decisions? Do others seek their advice? Can they work things out on their own, or do they continually need reassurance and guidance? If you would trust a potential leader's advice, chances are good that others would as well.

6. THE ATTITUDE TEST

The last requirement of the seven was that they have the right attitude toward serving their peers. Peter described them as being "full of faith."

True leadership requires a willingness to serve others full-time. How do your potential leaders view leadership? Are they unselfish? Are they team players? For any leader to be an asset to you and the team, he must be ready and willing to serve.

How do you think the people you spend your time with would stack up using these criteria? Do they pass these tests? Do they turn around and give to others, or do they at least have the potential to do so in the future? If not, you may need to rethink the way you allot your time with people.

TODAY'S QUESTION FOR REFLECTION:
*Have you positioned yourself and your people
for maximum effectiveness?*

Day 5

Bringing the Law to Life

TAKING IT IN

In leadership, priorities should be a matter of principle, not preference. Review the following leadership statements concerning the Law of Priorities:

1. Leaders put first things first.

2. Leaders see everything but focus on the important things.

3. Leaders invest their time in what produces the greatest return.

4. Leaders position people where everybody wins.

Have you been using specific criteria for determining what's most important in your organization? Do you prioritize the way you do your work, spend your money, and invest your time with people? If you're not as effective or efficient as you would like to be, it may be time for you to reevaluate.

SORTING IT OUT

If you're not sure where you stand when it comes to understanding and applying the Law of Priorities, visit the Web site www.injoy.com/21 Minutes to take a free twenty-five-question assessment quiz that will help you measure your ability.

PRAYING IT THROUGH

Use the following words to begin your time of prayer:

Dear God, You know what's best for me. Please help me order my life according to Your will, not my own. Show me the people in whom I should invest, and help me be an effective leader in their lives and my own. Amen.

LIVING IT OUT

When was the last time you did some real soul-searching about your priorities? If you're like most people, it has been a long time—or you've never really done it at all.

Schedule a retreat for yourself where you will reevaluate your mission and priorities. You may want to review your life and make a list of the major milestones and regrets you have from the last one to five years in order to get some gut-level indications on how you're doing. Then spend significant time in reflection and prayer. After you've determined what your priorities *should be*, review your mission, projects, to-do lists, and people development methods in light of what you learned.

PASSING IT ON

Which one leadership concept, insight, or practice that you've learned this week will you pass on to another leader in the next two days?

Week 18

THE LAW OF SACRIFICE

A LEADER MUST GIVE UP TO GO UP

Many people today want to climb up the corporate ladder because they believe that freedom and power are the prizes waiting at the top. They don't realize that the true nature of leadership is really sacrifice . . .

Leaders who want to rise have to do more than [be willing to] take an occasional cut in pay. They have to give up their rights . . . That's true of every leader regardless of profession. Talk to any leader, and you will find that he has made repeated sacrifices. Usually, the higher that leader has climbed, the greater the sacrifices he has made. Effective leaders sacrifice much that is good in order to dedicate themselves to what is best . . .

Sacrifice is a constant in leadership. It is an ongoing process, not a one-time payment . . . The circumstances may change from person to person, but the principle doesn't. Leadership means sacrifice.

FROM "THE LAW OF SACRIFICE" IN *The 21 Irrefutable Laws of Leadership*

Day 1

Moses
and the
Law of Sacrifice

LEADERSHIP THOUGHT FOR TODAY:
There is no success without sacrifice.

Read
Exodus 2:1–4:31; 12:31–42; Hebrews 11:23–29.

What price are you willing to pay to be a more effective leader? Have you ever thought about that? Many leaders are so busy pursuing their vision and rallying their people that they give it little thought. But leadership always requires sacrifice. Leader or not, no one achieves success without it.

WHAT THEY GAVE UP

If you doubt that sacrifice can be separated from leadership, just read Scripture. Time after time, leaders had to make sacrifices to be the leaders God created them to be. Often, the greater the calling, the greater the sacrifice required. Here are a few examples:

- *Noah.* He was the first person to make great sacrifices to become a leader. How would you feel if you were required to give up every place and every person you had ever known (other than seven family members) to be the leader God wanted you to be? That's what Noah did. He started the world over from scratch. Many people faced with the same prospect would have said, "Forget it," and lain down to die.

- *Abraham.* The calling of Abraham involved his leaving his family and home in Ur to go to a land he'd never seen. As Hebrews 11:8 states, he went "not knowing where he was going" (NKJV). And after he got there, he didn't get to establish himself. He lived in tents all his life.

- *Joseph.* The Law of Process gave you insight into his life and what he gave up—his comfort, his home, and his freedom. How many people would faithfully endure slavery for the promise of leadership later in life?

- *Nehemiah.* The leader who demonstrated the Law of Navigation gave up a cushy job in the palace of a king to travel several hundred miles to a broken-down city in the boondocks. And when he got there, he faced opposition and death threats.

- *Paul.* The greatest of Jesus' apostles gave up his secure life as a Pharisee of Pharisees to become an itinerant worker who was persecuted, beaten, whipped, stoned, shipwrecked, and ultimately executed because of his leadership for the cause of Christ.

ANOTHER LEADER, ANOTHER SACRIFICE

One of the finest examples of sacrifice by a leader in the Bible is the life of Moses, the greatest prophet of the Old Testament. He could easily be the poster child for leadership sacrifice.

The Dreamworks movie *The Prince of Egypt* captured his situation well. He grew up like a son of Pharaoh, a prince. As a boy, he enjoyed every pleasure of the palace. He possessed power, privilege, and possessions. But not only did he receive the best of what Egypt offered physically, he also received its intellectual benefits. Scripture explains, "Moses was learned in all the wisdom of the Egyptians, and was mighty in words and deeds" (Acts 7:22).

Yet Moses was willing to risk losing all of that to try to help his people. And he did lose it all. After murdering an Egyptian, he faced a forty-year exile in the desert of Midian. He went from privilege to poverty, from the world's capital to the wilderness, from adopted son to obscure shepherd.

When Moses fled Egypt, he probably thought he had risked and lost everything for nothing. For forty years he lived with the sacrifice he had made before learning that God intended to use him as a leader. By then, Moses had undergone the breaking and remaking process required for him to be used by God. He had gone from an arrogant child of privilege who thought he could deliver the Hebrews single-handedly to a man of God who, as Scripture says, "was very humble, more than all men who were on the face of the earth" (Num. 12:3 NKJV).

Leadership *always* has a cost. To be a leader, you may not be asked to leave your country or give up all your possessions, as Moses was. But you can be sure that leading others will have a price.

> Leadership always has a cost.

TODAY'S QUESTION FOR REFLECTION:
Are you willing to sacrifice to succeed?

Day 2

Nothing is a sacrifice unless it costs you something.

Jesus, walking by the Sea of Galilee, saw two brothers, Simon called Peter, and Andrew his brother, casting a net into the sea; for they were fishermen. Then He said to them, "Follow Me, and I will make you fishers of men." They immediately left their nets and followed Him.

Matthew 4:18–20 (NKJV)

In 1856, poet John Greenleaf Whittier wrote the following words in his poem "Maud Muller." You may have heard them quoted before:

> For of all sad words of tongue or pen,
> The saddest are these: "It might have been!"

"It might have been." Just about every day you can hear someone mention what could have happened in life: "I could have married anyone I wanted, but I gave it all up by marrying you." "I could have been the CEO, but I sacrificed my career for my family." "I sacrificed wealth and fame to serve the Lord."

The problem with that thinking is that it's pie in the sky. You can't sacrifice something you don't have. You can give up only what you possess. Nothing is a sacrifice unless it actually *costs* you something.

> Nothing is a sacrifice unless it actually costs you something.

A WILLING SACRIFICE

As I've already pointed out, Moses gave up a lot. He truly made great sacrifices because he had something to give and he gave it up. How was he able to give all that up without being bitter or resentful toward God? And what made him willing to return to Egypt as God's servant after he had enjoyed the best that the country had to offer? Look at Moses' actions, and you can see how God molded him into a leader He could use:

1. Moses Was Alone with God

If Moses had stayed in Egypt, who knows whether he would have paid attention when God called to him. His life was filled with distractions. But after Moses departed for Midian, he had a lot of time to reflect—forty years! By the time he passed near the burning bush, he was ready to listen to God, and he was quiet enough to hear God's voice.

In our culture, leaders take too little time to get alone with God. Most people are continually on the go and rarely quiet themselves. If you are constantly on the run and don't set aside time alone with God, change your habits. You don't want to force God to send you to the desert to get your attention.

2. Moses Was Honest with God

By the time Moses met God at the burning bush, there was no trace of the cockiness that had been part of his life in Egypt. He was weak, and he knew it. To God's announcement that he would bring the people out of Egypt, Moses responded, "Who am I that I should go to Pharaoh, and that I should bring the children of Israel out of Egypt?" (Ex. 3:11 NKJV).

Ironically, when Moses was young, he thought he was strong, but he really wasn't. Only as an older man humble before God was he of any use to God. If you are willing to look at yourself honestly, admit your weakness, and humble yourself before God, He will be able to use you.

3. Moses Was Hungry for God

What does it take before a person *really* becomes hungry for God in his life? It's different for each individual. Some people seem to possess a desire to know God from the time they are children. For others, a personal tragedy realigns their priorities. Others *never* turn to God. For Moses, it took four decades in the wilderness.

> A person can't be staunchly self-reliant and hungry for God at the same time.

I can't help wondering if Moses had given up all hope of doing something worthwhile with his life when God finally spoke to him. I imagine he probably had. I say that because a person can't be staunchly self-reliant and hungry for God at the same time. That's something we should remember too.

4. MOSES WAS BROKEN BY GOD

God did not force Himself or His will on Moses. God waited for Moses to willingly come to Him: "When the LORD saw that he turned aside to look, God called to him from the midst of the bush and said, 'Moses, Moses!'" (Ex. 3:4 NKJV). Once Moses had turned to God, he could be broken.

Brokenness involves two things: removing inappropriate pride and self-reliance and building healthy God-reliance. For Moses, his self-reliance and pride were tamed in the desert during his years of exile. But shifting his trust to God involved breaking his doubts and fears. In his encounter with God, he dealt with different kinds of fear:

- *Fears concerning himself.* Moses' first concern was his own value. In humility, he asked, "Who am I that I should go to Pharaoh, and that I should bring the children of Israel out of Egypt?" (Ex. 3:11 NKJV). God's response was to assure him of his purpose.

- *Fears concerning God.* Moses' next fear related to God's identity. He wanted to know His name and who He was (Ex. 3:13). God's response was to overwhelm Moses with His presence.

- *Fears concerning others.* Moses then worried about how God's people would respond (Ex. 4:1). As a younger man, Moses had already experienced the Hebrews' rejection. God's response was to assure him by demonstrating His power.

- *Fears concerning his ability.* Moses had doubts about himself—his speech (Ex. 4:10) and ability (Ex. 4:13). God's response was to provide him with a partner, Aaron, his brother.

Having his willfulness broken, his fears overcome, and his purpose reaffirmed, Moses placed himself in the hands of God.

Life is filled with trade-offs. But you can trade up only if you have something to sacrifice. To be prepared for his life purpose, Moses had to sacrifice his status and all of his material posses-

> Life is filled with trade-offs. But you can trade up only if you have something to sacrifice.

sions. Then to fulfill it, again he had to sacrifice. The second time he relinquished the security and safety of obscurity in the desert to return to his boyhood home.

If you desire to lead, and you hope to find and fulfill the purpose for which God created you, then you must have something to give. Keep growing and building your personal assets, and hold lightly the things God gives you because you may need to sacrifice them at any time to answer His call.

TODAY'S QUESTION FOR REFLECTION:
What enables you to make the needed sacrifice for success?

Day 3

What things were gain to me, these I have counted loss for Christ.

Philippians 3:7 (NKJV)

A few years ago, American Express ran an ad campaign that used the slogan, "Membership has its privileges." The implication was that if you possess an American Express card, you've made it. You've moved up to a position in life where you have certain rights and can enjoy particular perks not available to the rest of the population—to merely "ordinary" people.

Many people view leadership in a similar fashion. They associate it with privilege. They see only positives. The power is appealing. So are the relationships with other leaders

> **Sacrifice is the true nature of leadership.**

and high-profile people. And who wouldn't enjoy being on the inside track in terms of information and planning? But people who idealize the privileges of leadership often fail to notice the sacrifice involved. Sacrifice is the true nature of leadership.

ACHIEVING LEADERSHIP POTENTIAL

After forty years in the desert of Midian, Moses learned the first hard lesson of leadership:

1. LEADERS HAVE TO GIVE UP TO GO UP

As I've already explained, Moses made great sacrifices in his life. To step up to leadership and become the man the Hebrews would follow, Moses had to give up his home, his old life, and his right to do whatever he wanted. The path to leadership is narrow. But when Moses gave up all the riches of Egypt and the security of life as a shepherd, he was just getting started.

2. LEADERS HAVE TO GIVE UP TO GROW UP

Moses' time in the desert of Midian molded his character. It qualified him to become God's chosen instrument for delivering his people. But it didn't teach him leadership. To become an effective leader, Moses had to give up more of himself.

Becoming a leader takes time. Moses' early efforts at leading the children of Israel weren't always successful. For example, after he first led the people out of Egypt, he tried to do everything by himself. It took the instruction of his father-in-law, Jethro, to teach him how to delegate authority (Ex. 18). When he tried to lead the people at Mount Sinai, they were unrestrained and worshiped a golden calf (Ex. 32). And when he tried to lead them into the promised land, they refused to follow and obey him (Num. 14). It took God years to raise up Moses to become the great leader he finally became—the kind of leader the people loved and for whom they would weep and mourn for thirty days following his death (Deut. 34:8).

3. LEADERS HAVE TO GIVE UP TO STAY UP

There's no arriving as a leader. No good leaders reach a place where they can afford to stop learning, growing, and improving—if not for themselves, then for the sake of their organization and people. To remain effective, they have to keep sacrificing. Besides, what takes an organization to the top is never enough to keep it there. Life is change.

It takes incredible stamina to keep giving up. Even Moses wasn't able to stay the course. Although he dedicated his life to God and leading the children of Israel, he disqualified himself in the eyes of God before he finished leading. Because of his disobedience, he didn't get to take his people the last leg of the journey. If you want to finish well, keep practicing the Law of Sacrifice.

As you become aware of the long leadership journey ahead of you, try to measure the sacrifices that will be involved. The greater the calling, the greater the sacrifice. The higher you intend to go, the more you will need to give up.

TODAY'S QUESTION FOR REFLECTION:
To become a more effective leader, what are you willing to give up?

Day 4

For everything you gain, you lose something.

> I do not count myself to have apprehended; but one thing I do, forgetting those things which are behind and reaching forward to those things which are ahead, I press toward the goal for the prize.
>
> Philippians 3:13–14 (NKJV)

Earlier this week I advised you to hold on lightly to what God gives you because you may need to sacrifice it at any time to answer His call. But most people seem to have a very hard time letting go of things. You see proof of that in their garages, attics, or basements.

To gain anything, you have to be willing to lose whatever you have. Of course, I'm not speaking of sacrificing your values, your self-respect, or your family. I'm speaking of giving up material possessions, opportuni-

> If you want to keep moving up to your potential, you can't cling to the security of what you now possess.

ties to do other things, and even your rights. If you want to keep moving up to your potential, you can't cling to the security of what you now possess. It's like trying to climb a ladder while both of your arms are full of junk. You have to put something down to reach up. That's the only way up to the next level.

KEEP YOUR GRIP LIGHT, NOT TIGHT

How do you cultivate a willingness to sacrifice so that you can become all you can be? You can start by practicing the following six habits:

1. APPRECIATE TIMING

In Ecclesiastes, Solomon wrote that there is "a time for every purpose under heaven" (3:1 NKJV). Moses might not have understood this concept when he fled into the desert, but he certainly did later, beginning with the day he saw the burning bush. And his understanding of the concept increased during his years leading the children of Israel.

When we're children, we readily recognize that there are seasons of life. We look forward to life's milestones and the next step: moving up a grade, staying home alone the first time, getting a driver's license, graduating from high school, getting married, and so on. We are anxious to put away childish things as we move on. But as adults, we often lose that perspective. Life is a journey, not a destination. Try to remember that there are going to be times when it's appropriate to move on. Be ready for them.

2. PUT PEOPLE FIRST

People's reluctance to sacrifice is often cultivated by their tendency to focus too much on themselves. It's hard to let go of anything if your view is continu-

> "A person starts to live when he can live outside of himself."
> —ALBERT EINSTEIN

ally filtered through your needs and wants. But as Albert Einstein observed, "A person starts to live when he can live outside of himself." Putting others first has a way of shifting priorities and putting things back into proper perspective.

3. DEVELOP THE HABIT OF GIVING

Nothing loosens a person's grip like giving things away. It purifies motives and lightens the heart. And once you're in the habit of being free with your money, time, talents, and possessions with no expectation of anything in return, it's not difficult to make a sacrifice that will bring something greater in return.

4. LEARN TO ENJOY THINGS WITHOUT OWNERSHIP

Author Richard Foster insightfully remarked, "Owning things is an obsession in our culture. If we own it, we feel we can control it; and if we can control it, we feel it will give us more pleasure. The idea is an illusion. Many things in life can be enjoyed without possessing or controlling them." The more things you can enjoy without having to control or own them, the lighter hold things will have on you.

5. EXPRESS GRATITUDE FOR YOUR BLESSINGS

If we're really honest with ourselves, we will admit that we don't deserve any of the things God has given us: not our gifts or talents, not our material possessions, not even the grace we enjoy. James reminded us, "Every good gift and every perfect gift is from above, and comes down from the Father of lights" (James 1:17 NKJV). When you recognize that what you have is a gift to begin with, it's easier to give it up or give it away.

6. MAINTAIN AN ETERNAL PERSPECTIVE

Sacrifice is never painless, even when we try to maintain an attitude of gratitude and a giving heart. That's why it's important to try to see things from God's perspective. In those moments when you are reluctant to endure the pain of giving something up and making a transition, try to see the bigger picture. Moses spent a total of eighty years in the desert, and he still didn't get to enter the promised land. But his people did, the Davidic dynasty was established, and the Hebrews were given the Messiah. That's the bigger picture. If a temporal sacrifice will bring an eternal reward, make the trade.

No matter what your personal history, you can become someone willing to sacrifice. It may not be easy, but it is possible. And if you want to become a leader, it's imperative. That's the nature of leadership.

> Moses spent a total of eighty years in the desert, and he still didn't get to enter the promised land. But his people did.

TODAY'S QUESTION FOR REFLECTION:
Which habit do you need to work on the most?

Day 5

Bringing the Law to Life

TAKING IT IN

What is your mind-set when it comes to leading people? Is the focus of your energy on what you get or what you give? Which one you focus on will determine whether you're in leadership for the short gain or the long haul.

Review the four leadership truths related to the Law of Sacrifice:

1. There is no success without sacrifice.

2. Nothing is a sacrifice unless it costs you something.

3. Effective leaders know the value of sacrifice.

4. For everything you gain, you lose something.

If you can learn to live a life of sacrifice, you will be in a better position to take your people where they need to go.

SORTING IT OUT

If you're not sure where you stand when it comes to understanding and applying the Law of Sacrifice, visit the Web site www.injoy.com/21 Minutes to take a free twenty-five-question assessment quiz that will help you measure your ability.

PRAYING IT THROUGH

Use the following words to begin your time of prayer:

Dear God, give me the heart of a giver. Help me to understand Your timing, to see what I should sacrifice for the sake of my people, and to relinquish anything

I possess for the betterment of others. And if the best sacrifice I can make for my organization is to step aside and allow someone else to lead, give me the courage and the heart to do that. Amen.

LIVING IT OUT

Have you begun to plateau in your leadership, or are you still climbing? Whether you are in the early stages of sacrifice or you have been leading for forty years, you need to identify the next step in your leadership and what it will take to get there. What is the cost? What are you being called to sacrifice? Take some time to define the step and the cost right now.

PASSING IT ON

Which one leadership concept, insight, or practice that you've learned this week will you pass on to another leader in the next two days?

Week 19

THE LAW OF TIMING

WHEN TO LEAD IS AS IMPORTANT AS WHAT TO DO AND WHERE TO GO

When leaders do the right things at the right time, success is almost inevitable. People, principles, and processes converge to make an incredible impact. And the results touch not only the leader but also the followers and the whole organization.

When the right leader and the right moment come together, incredible things happen . . . Winston Churchill . . . described it like this: "There comes a special moment in everyone's life, a moment for which that person was born. That special opportunity, when he seizes it, will fulfill his mission—a mission for which he is uniquely qualified. In that moment he finds greatness. It is his finest hour." . . .

Reading a situation and knowing what to do are not enough to make you succeed in leadership. Only the right action at the right time will bring success. Anything else exacts a high price.

FROM "THE LAW OF TIMING" IN *The 21 Irrefutable Laws of Leadership*

Day 1

Esther
and the
Law of Timing

LEADERSHIP THOUGHT FOR TODAY:
Right timing makes a good decision a better decision.

Read
Esther 2:1–23; 4:1–17; 5:1–5; 7:1–8:8

If you've ever had to drive in rush-hour traffic in a big city, you know that timing is everything. My good friend Josh McDowell often tells about a time when he and a local resident were touring the streets of Buenos Aires, Argentina, a few years ago. It illustrates the importance of timing.

At one point in their drive they came to an intersection in the middle of downtown where sixteen lanes of traffic converged. But that wasn't the half of it. It was rush hour, there were no traffic lights, and no one was directing traffic! It was definitely not a place for the timid.

The only way to make it through the intersection was to find one small space in traffic, then punch the gas without hesitation—knowing that if you missed the opportunity, you could be stuck for another fifteen minutes. If your timing was on, you made it through unscathed. But if your timing was off, you could expect a trip to the local body shop. Fortunately the man driving the car had driven there before and had a good sense of timing. Otherwise, they might not have made it through in one piece.

For a leader, timing works much the same way. There are certain windows of opportunity when—if you don't take a risk and move forward—your effectiveness could come to a standstill. Or worse, you could permanently damage your ability to lead your people. And the greater the risk you take, the more critical it is that you have the proper timing.

But when you are able to discern a prime opportunity and take initiative to seize it at the right time, success is almost inevitable.

ESTHER'S RISE

I've always maintained that ultimately leaders are not successful
unless other people want them to
be. Esther was fortunate to have a
mentor like Mordecai, who con-

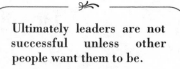

> Ultimately leaders are not successful unless other people want them to be.

stantly reminded her of the Law of Timing. As a result, Esther learned to seize the opportune moments in her life and transform a people on the verge of annihilation to become the most respected in the land. When you read the story of Esther, you can see that her entire life is a study of timing.

THE RIGHT PLACE

Esther was born into a period of Jewish history when her people were in distress and had fallen away from God's commands. In short, they were in need of leadership. While a remnant of Jews had returned to Israel after seven decades of captivity, many remained in the cities of their exile. Some were welcomed as valuable members of their communities, while others were despised. Esther's family had chosen to remain in Persia, the place where she would later be needed the most.

A leader can't afford to overlook the big picture. You may tend to spend your time thinking about current events—how to better provide for your
family or how to grow your com-
pany—and there's nothing wrong
with that. But when you believe as
I do that God has arranged the
events of your life in such a way
for you to accomplish something
bigger—a purpose with as much

> It's easy to think that a person being in the right place at the right time was coincidence. But when a leader is following God, nothing is coincidental.

significance as Esther's—the timing of events begins to make more sense, and the way you approach decisions becomes more important.

In hindsight, it's easy to think that a person being in the right place at the right time was coincidence. But when a leader is following God, nothing is coincidental. In the case of Esther, it's not hard to imagine what might have been for the Jewish people if she hadn't been born at that time and in that place. The Jewish people might have experienced something more devastating than what happened during Hitler's Nazi regime.

THE RIGHT PEOPLE

At first, Esther probably didn't think too much of Queen Vashti's removal from the throne or of King Ahasuerus's empirewide beauty contest to find a new queen. After all, she was an orphan, and like most of her people, she lived a very common existence. She had no reason to suspect she'd have a chance to win the contest. But soon she found herself in the king's palace, and with the advice of the king's eunuch and her cousin Mordecai, she took advantage of the opportunity and won the king's favor.

THE RIGHT POSITION

Esther probably started to catch on to God's purpose for her when the king selected her as his next queen. In a short period of time she had gone from an orphaned commoner, living in the land of her captivity, to the highest position in the land for a woman.

THE RIGHT PLAN

Fortunately Esther was humble enough and discerning enough by the time she was queen that she readily listened to Mordecai's advice. Together they had already decided to hold off on telling the king about her background— that she was an exiled Jew. But when Mordecai learned of Haman's plot to carry out a Jewish holocaust, he knew that someone needed to act immediately on the Jewish people's behalf—and he knew it had to be Esther. And she was obedient to God's calling.

After the dust settled, Esther discovered the value of timing in every decision. She learned that when leaders have God on their side and continually strive to do the right thing at the right time, success follows them everywhere.

❧

TODAY'S QUESTION FOR REFLECTION:
Do you consider timing when you make a decision?

Day 2

LEADERSHIP THOUGHT FOR TODAY:
When leaders fail to seize the moment,
they undermine their leadership.

Do you not say, "There are still four months and then comes the harvest"? Behold, I say to you, lift up your eyes and look at the fields, for they are already white for harvest!

John 4:35 (NKJV)

When you don't take initiative and seize an important opportunity, you limit your ability to lead. Like Esther, many leaders have obstacles that keep them from seizing the moment—the most common being fear of failure. But other obstacles include pride, selfish motives, wrong priorities, lack of discernment, and not paying attention.

LEARNING TO TAKE INITIATIVE

To be an effective leader, you must take steps to acknowledge and overcome whatever keeps you from moving forward when opportunity knocks. Like Esther, you must learn that if you don't seize the moment . . .

1. YOUR FATE WILL BE LIKE THAT OF THE REST OF THE CROWD

Sometimes it's easy to buy into the notion that we are special and won't have to take the risks that earlier generations have had to take. We feel we can maintain the status quo, and God will do the rest to make sure we accomplish the mission. But that notion is a myth. If we don't take risks, we can never expect to rise to the occasion. Mordecai reminded Esther that even though she was queen, her future would be no better than that of the rest of the Jews if she didn't capitalize on the opportunity to talk to the king.

> When God is involved, it's not necessarily the giftedness of the leader that prompts God's blessing; it's more often the leader's willingness to move when and where He indicates.

2. GOD WILL REPLACE YOU WITH SOMEONE ELSE TO DO THE JOB

Esther was motivated by Mordecai's reminder that God's purposes would be accomplished—even if she sat on the sidelines and watched. You see, when God is involved, it's not necessarily the giftedness of the leader that prompts God's blessing; it's more often the leader's willingness to move when and where He indicates.

3. YOU COULD LOSE MORE THAN AN OPPORTUNITY

Mordecai reminded Esther that if she sat back and did nothing with the opportunity in front of her, she could lose more than a chance to do the right thing—she could lose her life. Although doing the right thing at the right time can sometimes require a big risk, in the long run, leaders incur a greater risk by *not* taking action. In leadership, the risk of failing is usually far less than the risk of missing an opportunity.

4. YOU COULD MISS OUT ON YOUR MISSION IN LIFE

Eventually Mordecai posed the ultimate question to Esther. He speculated that the opportunity before her might be the very reason she was given her royal position in the first place. In other words, if she failed to follow through, she might miss out on God's entire purpose for her life. She took Mordecai's advice and experienced great success.

That same advice holds true for all leaders. You will never accomplish your mission—whether short-term or lifelong—by being idle. For some leaders like Esther, fear of failure paralyzes them. For you, it may be something different. But regardless of what keeps you from pursuing an

> In leadership, there's no such thing as zero risk.

opportunity, you can overcome that hurdle only by making one timely decision after another.

You see, in leadership, there's no such thing as zero risk. If your mission is great, you will have to incur great risk to fulfill it. You will never get to a place where you don't sense any risk at all. But when you accept that as fact and determine to seize a right opportunity despite the risk, you build momentum for the next opportunity that comes your way. Remember that Esther wasn't quick to jump at opportunity in the beginning. But the more opportunities she seized, the more comfortable she became with risk. The same will be true for you.

᪣

TODAY'S QUESTION FOR REFLECTION:
What prevents you from seizing your opportunity to lead?

Day 3

To everything there is a season,
A time for every purpose under heaven.
Ecclesiastes 3:1 (NKJV)

Many times, a leader's failure to seize an opportunity has nothing to do with lack of determination or willingness, but everything to do with an effort that was out of sequence—too early or too late. Consider what might have happened if Esther had revealed her background to the king too soon. She probably wouldn't have been crowned queen. As a result, she might not have been in the place to intercede with the king for her people. But because she waited for the proper time, Esther was able to pave the way for her people's success.

Like winter, spring, summer, and fall, specific seasons of a leader's life indicate the proper time to take certain actions. Based on the following five observations, notice the similarities between the seasons in a leader's life and the earth's seasons:

- The seasons are not all the same length.

- Each season has a beginning and an ending.

- The seasons always come in sequence.

- Crops of success may be cultivated in several areas simultaneously yet harvested at different times.

- Every season must be managed effectively to reap an abundant harvest.

THE FOUR SEASONS OF A LEADER'S LIFE

To always produce a successful harvest, you must learn the secret to mastering the seasons of leadership. While every leader is subject to the same set of rules with regard to the seasons, not every leader manages each season with the same effectiveness.

To help determine what direction you should be moving as a leader, consider the four seasons:

1. WINTER IS THE SEASON FOR PLANNING

For the unsuccessful leader, winter is a time to hibernate. But for the successful leader, winter is a time to envision the upcoming harvest. It's a time for brainstorming, revisiting your dreams, setting new goals, and making plans about how to fulfill your dreams.

Esther had a long winter season before God elevated her to queen of Persia. She spent several years in exile with her people—plenty of time to connect with their desires and needs. When she was crowned queen, she already had the heart of her people and knew exactly what they needed.

2. SPRING IS THE SEASON FOR PLANTING

In spring, the unsuccessful leader has spring fever. It's a time to daydream and take long afternoon naps. But the successful leader knows that spring is prime time to plant the ideas from the winter season. It's a time for sowing seeds and paying the price for future success.

Before Esther was crowned queen, Scripture says the law required her to spend an entire year in preparation to appear before the king (Est. 2:12). During that time, Esther gained so much favor with Hegai, the king's eunuch, that he told her how to win the king over when she appeared before him.

3. SUMMER IS THE SEASON FOR PERSPIRATION

To the unsuccessful leader, summer is for vacation. It's a time to forget about work and let go of responsibilities. But to the successful leader, summer is the key time for work. It's the right time for regular cultivation and fertilization—a time for personal growth. The wise leader knows that to produce success, he has to sweat a lot during the summer season.

Esther's summer began when she realized that she had to appear before the king and request that he reverse his decree. Knowing that the wrong timing could lead to her death, she spent three days praying and fasting.

4. FALL IS THE SEASON FOR PRODUCTION

In fall, unsuccessful leaders begin to feel a sense of loss and regret for their missed opportunities and poor planning. However, to successful leaders, fall is the time to produce the rewards of their planning, planting, and perspiring. It's the time to celebrate the accomplishments of their hard work.

For Esther and her people, the celebrating began when the king reversed his decree and Mordecai was made second in command, and the party continued to grow until every enemy of the Jews had been destroyed or become their ally. In fact, Esther had led her people so successfully that they set aside specific days to celebrate this episode of deliverance.

Esther learned that a key to making right decisions was accurately discerning the season. She knew that when she understood the times, she would better understand what needed to be done. As a result of her discernment, she found confidence in her decisions to capitalize on each opportunity.

TODAY'S QUESTION FOR REFLECTION:
Are your decisions consistent with the season?

Day 4

Make hay while the sun shines—that's smart;
go fishing during harvest—that's stupid.
Proverbs 10:5 (*The Message*)

If you're a leader, it's not enough to know *what* to do. You have to know *when* to act. Within each season of life, there can be several important decisions to make, and each one requires proper timing to ensure

> *If you're a leader, it's not enough to know what to do. You have to know when to act.*

success. How do you judge timing in your life? Are there certain signs that you look for? Do you ask others? Do you spend time in prayer? Do you guess and hope you're right? The answer is that you use discernment.

Esther wasn't strong in the area of discernment at first, but Mordecai was. And in the beginning of Esther's reign as queen, he was always quick to share his insight concerning her decisions. I'm sure Esther never forgot his most significant words to her: "For if you remain completely silent at this time, relief and deliverance will arise for the Jews from another place, but you and your father's house will perish. Yet who knows whether you have come to the kingdom for *such a time as this*?" (Est. 4:14 NKJV, emphasis added).

Eventually Esther became very good at discerning the times. And she was able to make confident decisions as Persia's queen.

THE TEST OF TIMING

Despite any poor decisions you might have made in the past, you can become more discerning, as Esther did. The key is making sure that each decision stands the test of timing before you take action. To help determine if it's the *right* time to seize an opportunity, consider the following:

1. THE NEEDS AROUND YOU

The Greyhound bus company once posted an ad that read, "When you deal in basic needs, you're always needed." That's also true for leaders. When you keep a finger on the pulse of your people's basic needs, you will always find opportune times to lead.

Esther understood the needs of her people. Before she was crowned queen, she lived and worked among them; she was one of them, and she never lost touch with that. Her heart was knit to theirs, and she understood not only what they needed, but also what they needed *from her*. As a result, she saved their lives, and she gave them back their dignity as a nation.

To discern opportune times to lead, get in touch with your people's needs. Then make a point to continually ask: What is their mood? What do they desire to accomplish? What do they need from me, their leader?

2. THE OPPORTUNITIES BEFORE YOU

Authors Helen Schucman and William Thetford declare, "Every situation, properly perceived, becomes an opportunity." In other words, the way to find ripe opportunities is to look for them. So often we make the mistake of thinking that opportunities—and therefore, the right timing—will be obvious to us. But that's not the case.

Early in Esther's leadership, Mordecai did much of the "spotting" for her. Each time he discerned a small window of opportunity, he let her know about it. Esther learned from Mordecai's insight, and later, she was able to discern the opportune time to promote Mordecai's actions in front of the king. Mordecai was immediately given a leadership position, second to the king.

As a leader, you may get overly busy and miss the right timing on a decision. But when you take time to be more purposeful about spotting golden opportunities in every endeavor, they start to stick out to you.

3. THE INFLUENCERS BEHIND YOU

Remember the Law of the Inner Circle: a leader's potential is determined by those closest to him. When trying to discern the right time to take action, you must get feedback from your key people.

Esther was fortunate to have a key influencer like Mordecai. He was like a built-in alarm clock. Most of the time she didn't have to ask for his insight—he volunteered it. In fact, Esther came to value Mordecai's opinion so much that she made sure he would remain by her side throughout her reign as queen. She knew that his trustworthy discernment would help her to be confident in her decisions.

Before you make an important decision, ask your key influencers what they are feeling. Do they see the same opportunity as you do? Are they discerning the same timing? When do they think you should act? What do they think you should do? Their answers could provide insight that you might otherwise overlook.

4. THE SUCCESSES UNDER YOU

Experience provides practical advice. When you're determining whether it's the right time to seize an opportunity, take a minute to recall your past successes. Have you done anything like this before? Is it reasonable to expect the same outcome from this decision? Is there something you can learn from your past successes to help you determine the best time to move forward?

The first time Esther was to approach the king, Mordecai had to convince her that the timing was right. When Esther found favor with the king and the outcome was successful, she banked on that success for the future. The next time she approached him, she spoke with more confidence and was able to persuade the king to reverse his decree. Before long, Esther had gained so much influence with the king that he was asking her for advice. To gain confidence that the time is right to move forward, evaluate the successful decisions you've made in the past.

> The word courage comes from a French word that means "heart." In other words, taking advantage of an opportunity at the right time requires heart.

5. THE COURAGE WITHIN YOU

Leadership requires courage—the courage to risk, to reach, and to put yourself on the line to seize an opportunity. The word *courage* comes from a French word that means "heart." In other words, taking advantage of an opportunity at the right time requires heart.

Esther demonstrated tremendous courage time after time. To stand before the king and risk death took great heart. So did her request of the king to reverse his decree, especially in the presence of Haman.

As a leader, you will experience times when fear will try to get the better of you. But good leaders understand that ripe opportunities are never completely devoid of fear. And they move forward despite the hesitation they may experience.

Effective leaders learn to overcome the fear of making a wrong decision by carefully considering all the influencing factors. They know that is the best way to set themselves up for success. It's what Esther learned to do from Mordecai's example. And if you desire to become a more confident leader, I encourage you to do the same.

TODAY'S QUESTION FOR REFLECTION:
Does your decision stand the test of timing?

Day 5

Bringing the Law to Life

TAKING IT IN

Has your leadership displayed a pattern of missed opportunities? Do you often wish you had done something after it's too late? If you do, you probably need to improve when it comes to the Law of Timing. Spend a few minutes reviewing the following leadership thoughts:

1. Right timing makes a good decision a better decision.

2. When leaders fail to seize the moment, they undermine their leadership.

3. There is a right season for everything.

4. Good discernment precedes good decisions.

You can improve your sense of timing by observing the timing of others, learning from it, and then applying it to your life.

SORTING IT OUT

If you're not sure where you stand when it comes to understanding and applying the Law of Timing, visit the Web site www.injoy.com/21 Minutes to take a free twenty-five-question assessment quiz that will help you measure your ability.

PRAYING IT THROUGH

Use the following words to begin your time of prayer:

Dear God, I recognize that You have provided a season for everything and that I fit into Your divine purpose. I ask for discernment to understand Your timing.

Give me wisdom and courage to make the right decisions regardless of the cost,
for I don't want to miss out on the plan You have for my life. Amen.

LIVING IT OUT

Based on what you read in Day 3, what season of life would you say you are
in right now?

- *Planning*—the season to capture God's vision for you and your
  people.

- *Planting*—the season to cast your vision to the people and lay the
  groundwork to carry it out.

- *Perspiring*—the season to work toward the completion of your
  vision.

- *Producing*—the season to realize and celebrate the completion of
  your vision.

Based upon the season in which you find yourself, what one thing can
you do to best fulfill that season and bring it to fruition for the development
of your potential and purpose?

PASSING IT ON

Which one leadership concept, insight, or practice that you've learned this
week will you pass on to another leader in the next two days?

Week 20

THE LAW OF EXPLOSIVE GROWTH

TO ADD GROWTH, LEAD FOLLOWERS— TO MULTIPLY, LEAD LEADERS

Leaders who develop followers grow their organization only one person at a time. But leaders who develop leaders multiply their growth, because for every leader they develop, they also receive all of that leader's followers. Add ten followers to your organization, and you have the power of ten people. Add ten leaders to your organization, and you have the power of ten leaders times all the followers and leaders *they* influence. That's the difference between addition and multiplication. It's like growing your organization by teams instead of by individuals. The better the leaders you develop, the greater the quality and quantity of followers.

To go to the highest level, you have to develop leaders of leaders. My friend Dale Galloway asserts that "some leaders want to make followers. I want to make leaders. Not only do I want to make leaders, but I want to make leaders of leaders. And then leaders of leaders of leaders." Once you are able to follow that pattern, there is almost no limit to the growth of your organization.

FROM "THE LAW OF EXPLOSIVE GROWTH" IN *The 21 Irrefutable Laws of Leadership*

Day 1

Paul
and the
Law of Explosive Growth

LEADERSHIP THOUGHT FOR TODAY:
Leaders developing leaders equals explosive growth.

Read
Acts 15:36–16:5; 18:1–11; 19:8–10;
1 Timothy 4:12–16; 2 Timothy 2:1–10, 14–26

A fascinating irony of leadership is that if you want to do something *really* big that involves a lot of people, you need to narrow your focus to a few people. That may not seem to make sense. It goes against the grain of our natural inclinations. But it's true nonetheless. Great things aren't achieved by the crowd. They're accomplished by the core. If you think huge, you need to learn to act narrow.

Ninety percent of all leaders don't work this way. They gather followers, not leaders. Why? Because focusing on leaders isn't easy. Leaders are hard to find, hard to gather, and hard to hold. Where followers are waiting around looking for someone to lead them, leaders are out making things happen. Where followers readily fall in line behind a leader, other leaders need compelling reasons before they are willing to follow. Leading other leaders is no easy task.

> A fascinating irony of leadership is that if you want to do something really big that involves a lot of people, you need to narrow your focus to a few people.

If it's so difficult, then why bother? Why go to all the trouble? Why did Paul do it in the first century, and why should we bother to do it now? Because the *only* way to experience explosive growth in your organization—and to sustain that growth over the long haul—is to lead leaders. It is the only way to multiply your leadership.

PARADIGM SHIFT

Moving yourself from the 90 percent who lead followers to the 10 percent who lead leaders requires a whole new way of thinking. Leading leaders means . . .

1. NOT JUST DOING THINGS RIGHT— BUT DOING THE RIGHT THINGS

If you've relied heavily on your ability to perform your job well to attract people, that won't be enough. In addition to being highly competent, you have to be highly strategic to locate and attract leaders for your organization.

2. NOT JUST PRIORITIZING YOUR SCHEDULE— BUT SCHEDULING YOUR PRIORITIES

All leaders are busy people, and as they prioritize their schedules, developing others often goes to the back burner. But to employ a team of good leaders, you will have to make developing people a top priority. You cannot lead leaders unless you teach leadership and mentor people all the time.

3. NOT SEEKING FULFILLMENT— BUT FULFILLING YOUR DESTINY

Our culture places an extremely high price on personal fulfillment. But fulfillment is a lot like happiness: it's a function of attitude. The higher calling is to reach your potential and fulfill your destiny. When you do, you can develop leaders out of the overflow.

4. NOT LEADING WITH POWER—BUT EMPOWERING LEADERS

People who lead followers don't share their power. Weak leaders in that situation are afraid to share it, and they often rely on their position or title to protect them. But even strong leaders who lead followers don't need to share their power. Why would they? Followers wouldn't know what to do with it if they had it.

On the other hand, leaders who lead other leaders *must* share their power. The only way to make leaders effective—and to keep them—is to empower them. The more power you give away, the more effective the entire organization can become.

Adding followers is fairly easy. The better the leader, the greater the number of followers he can recruit. On the other hand, recruiting or developing leaders is a slow process. But once you dedicate yourself to it, your leadership builds over time. And for each leader you gain, you gain all the people who follow him. It has a multiplying effect.

That's the method Paul used to multiply his leadership. He started with a few potential leaders, and he devoted his life to developing them to reach their potential. And because he did, the church experienced explosive growth during the first century unlike anything the world had ever seen. Paul didn't settle for addition. He couldn't afford to. And neither can you.

TODAY'S QUESTION FOR REFLECTION:
As a leader, are you adding or multiplying?

Day 2

Leaders commit themselves to people
and activities that provide explosive growth.

For though I am free from all men, I have made myself a servant to all, that
I might win the more . . . I have become all things to all men, that I might
by all means save some.

1 Corinthians 9:19, 22 (NKJV)

The apostle Paul had a lot of things going for him. He was an adroit apologist, able to reason with the best contemporary philosophers of Athens (Acts
17:18–34). He was a bold preacher of the gospel, helping spread the Word of
God to all of Asia (Acts 19:10). And he was an incredible instrument of healing, miracles occurred even when people touched an apron he had worn
(Acts 19:11–12). But none of these things can compare to his contribution as
a leader. Of all the apostles, he was unmatched as a developer of pastors and
church leaders, such as Titus, Luke, Apollos, Timothy, Silas, Priscilla, and
Aquila. Without the leadership of Paul, the world would have been a very different place during the first century.

A STRATEGY FOR EXPLOSIVE GROWTH

Paul was a master of explosive growth. He dedicated himself to people and
activities that would impact the world. His time was limited, but his influence
seemed limitless. And his actions changed not only his world, but also ours.

The strategy Paul used is as effective today as it was two thousand years
ago. To promote explosive growth . . .

1. ATTRACT AND EQUIP PEOPLE
Everywhere Paul went, he gathered people who would listen, and he

taught them. The book of Acts shows how Paul would enter a town and begin teaching large numbers of people—for days, months, and sometimes years. For example, at Ephesus, he taught for three months in the synagogue and then another two years at a school (Acts 19:8–10). No matter where he went or what else he was doing, he continually equipped as many people as he could.

2. FIND AND MENTOR EMERGING LEADERS

Besides the value of helping others reach their potential, an advantage of equipping so many people is that it provides a pool of individuals from which to find potential leaders. That was certainly true for Paul. He mentored too many leaders to count. Some of them, such as Silas, came to him already possessing influence and leadership skills (Acts 15:22). Others were homegrown, such as Timothy, the man Paul called "a true son in the faith" (1 Tim. 1:2 NKJV). But no matter what their background was, Paul took them with him as he worked, preached, and led. He taught them what they needed to learn. Then he turned them loose, giving them responsibility and authority.

As a leader, if you can follow a similar pattern—you continually attract and equip followers and then find and develop potential leaders—you will multiply your leadership in ways you never dreamed possible.

3. CREATE NEW ORGANIZATIONS

As Paul developed leaders, he didn't hoard them. He didn't mentor people with the sole purpose of making his life easier. He raised up leaders to multiply and extend his influence. And he did it with a strategy.

In his travels, Paul continually planted churches. The list of cities where he visited and started churches is extensive and covers all of Asia Minor and a good part of Europe. Tradition states that he traveled as far as the British Isles,

> As Paul developed leaders, he didn't hoard them. He didn't mentor people with the sole purpose of making his life easier.

though no evidence exists to support that assertion. But wherever he *did* travel, he left a church with leaders who would carry on after he was gone.

You cannot make a great impact with a maintenance mind-set. Instead, you must possess a vision and then think big as Paul did.

4. ENGAGE IN THE ONGOING DEVELOPMENT OF LEADERS

Leadership development is a lifelong process. Paul knew that. Once he had developed people to the point that they could lead others on their own, he didn't abandon them. Paul visited the leaders in his churches to follow up with them, encourage them, and give them direction. Scripture tells us that Paul's second missionary journey began with the following suggestion: "Then after some days Paul said to Barnabas, 'Let us now go back and visit our brethren in every city where we have preached the word of the Lord, and see how they are doing'" (Acts 15:36 NKJV).

Paul continued to develop his leaders through the letters he wrote. In particular, the letters to Timothy and Titus reveal the kind of instruction and encouragement he gave. And those letters, along with the others Paul wrote, continue to instruct and develop leaders today, nearly two thousand years later.

If your vision is large—so large that it will require multiplied leadership—then there's only one way you will be able to achieve it: through explosive growth. Anything less will leave you far short of your dreams.

TODAY'S QUESTION FOR REFLECTION:
Have you identified the people and activities
that provide explosive growth?

Day 3

Leaders recognize the qualities needed for explosive growth.

> You therefore, my son, be strong in the grace that is in Christ Jesus. And the things that you have heard from me among many witnesses, commit these to faithful men who will be able to teach others also.
>
> 2 Timothy 2:1–2 (NKJV)

People frequently ask me, "John, how can I recognize a potential leader? What should I look for?" When I hear leaders ask that, I get excited because I know that they're starting to think in terms of multiplication instead of addition. They want to lead leaders, not just gather followers.

Over the years, I've taught a lot of lessons on that subject because I'm constantly exploring it. And it's a subject that Paul often taught about too. For example, twice in Scripture he gave spiritual guidelines for the selection of elders (1 Tim. 3:1–10; Titus 1:5–9) He also provided insightful instruction to Timothy that reveals his view of what it takes to be a good leader.

PAUL'S PICTURE OF A LEADER

On Day 1 of the Law of Explosive Growth, you read passages from 2 Timothy 2. In them, Paul noted four images that characterize a good leader. And we can use them to measure ourselves and the potential leaders we desire to develop. A good leader needs to be the following:

1. A TEACHER

The first and most important quality of a leader is the ability to teach and develop other leaders. Paul told Timothy to reproduce

> The first and most important quality of a leader is the ability to teach and develop other leaders.

341

himself in others. That, after all, is the secret to explosive growth. Paul said, "Commit these [things that I've taught you] to faithful men who will be able to teach others also" (2 Tim. 2:2 NKJV).

If you desire to be an explosive-growth leader, you must be willing to share your knowledge, authority, and experience. And you must wisely select potential leaders who are loyal, faithful, and capable of carrying on the value of leadership development in others.

2. A SOLDIER

A good leader should be like a soldier. A good soldier is many things: committed, courageous, and resilient. But Paul focused primarily on two major characteristics in his message to Timothy. First, soldiers are focused on the priority of their work; they don't entangle themselves in affairs that will distract them from the battle they are fighting. The second quality is their desire to please their leader. That implies a deep loyalty and a willingness to sacrifice.

One reason so many soldiers are able to become good leaders is that they learn what it means to follow before being given the opportunity to lead. That's why my friend Lynd Fitzgerald, who serves as a consultant with one of my companies, INJOY Stewardship Services, calls the United States military "the greatest leadership training ground in the world." He would know: he was a pilot with the U.S. Navy who rose to the rank of captain before retiring. As you search for people to develop, find those who exemplify the qualities of a good soldier—a willingness to follow and the ability to carry through on their responsibilities.

3. AN ATHLETE

A good leader is like a winning athlete. Paul stated that "if anyone competes in athletics, he is not crowned unless he competes according to the rules" (2 Tim. 2:5 NKJV). The two characteristics he was highlighting were integrity and discipline. People without integrity *won't play* by the rules. And people without discipline *can't win* by the rules. It takes both qualities.

> People without integrity won't play by the rules. And people without discipline can't win by the rules. It takes both qualities.

Today we live in a culture that tells us to win at all costs—regardless of rules or the promptings of conscience. But nothing is more important in a potential leader you select than integrity. And discipline will guard a person's integrity and will make it possible for him to keep growing, competing, and winning.

4. A FARMER

The final image Paul used to teach about leadership was that of a farmer. Most people today in the United States don't understand what it means to be a farmer or what it takes. I grew up in a small town in Ohio, and even though I lived fairly close to a lot of farms, I didn't really understand anything about farming until I led my first church in rural Indiana. There I learned what hard work farming is. Farmers are up before the sun, work until they are exhausted, and live at the mercy of the seasons.

Farmers are patient too. There's no instant gratification when you work the land. Farmers work, then wait. If you can find potential leaders with a farmer's patience and work ethic, you've got people with the right attitude to go far as leaders.

Leadership is difficult. Leading leaders is even more difficult. That's why it's important for you to be the kind of leader Paul described and for you to select the right people to be developed in your organization. If they are unable to lead and to be effective on their own, you will never be able to achieve explosive growth.

❦

TODAY'S QUESTION FOR REFLECTION:
*Do your potential leaders possess the qualities needed
for explosive growth?*

Day 4

There are major differences between leaders who gather followers and leaders who develop leaders.

Most assuredly, I say to you, unless a grain of wheat falls into the ground and dies, it remains alone; but if it dies, it produces much grain. He who loves his life will lose it, and he who hates his life in this world will keep it for eternal life.

John 12:24–25 (NKJV)

Becoming an explosive-growth leader requires more than a change in the way you work. It requires a change in the way you think. It's an entirely different mind-set from that needed to gather followers.

LEADERS WHO GATHER FOLLOWERS VERSUS LEADERS WHO DEVELOP LEADERS

There are seven major differences between leaders whose focus is on gathering followers and leaders who dedicate themselves to developing other leaders:

1. LEADERS WHO GATHER FOLLOWERS NEED TO BE NEEDED— LEADERS WHO DEVELOP LEADERS WANT TO BE SUCCEEDED

Many people who desire to lead only followers do so because having followers strokes their egos. They feel indispensable. But leaders who develop leaders are *working* to make themselves dispensable. They raise up leaders to replace them. They don't want to have a following; they want to leave a legacy. That's what Paul valued. He developed leaders, such as Timothy and Titus, who would carry on after he was gone.

2. LEADERS WHO GATHER FOLLOWERS FOCUS ON PEOPLE'S WEAKNESSES—LEADERS WHO DEVELOP LEADERS FOCUS ON THEIR STRENGTHS

Ineffective leaders focus on their followers' weaknesses. Sometimes they do it because they don't understand the way development and encouragement work. Other times they do it because of insecurity. (Weak leaders want to keep their followers off balance.) But strong leaders—the ones capable of leading other leaders—focus on their people's strengths because they know that is the key to developing people.

Read through Scripture and then tell me: What were Timothy's weaknesses? The answer is that we don't really know. Why? Because Paul's letters encouraged his protégé to build his strengths and develop his potential. His admonition to Timothy to "stir up the gift of God which is in you" (2 Timothy 1:6 NKJV) summed up Paul's attitude. If you desire to develop leaders, turn your focus to people's strengths to help them reach their potential.

3. LEADERS WHO GATHER FOLLOWERS FOCUS ON THE BOTTOM 20 PERCENT—LEADERS WHO DEVELOP LEADERS FOCUS ON THE TOP 20 PERCENT

Explosive-growth leaders focus on the best in their leaders; they also focus on the best potential leaders. In contrast, leaders of followers usually give their attention to the loudest and most difficult people, the ones who take and take, giving nothing in return to anyone else.

As you develop leaders, do what Paul did. Teach and love everyone. But focus your attention on developing the best leaders. Do that, and the leaders you develop will help you take care of the rest of the people.

> Explosive-growth leaders focus on the best in their leaders; they also focus on the best potential leaders.

4. LEADERS WHO GATHER FOLLOWERS TREAT EVERYONE THE SAME—LEADERS WHO DEVELOP LEADERS TREAT PEOPLE AS INDIVIDUALS

When Paul went on his missionary journeys, he didn't try to take everybody with him. Nor did he give everyone an equal chance to oversee the churches he started for everyone was not equally qualified for or called to the task. Accordingly, he was strategic with his time and attention. He treated each person he encountered according to his gifts, calling, and willingness to grow. As a leader who develops other leaders, you must do the same.

5. LEADERS WHO GATHER FOLLOWERS SPEND THEIR TIME— LEADERS WHO DEVELOP LEADERS INVEST THEIR TIME

In the early years after his conversion, Paul spent time alone. Like many other biblical leaders, he was laboring in obscurity to be prepared to fulfill his calling. But once he traveled to Jerusalem for the first time and began leading others and planting churches, he never worked alone again. Everywhere he went, he took companions. He considered the time he spent with them an investment. And if he didn't see a return, for example, in the case of John Mark who didn't accompany him to Antioch (Acts 13:13), Paul was reluctant to keep investing in him (Acts 15:37–40).

As you lead others, think of your work with emerging leaders as an opportunity to invest in them. Be strategic with your time. Keep a leader you are mentoring by your side as much as possible as you work. Show him how to do everything you do, and always explain why. Invest in him with the intention of working yourself out of a job.

6. LEADERS WHO GATHER FOLLOWERS ASK FOR LITTLE COMMITMENT—LEADERS WHO DEVELOP LEADERS ASK FOR GREAT COMMITMENT

Following a leader takes commitment. But it's nothing compared to the commitment of a follower who is asked to lead others. Leadership requires sacrifice, and sacrifice requires commitment. Paul, as a follower of Christ, committed his life. So did his close companions, who suffered the same kind of persecution and hardship he did.

As you ask people to step up to leadership, don't treat that request lightly. Let them know what you are asking them to commit to. Certainly tell them about any potential rewards, but also acquaint them with the sacrifice and the service that come with leadership.

7. LEADERS WHO GATHER FOLLOWERS IMPACT THIS GENERATION—LEADERS WHO DEVELOP LEADERS IMPACT FUTURE GENERATIONS

People who lead followers are able to make an impact only on the individuals whose lives they touch personally. But people who develop and lead leaders can extend their reach. Paul extended his reach beyond his circle of influence and beyond his lifetime. His leadership created a legacy that has continued to the present day.

I may sound as if I'm disparaging leaders of followers. That's not my intention. It takes a good leader to gather a group of followers and lead them to achieve a worthy goal. But it takes a great leader to lead other leaders. And that's the only kind of leader who is able to take an organization to the highest level and achieve explosive growth.

❧

TODAY'S QUESTION FOR REFLECTION:
Are you developing followers or leaders?

Day 5

Bringing the Law to Life

TAKING IT IN

Review the four statements related to the Law of Explosive Growth:

1. Leaders developing leaders equals explosive growth.

2. Leaders commit themselves to people and activities that provide explosive growth.

3. Leaders recognize the qualities needed for explosive growth.

4. There are major differences between leaders who gather followers and leaders who develop leaders.

Which way do you lean—toward gathering followers or developing leaders? If you're not sure, honestly examine the people who follow you in your organization. Are you surrounded by people of influence who make an impact every time they get the opportunity? Or are people continually waiting for you to initiate everything and give them instruction, inspiration, and direction?

SORTING IT OUT

If you're not sure where you stand when it comes to understanding and applying the Law of Explosive Growth, visit the Web site www.injoy.com/21 Minutes to take a free twenty-five-question assessment quiz that will help you measure your ability.

PRAYING IT THROUGH

Use the following words to begin your time of prayer:

Dear God, I want to make an impact. I want to lead beyond my capabilities and my circle of influence. Teach me to be a leader of leaders. Give me favor with people, and bring me people with great leadership potential. And help me learn how to invest my life in them so that the result is explosive growth. Amen.

LIVING IT OUT

Set aside time in the next few days to analyze the people in your organization. Write down the names of all the people with whom you have influence. (If your organization is very large, then focus on a smaller, more manageable group, such as the top thirty to fifty.) Next to the name of each person, write a number from 1 (low) to 10 (high) representing their leadership potential. For criteria, think about the images Paul equated with good leaders: they must be teachers, soldiers, athletes, and farmers. Now select the top one to five people to develop personally. (If you've never done this before, start small.) Teach them. Take them with you as you work. Let them sit in on important meetings. Do whatever it takes to raise them up as leaders.

PASSING IT ON

Which one leadership concept, insight, or practice that you've learned this week will you pass on to another leader in the next two days?

Week 21

THE LAW OF LEGACY

A LEADER'S LASTING VALUE IS MEASURED BY SUCCESSION

Just about anybody can make an organization look good for a moment—by launching a flashy new program or product, drawing crowds to a big event, or slashing the budget to boost the bottom line. But leaders who leave a legacy take a different approach. They lead with tomorrow as well as today in mind . . .

Achievement comes to someone when he is able to do great things for himself. Success comes when he empowers followers to do great things *with* him. Significance comes when he develops leaders to do great things *for* him. But a legacy is created only when a person puts his organization into the position to do great things *without* him . . .

When all is said and done, your ability as a leader will not be judged by what you achieved personally or even by what your team accomplished during your tenure. You will be judged by how well your people and your organization did after you were gone . . . Your lasting value will be measured by succession.

FROM "THE LAW OF LEGACY" IN *The 21 Irrefutable Laws of Leadership*

Day 1

Jesus
and the
Law of Legacy

LEADERSHIP THOUGHT FOR TODAY:
More important than leaving an inheritance is leaving a legacy.

Read
Luke 5:1–11; 6:12–16; 9:1–6, 10–20; 9:57–10:12;
Matthew 28:16–20

When most people think about Jesus, the first things that come to their minds are miracles He performed. I was reminded of that recently when one of the television networks produced and aired a miniseries called *Jesus*. It explored His early life and gave a significant amount of attention to His crucifixion, but the part that covered His three years with the apostles focused almost entirely on His teaching and His miracles. The producers missed the most important part of His ministry. They left out the way Jesus strategically created a legacy.

LEFT BEHIND

Deep down, all people would probably like to leave something behind that will live on after them. That desire is stronger for leaders than it is for the average person. But not everyone sees the issue the same way. People are most likely to leave behind three kinds of things as they finish the most productive period of their lives:

1. SOUVENIRS

No one wants to depart from this world without leaving a trace of having been in it. But some people are so preoccupied with surviving or with pursuing happiness that they don't accomplish anything. They satisfy themselves by collecting souvenirs.

Souvenirs are little more than markers—they commemorate events, milestones, or activities that people engage in. There's nothing wrong with having souvenirs. My office contains many from my life: a picture of me with my son, Joel Porter, at the grave of my hero, John Wesley; a walnut-sized chunk of brick and mortar that was once part of the Berlin Wall; a photo of the board members who served with me at Skyline Church, taken on the property purchased for its new campus. I like souvenirs as much as anyone, but alone they contain no intrinsic value. They're like graffiti or the infamous "Kilroy was here" message that GIs wrote everywhere during World War II.

2. TROPHIES

Other people strive to capture trophies to leave behind. Where souvenirs are records of existence, trophies are records of achievement. They show that we were once here, and we did something that separated us from the rest of the pack.

Trophies have many forms. Some are actual trophies or awards: the Stanley Cup, the Nobel Prize, an Olympic gold medal. Others are trophies of a different (and sometimes more impressive) kind: Trump Plaza, a million-selling novel, the Microsoft Corporation. Trophies give their winners prestige and recognition, but of themselves they have no real, lasting value.

3. LEGACIES

People also strive to leave behind legacies. A legacy is different from a trophy or souvenir in that it doesn't just mark something that happened in the past: it lives on and continues to make an impact in the present. It's a gift given to the next generation.

If you look up the word *legacy* in a dictionary, you will see that one definition is "inheritance." But when a legacy is created by a leader, it is more than the giving of an inheritance. It specifically includes the passing of the leadership baton. It means succession from the leader to his replacement. That makes a leader's legacy a tremendous gift.

CARRYING ON

The reason it is such a disservice to Jesus' ministry to show only His miracles and His teaching to the crowds is that it disregards the work He did to create His legacy. Jesus spent most of His time during those three years with His twelve disciples, not the crowds who sought Him out. He strategically prepared them to carry on His ministry after He would depart. The gospel was His message, but legacy was His method. *Everything* depended on the job He did with those twelve men.

People believe in Jesus today and call Him Lord because Jesus made it possible for the disciples to carry on His work. And they in turn trained others to continue in their place. He practiced the Law of Legacy, and so did they. If He hadn't, then the message of the gospel and its method of transfer would have ended in the first century A.D.

>
> The gospel was His message, but legacy was His method. Everything depended on the job He did with those twelve men.

TODAY'S QUESTION FOR REFLECTION:
What are you leaving behind?

Day 2

Legacies are not left by accident.

Abide in My love. If you keep My commandments, you will abide in My love
. . . These things I have spoken to you, that My joy may remain in you, and
that your joy may be full. This is My commandment, that you love one
another as I have loved you.

John 15:9–12 (NKJV)

Have you ever been asked how you want to be remembered? You may not
have, depending on your age. I think it's the kind of question most people
don't hear much before they turn fifty. When most people are asked what
they will be remembered for, they fumble for a moment and say something
like, "Well, I don't know. I've tried to do my best. History will have to answer
that. I hope history will be kind to me."

While it may be true that history
judges the results of our actions, we
are responsible for our efforts. No
one leaves a legacy by accident. We
can't hope for the best. Every positive
legacy ever created by a leader was
planned and pursued with purpose.

>
> **While it may be true that
> history judges the results of
> our actions, we are respon-
> sible for our efforts. No one
> leaves a legacy by accident.**

PREPARING THE WAY

If you desire to create a legacy, you need to be strategic and intentional. These
guidelines can help you get started:

1. DECIDE AHEAD WHAT YOU ARE WILLING TO GIVE UP

The Law of Sacrifice states that a leader must give up to go up. Being a leader has a price. Being a leader who leaves a legacy has an even greater price because when you work to create a legacy, your life is no longer your own.

That's why it's so important to *know* what you are willing to give up so that others can go up. Jesus taught this principle. He told this to His disciples, the very ones who would be required to continue His legacy: "For which of you, intending to build a tower, does not sit down first and count the cost, whether he has enough to finish it" (Luke 14:28 NKJV).

What are you willing to give up? How much of your time? How much of your money? How many opportunities will you forgo? You probably have a lot of dreams. How many are you willing to set aside to ensure that one or maybe two of them survive in the lives of others? Don't go into the process blind.

2. TAKE THE INITIATIVE TO START THE PROCESS

If you're a great leader, good leaders will flock to you. Resources will come your way. People will come to you with ideas they want to see fulfilled. But no one will create your legacy for you.

Jesus' followers had various agendas. Some, like Simon the Zealot, wanted Him to lead a revolt against Rome. Others, like James and John, wanted positions of power for themselves (Mark 10:37). Even Peter, whom Jesus called "the rock," tried to dissuade Jesus from the very act that would release Peter and the other disciples to follow in Jesus' footsteps (Matt. 16:22).

If you want to create a legacy, you will have to initiate the process. And there will be times when you have to fight for it.

3. KNOW YOUR GOALS WITH EACH PERSON

The process of creating a legacy relies primarily on people, a concept so important that it is tomorrow's subject. It requires the selection of the right people and the right development process for each individual.

Jesus carefully chose His legacy carriers. Scripture says He picked the twelve He wanted very intentionally. He didn't take the first guys who showed up. And He didn't treat all of them the same. I believe that He had a specific development process for each person. For some of those men, we know what Jesus was trying to overcome:

- Peter—impetuosity
- James and John—ambition
- Matthew—materialism

As you find the right people to whom you will entrust your legacy, remember that you have a different job with each person. You want to help all of them become better leaders, but you will need to develop strengths specifically and address particular character issues.

4. PREPARE TO PASS THE BATON WELL

Once you have prepared your people, then you need to prepare for the upcoming transition. There's a real art to preparing a successor for a transition. And it doesn't always go smoothly.

Jesus had trouble handing the baton to His followers. He appeared to them after His resurrection and gave them the Great Commission, yet some of them still didn't get it. John, the apostle Jesus loved, admitted that he, Peter, and James returned to fishing *after they saw Jesus resurrected!* As you prepare to hand off your leadership to a successor, do everything you can to make for a smooth transition, and even then, plan to offer additional assistance without getting in the way.

It's never too soon to start thinking about leaving a legacy. If you feel that you don't have something worth handing off, then work harder on your contribution

> **What are you doing today to leave your legacy tomorrow?**

today. But as you do, keep your eyes open for the people who will someday carry on the work you've begun. The only way to build anything of real value is to give it away.

TODAY'S QUESTION FOR REFLECTION:
What are you doing today to leave your legacy tomorrow?

Day 3

Leaders deposit their legacy in people.

He went up on the mountain and called to Him those He Himself wanted. And they came to Him. Then He appointed twelve, that they might be with Him and that He might send them out to preach.

Mark 3:13–14 (NKJV)

If you wanted to change the lives of people a hundred years from now, how would you go about it? What would you do? How about a thousand years from now? Two thousand? Would you create a time capsule? Would you build a library? Would you found a university? How would you touch the lives of people one hundred generations after your death?

That is the task Jesus faced—and accomplished. He did it without writing any books, building any schools, or founding any institutions. As professor Robert E. Coleman has stated, "Men were His method." Lasting success calls for successors.

JESUS' IDEA FOR LEAVING A LEGACY

It's one of the greatest of ironies that Jesus chose people as the instruments through which He would reach the world. Someday when I stand before God in eternity, I hope to ask Him why He chose to use fallible humans for such an important task. But until then, I accept that if Jesus chose to deposit His legacy in people, then I should learn His method and practice it as best I can.

Take a look at Jesus' IDEA for working in the lives of people:

INSTRUCTION

Jesus was constantly teaching, most often with parables. He taught the masses. He educated and rebuked the Pharisees. And He carefully instructed the disciples. More than half of the Gospels' content is concerned with Jesus' teaching.

The account of Jesus telling the parable of the sower gives us insight into how He worked. Using parables, He taught the masses and tested their hearts. But with the disciples, Jesus gave much deeper instruction. When they asked Him about the meaning of the parable, He explained:

> To you it has been given to know the mystery of the kingdom of God; but
> to those who are outside, all things come in parables, so that
> Seeing they may see and not perceive,
> And hearing they may hear and not understand;
> Lest they should turn,
> And their sins be forgiven them. (Mark 4:11–12 NKJV)

Then Jesus explained the parable, revealing the insightful truth contained in the story.

DEMONSTRATION

A shortcoming of the educational philosophy used in our schools and colleges today is that it relies too heavily on instruction alone. If Jesus had taught the disciples and done nothing more, they never would have carried on His legacy. But Jesus shared His life with them.

As you examine how Jesus did this, you can see that the disciples' proximity to Him went through three phases:

- *Come and see.* In the first phase, Jesus invited them to observe Him and His priorities. It was an invitation for them to evaluate Him (and themselves in light of what He was doing).

- *Come and follow Me.* During the second phase, Jesus asked for a greater level of commitment. For example, He asked the Galilean fishermen to leave their nets and follow Him. The disciples were to do more than observe; they were to associate with Him.

- *Come and be with Me.* The third and final phase, which occupied most of Jesus' three years of ministry, required the disciples' commitment and companionship.

The most important kind of teaching Jesus did was modeling, for some things can only be caught, not taught. Once the Twelve moved to the highest level of connection with Jesus, they were present with Him always. They were present with

> The disciples saw that there was consistency between His teaching and His actions, and they learned the how and why of all He did.

Him as He taught, traveled, prayed, ate with "sinners," healed the sick, and raised the dead. They saw that there was consistency between His teaching and His actions, and they learned the *how* and *why* of all He did.

EXPERIENCE

After Jesus had modeled good leadership to the disciples and taught them spiritual truths, He didn't turn them loose and move on. He gradually worked them into positions of independent leadership by giving them valuable experience.

You can see the way Jesus progressively involved the disciples in His ministry. After they had spent enough time with Him, He gave instructions to the Twelve, invested them with authority, and then sent them out to do ministry in His place (Luke 9:1–6). Not long after that, He sent out seventy disciples in similar fashion (Luke 10:1–16). Though Scripture does not state it, my opinion is that the Twelve were probably included in that group. I believe Jesus was giving them an opportunity to practice what He had taught and to practice leadership of other disciples as they did.

ASSESSMENT

Jesus repeatedly evaluated the progress of His disciples. For example, after the return of the seventy whom He had sent out, He debriefed them, gave them instruction concerning priorities, and celebrated with them (Luke 10:17–24). Jesus also gave individual assessment to His disciples, which included specific feedback concerning their character and their capabilities. Such was the case with Peter, whom He praised for his great faith (Matt. 16:17–19) and also rebuked for the great weakness of his denial (Matt. 26:33–34).

The disciples might not have always understood everything Jesus told them, but they knew where they stood with Him. And when they weren't act-ing in a way that was consistent with what they had been taught, Jesus let them know.

If you possess the desire to leave a legacy, then you must look to people to carry it for you. You need the right people and the right process of prepa-ration for them. Only as you have poured into them will they be able to pour out themselves for others. No one can give what he does not have.

≫

TODAY'S QUESTION FOR REFLECTION:
Who will carry your legacy?

Day 4

> I tell you for certain that if you have faith in me, you will do the same things
> that I am doing. You will do even greater things.
>
> John 14:12 (CEV)

Many leaders who leave a legacy never get the privilege of seeing it carried forward in their lifetimes. But I must say that God has been very gracious to me. After serving for twenty-six years in pastoral leadership, I have had the privilege of glimpsing something that I worked hard to hand off to a successor.

In *The 21 Irrefutable Laws of Leadership*, I wrote about the difficulty of trying to sustain momentum at Skyline Church while fighting to get permission to build a new campus. Between the local community's politics, San Diego County's bureaucracy, and California's environmental red tape, we couldn't move forward for eleven years. We started the process in 1984. The church didn't get the permits to build until 1995. It was a nightmare.

I wanted nothing more than to take the people of Skyline to "the mountain"—that's what we called the property because it was situated on a large hill near Mount San Miguel. I intended that to be part of my legacy, along with all the leaders I had developed over the fourteen years I was there. But that was not meant to be. The best I could hope to do was to help my successor, Jim Garlow, succeed in the task.

When Jim arrived at Skyline, he wholeheartedly embraced the vision of relocating the church to the new property. He put together a skilled team of people to carry the ball in the relocation. And anytime he asked for my help, I gladly gave it. For nearly five years he and the other leaders of the church worked diligently. They took the vision I had originally given the church and made it become a reality. On May 7, 2000, Jim dedicated the new facility, and he invited me to participate. It was an incredible day that I will never forget.

WHAT WILL IT TAKE?

When a leader wants to create a lasting legacy, a lot of things need to go right. The following table summarizes what can happen as a leader works on a successful succession:

IF MY LEADERSHIP FOCUS IS	AND THE RESPONSE OF MY PEOPLE IS	THEN THE RESULT IS	% WHO DO
Gathering Followers	They Leave	No One's Success	25
Gathering Followers	They Stay	My Limited Success	50
Developing Leaders	They Leave	Someone Else's Success	5
Developing Leaders	They Stay	Our Mutual Success	15
Developing Leaders of Leaders	They Stay and Develop Others	The Whole Organization's Success	4
Handing Off to Leaders of Leaders	They Stay and Lead Well After I'm Gone	A Legacy of Success for Everyone	1

Handing off the baton is never easy. A leader has to find the right leaders. He has to take them through an effective development process. He needs the buy-in of the people. He needs the favor of God. And then he has to *let go* and get out of the way.

THE FINAL LEG OF THE JOURNEY

I was very fortunate on Skyline's dedication day because I was able to fulfill a promise I had made a decade before to an old friend, and that act brought closure to my role of passing the leadership baton to Jim. Years ago while I was raising funds as the pastor at Skyline, Beth Myers asked that I make her a promise. She said, "Pastor, I believe in you and in your vision for the church. I will be glad to give to the relocation—on one condition. The day we move into the new building, I want you to take me by the hand and give me a tour."

Beth is in her eighties now, and I got the opportunity to fulfill that promise. I took her by the hand that day and showed her every part of the building. I felt as if I were walking around with Anna the prophetess, about whom Luke had written in his gospel (2:36–38).

Fulfilling a calling to leave a legacy is an incredible joy. I delight in seeing Jim Garlow succeed at Skyline. The church's greatest years are still ahead. But I also recognize that leaving a legacy is an unbelievably difficult challenge. You pay a high price to live for people other than yourself. But it is worth it.

If God has given you a vision for something that will outlive you, be willing to pay the price for it. A legacy is a dream that changes not only your life but also the lives of all the people it touches.

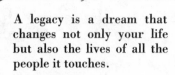

> A legacy is a dream that changes not only your life but also the lives of all the people it touches.

TODAY'S QUESTION FOR REFLECTION:
Can you imagine what your legacy will look like?

Day 5

Bringing the Law to Life

TAKING IT IN

Are you so focused on succeeding today that you haven't thought about any long-term contribution you could make? If so, spend some time thinking about these points:

1. More important than leaving an inheritance is leaving a legacy.

2. Legacies are not left by accident.

3. Leaders deposit their legacy in people.

4. A leader's legacy: your toughest job, your deepest joy.

Once your productive years as a leader are behind you, it's too late to *begin* thinking about leaving a legacy. The time to build your legacy is today, while you still have something to give and someone to give it to.

SORTING IT OUT

If you're not sure where you stand when it comes to understanding and applying the Law of Legacy, visit the Web site www.injoy.com/21 Minutes to take a free twenty-five-question assessment quiz that will help you measure your ability.

PRAYING IT THROUGH

Use the following words to begin your time of prayer:

Dear God, make me a leader of legacy. Give me a vision worthy of my life and legacy. Send the right leaders to fulfill it, and help me to pour myself into their lives. Give me Your favor and that of the people. And when it's time for me to pass the baton, help me to get out of my successor's way. Amen.

LIVING IT OUT

If you are determined to make your life one that leaves a legacy rather than souvenirs or trophies, then use the plan from Day 2 to start preparing your legacy today:

1. List what you are willing to give up for your legacy.

2. Describe how you will take the initiative to start the process.

3. List the people you will develop, and note your goals with each person.

4. Describe what it will mean to pass the baton.

PASSING IT ON

Which one leadership concept, insight, or practice that you've learned this week will you pass on to another leader in the next two days?

CONCLUSION

I hope you have enjoyed learning from the leaders of the Bible as much as I have enjoyed sharing the lessons I've learned with you. If you spend time in Scripture, you will continue to discover and learn leadership lessons, for the Bible truly is the greatest leadership book ever written.

Keep growing, keep developing other leaders, and do your best to enjoy the journey.

Books by Dr. John C. Maxwell
Can Teach You
How to Be a REAL Success

RELATIONSHIPS

Be a People Person (Victor Books)
Becoming a Person of Influence (Thomas Nelson)
The Power of Influence (Honor Books)
The Power of Partnership in the Church (J. Countryman)
The Treasure of a Friend (J. Countryman)

EQUIPPING

Breakthrough Parenting (Focus on the Family)
Developing the Leaders Around You (Thomas Nelson)
Partners in Prayer (Thomas Nelson)
The Success Journey (Thomas Nelson)
Success One Day at a Time (J. Countryman)

ATTITUDE

Be All You Can Be (Victor Books)
Failing Forward (Thomas Nelson)
The Power of Thinking (Honor Books)
Living at the Next Level (Thomas Nelson)
Think On These Things (Beacon Hill)
The Winning Attitude (Thomas Nelson)
Your Bridge to a Better Future (Thomas Nelson)
The Power of Attitude (Honor Books)

LEADERSHIP

The 21 Indispensable Qualities of a Leader (Thomas Nelson)
The 21 Irrefutable Laws of Leadership (Thomas Nelson)
The 21 Most Powerful Minutes in a Leader's Day (Thomas Nelson)
Developing the Leader Within You (Thomas Nelson)
The Power of Leadership (Honor Books)

The INJOY Group
A Lifelong Partner Dedicated to
Lifting Your Potential

The INJOY Group, founded in 1985 by Dr. John C. Maxwell, dedicates itself to adding value to individuals and organizations across America and around the world. It accomplishes its mission by forging lasting partnerships that foster personal growth and organizational effectiveness.

The INJOY Group consists of . . .

INJOY Resources—Equipping People to Succeed
INJOY Conferences—Empowering Leaders to Excel
INJOY Stewardship Services—Energizing Churches to Raise Funds for
    Financing the Future
EQUIP—Effecting Leadership Development in Emerging Countries,
    American Urban Centers, and Academic Communities

Each year, The INJOY Group partners with tens of thousands of people, dozens of church denominations, and countless business and nonprofit organizations to help people reach their potential.

To contact Dr. John C. Maxwell or any division of The INJOY Group, call, write, or E-mail us:

The INJOY Group
P.O. Box 7700
Atlanta, GA 30357-0700
800-333-6506
www.injoy.com